Missing & Murdered

Missing&
Murdered

A PERSONAL ADVENTURE IN
FORENSIC ANTHROPOLOGY

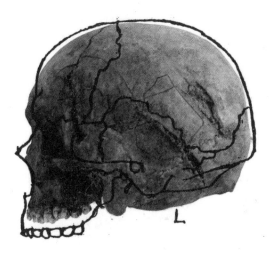

ALAN G. MORRIS

Published by Zebra Press
an imprint of Random House Struik (Pty) Ltd
Company Reg. No. 1966/003153/07
Wembley Square, First Floor, Solan Street, Gardens, Cape Town, 8001
PO Box 1144, Cape Town, 8000, South Africa

www.zebrapress.co.za

First published 2011

1 3 5 7 9 10 8 6 4 2

Publication © Zebra Press 2011
Cover image and text © Alan G. Morris

PUBLISHER: Marlene Fryer
MANAGING EDITOR: Ronel Richter-Herbert
EDITOR: Jane Housdon
PROOFREADERS: Beth Housdon and Ronel Richter-Herbert
COVER DESIGNER: Michiel Botha
TEXT DESIGNER: Monique Oberholzer
TYPESETTER: Monique van den Berg
PRODUCTION MANAGER: Valerie Kömmer

Set in 11.75 pt on 15.5 pt Granjon

Printed and bound by Paarl Media, Jan van Riebeeck Drive,
Paarl, South Africa

ISBN 978 1 77022 361 5 (print)
ISBN 978 1 77022 362 2 (ePub)
ISBN 978 1 77022 363 9 (PDF)

Contents

To Liz, for being both the anchor and inspiration in my life

Acknowledgements

There are so many people to thank, as there always is in a project of this scope. The key people are those I work with on a regular basis: Vince Phillips and Sean Davison of the University of the Western Cape, Maryna Steyn of the University of Pretoria, Madeleine Fullard of the Missing Persons Task Team, Mary Patrick of the Cape Archaeological Survey, Coen Nienaber of the Forensic Unit at the University of Pretoria, and Tim Hart and Dave Halkett of the Archaeological Contracts Office at UCT.

I need to give special thanks to Maryna Steyn, Vince Phillips and Madeleine Fullard for allowing me to happily steal from their research and publications on specific cases. I also could not have done any of the forensic work over the years without the forensic pathologists and their support team in the Western Cape: Diedré Abrahams, Sindisa Potelwa, Mariette Hurst, Yolanda van der Heyde, Linda Liebenberg, Lorna Martin, Shabbir Wadee, Omar Galant and June Mehl.

I mustn't forget the current crew of pathologists in training at UCT – Itumeleng Molefe, Steven Afonzo, Sipho Mfolozi, Sairita Maistry, Akmal Khan and Lekram Alli. I also need to acknowledge my own colleagues and students who have worked with me on forensic and archaeological cases over the past few years: Jacqui Friedling, Thabang Manyaapelo, Kundi Dembetembe, Belinda Speed, Laché Rossouw, Kavita Chibba, Nhlanhla Dlamini.

Many of these friends, students and colleagues have kindly offered to comment on sections of chapters that I have sent them. Names I haven't mentioned so far include Morongwa Mosothwane, Jatti Bredekamp, Jay Aronson, and Goran Štrkalj. Hendrik Swanepoel helped with some difficult Afrikaans translations from hand-written police records, and Steve Ousley and Ericka L'Abbé put up with my dissensions and arguments about the use of FORDISC.

The staff at the Hout Bay Medical Centre let me rent an office in their suite so that I could hide from the telephone and email while I put this book together. And of course I mustn't forget Bridget Elizabeth Shevlin-Morris, my long-suffering wife who drew the short straw and ended up reading the whole manuscript before any-one else. She not only told me where my writing style had bogged down to a state of boring, but also suggested a title that was way better than anything I had thought of.

ALAN G. MORRIS
SEPTEMBER 2011

List of Abbreviations

AAFS: American Academy of Forensic Sciences
AFAT: African Forensic Anthropology Team
AFIP: Armed Forces Institute of Pathology
AI: Amnesty International
ANC: African National Congress
ASSA: Anatomical Society of Southern Africa
BBC: British Broadcasting Corporation
CO_2: carbon dioxide
CSI: Crime Scene Investigation
CSU: Crime Scene Unit
CT: Computed Tomography
DJD: degenerative joint disease
DNA: deoxyribonucleic acid
DSO: Directorate of Special Operations
EAAF: Argentine Forensic Anthropology Team (Equipo Argentino de Antropología Forense)
FARC: Forensic Anthropology Research Centre
FBI: Federal Bureau of Investigation
FORDISC: Forensic Discriminant Analysis Program

FPS: Forensic Pathology Services
GNC: Griqua National Conference
IDASA: Institute for Democracy in South Africa
LODOX: low dose digital X-ray
LSA: Later Stone Age
MK: Umkhonto we Sizwe
MPTT: Missing Persons Task Team
mtDNA: mitochondrial DNA
NMB: National Museum Bloemfontein
NMC: National Monuments Council
NMHM: National Museum of Health and Medicine
NPA: National Prosecuting Authority
PAC: Pan Africanist Congress
Pebco: Port Elizabeth Black Civic Organisation
PCLU: Priority Crimes Litigation Unit
PCR: Polymerase Chain Reaction
PMI: postmortem interval
SAHRA: South African Heritage Resources Agency
SAP: South African Police
SAPS: South African Police Service
STR: short tandem repeat
SWAPO: South West African People's Organisation
TB: tuberculosis
TMJ: temporomandibular joint
TRC: Truth and Reconciliation Commission
UCT: University of Cape Town
UN: United Nations
UNESCO: United Nations Educational, Scientific and Cultural
    Organisation
USSR: Union of Soviet Socialist Republics
UWC: University of the Western Cape
Wits: University of the Witwatersrand

Introduction

This book is not a textbook on forensic anthropology. While I discuss some anthropological techniques, I have avoided technical jargon as far as possible, as I would like the forensically uninitiated to understand and enjoy it. There is some anatomical and medical discussion from time to time, but I promise not to bury anyone in detail prematurely.

There are, in fact, relatively few textbooks on forensic anthropology. The 'bible', Krogman and İşcan's *The Human Skeleton in Forensic Medicine*, is still the best technical book on the subject, but it is dense with detail, outdated in some areas and too rigid in interpretation in others. Other books, such as White and Folken's *The Human Bone Manual* and Blau and Ubelaker's *Handbook of Forensic Anthropology and Archaeology*, are more accessible but tend to be very anthropological.

There certainly is room for a new text for undergraduate university students, one that contains many pretty (and pretty gory) pictures, but that is not what I wanted to write.

One of the reasons that there are so few textbooks on the subject is because the practice of forensic anthropology is very much

experience-based. Each case brings its own complexities and analytical procedures, and nothing is more valuable than the experience
of the anthropologist. You can learn only so much from a book.

So what *did* I want to write? There are two things that I aimed
to put across to my readers when I started writing this book. Firstly,
I wanted to convey some impression of the experience of forensic
anthropology from a practitioner's perspective, but I didn't want
it to be purely a list of interesting cases. I wanted this book to reflect my experiences as a teacher, anthropologist, archaeologist and
forensic investigator. It is very personal because that is the nature
of the subject.

I have written about cases in which I have been involved and
those that have influenced my thoughts on forensic science and
anthropology, but I've aimed to go beyond the clinical cases. Thirty
per cent of the cases that are brought to me by the police are archaeological and don't involve anything more than a brief report to
the investigating officer so that he can close his file and move on
to the next inquiry. The investigating officer may have lost interest
in the old bones in question, but I remain fascinated by them. The
methods I use when working with skeletonised human remains all
come from physical anthropology and its specialised subdivision,
skeletal biology. My own training is much closer to 'bioarchaeology'
than it is to forensics. Although forensic anthropology is grounded
in the sciences of anatomy and medicine as applied to the law, it
cannot survive without an understanding of the nature of history,
politics and social anthropology. In this book I do not hesitate to
delve into all three when the occasion demands it.

Secondly, in this book I wanted to describe the nature and
importance of forensic anthropology in southern Africa. I know
that I run the risk of making the book too 'local', but I hope that not
all readers will see it that way. Nearly all of the forensic anthropological research that has been published to date is by European
or North American authors. Their work is very valuable: much of

it is ground-breaking and a source of wonderful information that is universally useful. But the experience of the practice of forensic anthropology is *not* the same everywhere. Human biology differs from region to region, and techniques that work well in Boston may not be applicable in Botswana. Laws and cultures also differ and, although the nature of police work and the gathering of evidence might be the same everywhere, the interpretation of the data may vary in different locations. There is almost nothing published about this from an African perspective.

In the context of forensic anthropology, South Africa is unique and can contribute to this field of study. Of critical importance is the depth of human presence on the continent. We have evidence of the remains of people who were alive tens of millennia before the ancestors of the modern North American First Nations set foot on the coastal plains of Alaska. At least a third of living people in Cape Town can track directly their own lineage back through mitochondrial and Y-chromosome DNA to forebears who lived in southern Africa a hundred millennia ago.

But such antiquity, although of interest in anthropological science, is of relatively little use in the practice of forensic anthropology. Much more important is the modern dynamic in South African society, which offers us a workshop of humanity that is rarely paralleled in other places. Capetonians proudly call their town the 'Tavern of the Seas', where mariners have stopped for over 300 years to obtain fresh supplies, rest in the lee of Table Mountain and weave their genes into the fabric of Cape society. Some came willingly as traders and settlers, while others were brought here against their will as part of the slave trade. In downtown Cape Town you will meet people whose ancestors hail from Batavia (now Jakarta) on the Indonesian coast, or Ceylon (Sri Lanka) or southern China. Their ancestors could be from the Hook of Holland, the villages of Cornwall, the principalities of Germany or the shtetls of Lithuania.

Some of our forefathers came in the holds of Portuguese or

Dutch slave ships from the Congo or Madagascar, while others arrived as free men from Bechuanaland or the Transkei as navvies needed for the industrial growth in the first half of the twentieth century. Still others came as Royal Navy 'Kroomen' – African sailors recruited from the Ghana coast by the Royal Navy in the nineteenth and early twentieth centuries – or as traders from the teeming lands of India and Pakistan via Durban and Johannesburg. And all of these people have mingled with the descendants of the original Khoekhoen (or Khoikhoi, historically referred to as 'Hottentots') and San, who lived in the region long before any of the 'foreigners' had ever heard of the Cape of Good Hope. This dynamic flow and intermixing of people is the reality of South African society.

This story alone would make southern Africa special, but our recent history, much of it unpleasant, has added other issues that have an impact on forensic anthropology. South Africans today are still celebrating the great events of 1994, which gave rise to a democratic society for the first time in our history, but the events of our past have not been erased by the political transformation.

We are still a society obsessed with race and racial identity, even if few of us really understand the meaning of biological variation. Even today we tend to cluster according to the groupings defined and separated during the years of apartheid. There is undeniably some progress towards a unified society, but the vast majority of us still see our identity in terms of 'white', 'coloured', 'Indian' and 'black' South Africans. This is not a biological classification but a 'folk' taxonomy or vernacular naming system based on biology and overlaid by culture, language, religion and history.

You might ask whether the practice of forensic anthropology is any different here from what it is overseas. Isn't crime the same everywhere? Surely murder is murder and it doesn't differ between the Cape and London? In fact, it is not different. The evidence of death is the same, but the context is local. We live in a society where it is easy to become invisible. Bureaucratic records are incomplete and many people here actually hide from bureaucracy. Therefore, when an unknown skeleton turns up (something that probably happens at least half a dozen times a month in South Africa), we don't have an easily manageable database to match with missing persons' records. Add to this the thousands of our fellow Africans who cross our borders undocumented each year and it becomes obvious that identification of unknown bodies is a special problem for South Africans. We are also a relatively under-studied population. Forensic anthropology standards of bone growth, maturation and variation are well documented for the populations of European origin, but there is far less information available for Africans.

In addition, we have particular local twists to murder. Favourite weapons in the rural districts include the knobkerrie, a knobbed stick of hard wood, and the panga, a broad-bladed bush knife. One of my first observations on the cadaver collection of skeletons when I was a student in Johannesburg was a deeply depressed skull fracture with a thin longitudinal depressed trough leading away from the frontal bone – the very clear mark of a knob and its shaft. Even more amazing was that the skull bones had healed, telling me that the poor man had survived the attack and lived on to die of something else later.

Politics and social beliefs are also local issues. We have the infamous 'necklace' of the apartheid years, when cooperation with the apartheid state could earn you a horrible death from having a burning tyre placed over your head and shoulders. Long after the end of apartheid, we now have the task of finding those who were killed and disposed of secretly by the apartheid state and the liberation armies. And we have the horror of muti murders, which deserves a chapter of discussion in its own right.

So these are the things I write about in this book. Call it a personal adventure in forensics. It is part text, part case list and part story. Above all, it is set in Africa and the experiences are South African.

I need to ask one last question: Why should I have written this? Who am I to wear the crown of forensic anthropology? I did not train as a forensic anthropologist; in many ways I fell into the field rather than followed a worn pathway. I arrived in South Africa as a freshly picked postgraduate student in January 1975 to study physical anthropology under Phillip Tobias in Johannesburg. In Canada, where I had spent my undergraduate years, this would have meant joining a Department of Anthropology, but at the University of the Witwatersrand (Wits), it meant working in anatomy in a medical school. The core knowledge was anatomical, but with Professor Tobias at the advisory helm, it could not stay that way. Anatomy intersected with fossil man, human variation, archaeology, social anthropology and politics. And every so often it overlapped with forensic medicine.

Yaşar İşcan, one of the pre-eminent figures in American forensic anthropology, has written about the rise of forensic anthropology as a discipline in the United States. He tells us that, in the early years, anthropologists filled an advisory role as anatomists and weren't recognised as forensic experts. A critical issue in the development of the science was the growth of large collections of human skeletons assembled for research by these anthropologists. Two collections in particular, the Terry Collection, originally in St Louis but now in Washington, and Cleveland's Hamann-Todd Collection, became major resources for sex, age and race determination of skeletons.

It was only after the creation in 1972 of a Physical Anthropology section of the American Academy of Forensic Sciences (AAFS) that things began to change. With the official recognition that physical anthropology had a role to play in forensic science, the forensic anthropologist changed from being an *advisor* to being an *authority*. No longer was the forensic anthropologist simply an anatomical 'fundi' who gave advice to pathologists; he became a specialist in his own right.

Although we are at least thirty years behind the United States, the same kind of process has occurred here. In the past, the training of forensic pathologists rarely included much information about skeletonised human remains, so when a 'bone case' appeared on the gurney, the pathologists frequently turned to their anatomical colleagues for help. All of my anatomical predecessors have assisted in this way and many have developed a great deal of expertise. Ron Singer published a very important paper in 1953 that showed how the cranial vault sutures (the joints between the flat bones of the skull) did not fuse like clockwork and that age estimations based on cranial suture closure were unreliable. In the same year, the young Phillip Tobias in Johannesburg wrote a paper on the problems of racial identification of human skulls. The paper outlined the very issues that we continue to struggle with today.

The earliest published paper I can find on South African forensic anthropology was published in 1948 by Matthew Drennan, a professor of anatomy at the University of Cape Town (UCT). Drennan was an obvious pick for the task. He had published a book on physical anthropology in 1930 and he was well known as an anatomist with an anthropological bent. Drennan had joined forces with the senior government pathologist in Durban to identify the remains of a body burnt beyond recognition in a car discovered on a country road near the city. Together, the pathologist and anatomist confirmed that the body was that of the late Michael Wolkersdorfer, a German immigrant, and they found solid evidence of cranial fractures that showed his end to have been no accident.

Drennan would never have called himself a forensic anthropologist. He was a classically trained anatomist who simply applied his knowledge of human osteology to forensic problems. All of the anatomists in South Africa did the same thing when requested.

Of greater importance in the development of forensic anthropology in South Africa, though, is the fact that we followed the

American lead by creating research collections of human skeletons. The largest of these, the Raymond A. Dart Collection in Johannesburg, has over 3 000 individual skeletons from cadaver dissections, and it has eclipsed in size the Terry Collection in the United States, on which it was modelled. These collections have become seedbeds for research on human variation, and this has opened up research on forensic questions.

Three institutions in South Africa have developed a tradition of skeletal biology research. The most important has been the University of the Witwatersrand under the influence of Raymond Dart and Phillip Tobias.

In the Department of Anatomy (now called the Department of Human Biology) at the University of Cape Town, some physical anthropology was a focus of research under Matthew Drennan and Ron Singer, but this has expanded with my involvement since the 1980s.

The third institution is the University of Pretoria, which has developed into a school of anatomical excellence with a forensic flavour under the able leadership of Maryna Steyn.

Maryna is the first of the anatomists/anthropologists to have made the move to forensic anthropology as a separate discipline from skeletal biology. Under her guidance, the University of Pretoria has launched a full slate of forensic anthropology research and invited forensic specialists of the calibre of Yaşar İşcan and Steven Symes to visit and share in research projects.

But one significant problem has prevented the full development of a forensic speciality in anthropology in South Africa: until recently, only a person with a medical degree was legally entitled to sign a postmortem report. A scientist, no matter how knowledgeable about pathology, could not hang out a shingle as a 'forensic anthropologist' because the state perceived the discipline of forensic anthropology to be a special division of pathology, and therefore demanded a medical degree as a minimum requirement for quali-fication. Only Maryna's department has been able to bridge the gap, because she is clinically qualified, but even her students faced this problem if their only qualification was the research PhD degree.

Unlike the United States, where change came in the form of professional recognition by the AAFS, the change in South Africa was unheralded and occurred at the stroke of an administrative pen. Under pressure from forensic pathologists, the Department of Health began to recognise this new kind of clinically allied creature in 2006 and 2007. As a result, students in the Departments of Anatomy in Johannesburg, Pretoria and Cape Town are start-ing to call themselves forensic specialists instead of anatomists, and those who are graduating with higher degrees are now taking on official roles as forensic anthropological scientists.

Important in this development has been the creation of the Missing Persons Task Team (MPTT) by the National Prosecuting Authority (NPA). They have been charged with finding the bodies left over from the apartheid era, and they have drawn heavily on students who have been trained in Cape Town, Pretoria and Johannesburg. This bodes well for the future and I am pleased to be part of it.

I started this long-winded talk about anatomists and forensics to explain why I am the person to have written this book. Certainly Maryna and her team in Pretoria have completed more cases than me. The part of my work that fills me with the most pride, how-ever, and the part that I believe qualifies me in some measure to have authored this book, is my teaching work and the group of students to whom I have taught the skills necessary to become forensic anthropologists. This is especially true of those who have passed through my office in the past half a dozen years or so. We have examined new cases, worked with the police in the field, argued about anatomy and pathology, and had a terrific time doing it. I suspect that I have learnt almost as much from them as they have from me, although they have attained the degrees. In the end, it is the students who will build the field of forensic anthropology in the future, and I hope to leave a legacy of forensic anthropology through them.

1

The Role of the Forensic Anthropologist

We need to start right at the beginning by defining the role of the person we call a forensic anthropologist. This should be straightforward, but it isn't. The catch is not in the anthropologist part, but in the forensic qualifier. 'Forensic' simply means 'pertaining to the law' and comes from the Latin word *forum*, which was the site in ancient Rome where court cases were heard. The forum was a place for robust debate (including the occasional knifing, like the incident that ended the career of Julius Caesar) but overall it would not have been very different from traditional courts in our own southern African context.

Two villagers have a dispute about a cow and the case is brought before the local headman in the designated court space – the *kgotla* in Setswana or the *imbizo* in isiZulu. This is not just a convenient spot under a tree, but a formally designated location. When the *kgotla* is in session, there are rules to be obeyed. The complainants each have a turn to tell their side of the story and the debate might go on for days if the issue is important. The chief, *nkosi* in isiZulu or *kgosi* in Setswana, acts as a judge, making decisions based on the advice of his *indunas*, his lieutenants or assessors. The *nkosi* has the power to invite other parties to join the discussion. These are expert witnesses – perhaps an old man who has memories of similar disputes in the past, or maybe someone who knows something about the markings on the cattle of the herds in the district.

This is no different from the South African court system. We have a judge (the *nkosi/kgosi*) and assessors (the *indunas*) who make the final call based on the testimony heard from both the complainants and the expert witnesses. The major difference is the addition of advocates, who act as official speakers in the court (the *kgotla/imbizo*), managing the testimony and supporting one specific view or other.

The forensic anthropologist is clearly one of the expert witnesses in this system. Sometimes we use the general term 'forensic scientist' to represent all of these expert scientific witnesses, but this is not technically correct. In my opinion, there is no such thing as a forensic scientist. There is only a scientist with knowledge of a specific field who, when called as an expert witness, gives his or her opinion about that subject in the court. Many scientific specialists can contribute to the legal debate: psychologists, demographers, geneticists, entomologists, physicists, chemists, archaeologists, toxicologists and pathologists, and even zoologists and botanists if the discussion involves rare or valuable animals or plants. There are even a few experts who are knowledgeable about several of these fields and come very close to being undifferentiated forensic scientists. Each of these authorities has a different expertise, but what they share is the approach to the presentation of their information to the courts. Each needs to be able to explain technical issues to non-specialists and each must also understand legal procedures.

In theory these expert witnesses are neutral, presenting the scientific facts so that the court can make an informed decision, but our legal system, unlike that of the traditional courts, is adversarial and the expert witness may be called by either the prosecution or the defence. This does present potential conflict. Although the facts are always the facts, a scientific witness called by the defence may concentrate on the unreliability of the data to sow doubt, whereas the same witness if called by the prosecution could emphasise his skill of observation in order to enhance the reliability of the data. This becomes critical when the case is being built on circumstantial evidence. The bottom line is that our expert is a specialist whose primary job is explaining his or her field of knowledge to the court.

Forensic anthropology is a specialist field that deals with the evidence that can be gleaned from human remains – both hard tissue in the form of dry bones and soft tissue in the form of dried flesh from desiccated or mummified bodies. The basic knowledge is of the anatomy, in particular the understanding of skeletal biology in humans as seen by anthropologists. The anthropologist who has specialised in skeletal biology understands a great deal about the growth, ageing, structure, function and variation of bone. The last-mentioned aspect of variation is something that makes anthropological understanding of anatomy different from that of clinically trained pathologists. Variation is studied not just as differences between individuals, but also as differences between populations and between species. The medically qualified pathologist focuses on the study of disease and the causes of death, but once decomposition of the body has advanced to the stage where organs are unrecognisable, the anthropologist steps in. When the body is down to bones, it is the anthropologist rather than the clinician who is better qualified to deal with the evidence.

Although the roots of forensic anthropology have grown from the anthropological study of skeletal biology, the application of this knowledge has become highly specific. Whereas the skeletal biologist working on the skeletons from an archaeological site will be interested in all sorts of questions about the ancient population, including historical demography, health issues and patterns of human behaviour, the forensic anthropologist restricts his or her inquest to only two key issues: the identification of the individual, and the evidence that relates to the events at death. The forensic focus also requires a different analytical viewpoint. The anthropological approach examines as many individuals as possible in order to quantify the range of variation within the group. It is inherently statistical in its analysis. By contrast, the forensic approach works with single individuals and uses statistics far less frequently. This difference may not seem terribly important, but it has major implications when the two approaches cross swords over racial identity and racial identification. But more of that later.

Not only is the anatomy of the bone important, but also the events that have led to the preservation of that bone. The archaeologists and palaeontologists call this the study of 'taphonomy'. It embraces the evidence of death, and the accumulation and preservation of bones over time. Forensic anthropology has borrowed this knowledge and applies it directly to forensic questions. Forensic anthropologists therefore speak of four taphonomic periods in relation to a dead individual: the antemortem period, which covers all of the time before the death of the person; the perimortem period, which is around the time of death; the postmortem period, which includes the time between death and discovery; and the post-recovery period, which includes the process of recovery, analysis and storage of the bony evidence. Each period provides different contexts for inquiry.

During the antemortem period, the skeleton records its own details of growth and development. These can be used to develop a biological profile of the individual and help in securing identification. The perimortem period is obviously important because it includes the events and cause of death, but the postmortem stage is significant as well because it gives the time context of the crime by revealing information about the postmortem interval (PMI). In the archaeological context, the post-recovery period seems the least valuable, but the forensic context demands a careful accounting of this too. Each and every event after the discovery needs to be recorded as part of the 'chain of custody' so that there are no questions about the data when the case is discussed in court.

As mentioned earlier, forensic anthropology is a relatively new field. It has been recognised only for the past thirty years or so, but it has become incredibly well known to the public in recent years as a result of the popularity of television programmes such as *CSI: Crime Scene Investigation*, *Silent Witness*, *Da Vinci's Inquest*, *Cold Squad*, *Waking the Dead* and *Bones*. I must admit that I enjoy watching programmes with anthropological or forensic themes. It is even more fun when the central hero is an anthropologist or a forensic scientist of some sort and he (or she) is able to bring superior knowledge into play to solve the crime or unravel the mystery. Indiana Jones is great, but I would have him arrested and shot for destroying archaeological sites if he were a member of my university department. I am sure that other archaeologists around the world feel the same way about Indiana Jones's predilection for site destruction, but that doesn't stop them wearing Indiana Jones–style hats and *Raiders of the Lost Ark* T-shirts as standard field attire.

I know that these programmes are only make-believe, but sometimes the characters do the most amazingly unscientific things. I watched in disbelief a couple of years ago when the 'professor' in the English television series *Primeval* reached down and counted the ribs in order to identify the sex of a skeletonised body that had been dispatched by a prehistoric creature. Come on, the guy is supposed to be a palaeontologist! Counting ribs doesn't identify sex. What misinformed writer managed to get that into the screenplay without the knowledge of the scientific advisor?

It would be laughable if it were only television, but you would be surprised to discover how much forensic and anthropological knowledge is being passed to the lay public by such sources. The American forensic specialists are starting to call it the '*CSI* effect' after the forensic science drama *CSI*. Now anyone who has a television set, goes to the movies or reads a good detective novel thinks he or she knows more about forensic science in general and forensic anthropology in particular than many of the practitioners in the field! The *CSI* effect is actually a dangerous phenomenon, because few of these media-educated investigators know much about solving crimes, and even less about the science that forms the backbone of investigative techniques.

The *CSI* effect causes problems by creating the misconception that forensic science can solve crime as quickly and as definitively as it is done in television crime shows. Not only that, but it creates the impression that scientific data are absolutely infallible. The public is therefore developing the unrealistic expectation that forensic science can solve all questions quickly and fully. In addition, no idea of the real cost of the tests and the time involved is given. Frequently the investigation, laboratory work and police interrogation all happen at the same time in these programmes and are carried out by the same individuals. The *CSI* investigator finds the evidence, analyses the data and interviews the suspects in just a day or two. This makes the stories dramatic and entertaining, but not very much like real life. The reality involves different teams of people and potentially long periods of investigation before a suspect is even identified, let alone interviewed. Certainly in South Africa a forensic pathologist will be brought out to a crime scene, but it is a rare occasion for a forensic *anthropologist* to be called out to the site of a crime.

In April 2009, the British Broadcasting Corporation (BBC) decided to film an episode of *Silent Witness* in Cape Town. The story was written by an English screenwriter who set the episode in the Western Cape. The producers really did want to get it right – Professor Lorna Martin, the head of forensic medicine at UCT, and I were asked to look at the script with a view to identifying any places where the story departed from what really would happen in modern South Africa. The plot involved the excavation of the skeletons of six anti-apartheid activists who had been murdered by the security police some twenty years before, so there were plenty of skeletons for me to enthuse over. There was also plenty for Lorna to examine, as the story had a sub-plot involving people-trafficking and several scenes were set in a mortuary.

There was indeed a scene that I believed to be problematic. It concerned the use of lead 210 for the dating of the skeletons. The technique is a new one and it evaluates the amount of radioactive isotope lead 210 in human bone. This is a common (and harmless) isotope found in the air that has a short half-life of only twenty-two years. Since the half-life is the time it takes for one half of the original material to decay into something else, it is perfect for measuring periods of time of less than fifty years or so, and there-fore has the potential accuracy to identify the time of death to within a year.

Rain washes the radioactive lead out of the air and the lead lodges in the soil. It is eventually taken up by plants and passed on to animals and humans, who eat the plants. However, not all plants pick it up at the same rate. Peanuts, coffee and seafood are all pref-erential lead 210 hoarders, so if a diet is heavy in these foods, there will be a higher lead 210 value in the tissues and biochemistry, which will indicate that a person is much younger than he or she really is. From the forensic perspective, the lead 210 analysis will show that this person died five years earlier, but in reality he or she has been dead for ten years. This will make a mess of the investigation. So, if we don't know a person's diet, we can't standardise their lead values and the date of death will be unreliable. The technique is still being refined and very few forensic laboratories use it.

Despite my concerns, the producers of the show decided to keep the scene in anyway. They showed a central character, Nikki, liter-ally taking a bone sample and putting it into some kind of gadget that read out the lead 210 value. It made a great scene, but it was plain wrong.

I could have blown the whistle on this little bit of reality-stretching, but I was bought by the producers: they offered me a bit part as a Canadian professor giving a talk at a conference where the two central *Silent Witness* characters, Nikki and Harry, are sitting in the audience discussing the case. All I had to do was sound professorial – something that I am actually quite good at. I was even able to write my own lines, and I delivered a 500-word treatise on the use of carbon 14 in forensic investigations. I had such fun that I decided to overlook the lead 210 anomaly, so I am probably guilty of spreading the *CSI* effect even further. I do have a secret, though, that was buried in the BBC production archives until I decided to reveal it here: the 'bone' that Nikki used to date the skeletons was, in fact, my lower left first molar. The producers asked if I had a specimen they could use for the scene and I offered them the tooth, which I keep in a jar on a shelf beside my desk. I had it extracted in 2005 and I keep it as a teaching specimen. It worked well in the scene. So technically I should have received two credits for the episode – one as the Canadian professor and the other as the unnamed body part analysed for lead 210 content.

But the real world is very different from the world of television make-believe. What happens, exactly, when human skeletons are discovered, and when is the forensic anthropologist called in? In South Africa, the process is usually initiated by the police.

The law and common sense dictate that if you are working in your garden and you dig up a skeleton, the first thing you should do is notify the police. The police will halt any further disturbance of the bones before creating a police investigation docket and assigning an investigating officer to the case. This officer may request a Crime Scene Unit (CSU) from the police to come to the site, but this isn't always necessary. If the located body has been part of a police search for a missing person or if the body is in a state of decomposition that suggests a death in the previous few weeks or months, then the CSU will be called. However, if the body is completely skeletonised and has been there for many years, the investigating officer may call only the Forensic Pathology Services (FPS). Forensic Pathology, which is part of the Department of Health, has the sole right to remove, examine and store the human remains. Each case will then be assigned a Clinical Forensic Medical Officer – the state forensic pathologist. This is the person who will phone me.

Under South African law, specifically the Inquest Act, anyone who dies of anything other than 'natural causes' must be the subject of an inquest. A magistrate is required to: 1) record the identity of the person; 2) determine the cause or likely cause of death; 3) confirm the date of death; and 4) determine if anyone is criminally responsible for the death. This makes absolute sense if the body is whole, slowly cooling and bleeding from a knife wound in the chest, but it is difficult to carry out these steps if the body is skeletonised, and impossible if the case is an old one. This means that the first question asked of the forensic anthropologist is whether the case at hand is a forensic one. Sometimes the answer is really obvious. A historic burial with an associated eighteenth-century clay pipe buried in the basement of a historic homestead is clearly not a forensic case. A report on the bones still needs to be done, but you can almost guarantee that the report included in the police docket will never be opened again by anyone for any reason. You can almost hear the sigh of relief from the investigating officer on realising that he or she won't have to do any more work on this one.

The forensic anthropologist becomes a gatekeeper for what happens next. If he or she identifies the body as being of forensic interest, then police protocol is continued and all evidence is sealed in evidence bags with the chain of custody carefully maintained. The report on the skeleton will go to the state pathologist, who will include it in his report to the investigating officer. This will be added to the paperwork needed for the inquest and any criminal case initiated afterwards. If, instead, the forensic anthropologist records the skeleton as coming from an archaeological context, then the dictates of the Inquest Act fall away and the report must be redirected to the South African Heritage Resources Agency (SAHRA), as it falls under the National Heritage Resources Act of 1999 (or the 'Heritage Act' for short).

On the rare (but thankfully increasingly common) occasion that the forensic anthropologist is called out to the site of discovery, this choice can be made earlier. If it is obvious that the remains are archaeological and still in context, then the police and State Pathology will close their investigation immediately and the site will be reported to SAHRA. Professional archaeologists will then be called to the scene and archaeological protocol of excavation will take over. Often the state museums, such as the Iziko South African Museum in Cape Town, have archaeological staff who can become involved right away, but, if there is a chance that the burial is from the historic period and living descendants may still have an interest, the Heritage Act demands a specific procedure.

The Act defines any graves older than sixty years before the present as part of its legal preserve. If such a grave is disturbed by construction, all construction work must stop and a sixty-day period begins in which an attempt is made to contact all possible descendants and descendent communities. A decision on whether or not excavation will continue is then made in consultation with all of these interested parties. This can be a complicated process and I will take you through some examples later in this book. Most important is that, if it is agreed that the skeletons can be moved, excavation must be done by a professional archaeologist and must include a physical anthropology report.

Historic burials that date between the period of European contact and sixty years before the present are managed by SAHRA, but pre-colonial graves are handled by the provincial heritage divisions. The only time that excavation can occur without the sixty-day contact period is if the skeletons are being destroyed by erosion or the damage caused by the construction is so great that the grave site cannot be stabilised.

FIGURE 1: Police and archaeological procedures on the discovery of skeletons

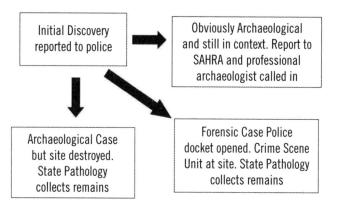

The two management pathways – forensic and archaeological – have different outcomes as far as the forensic anthropologist is concerned. Sadly, the hierarchical nature of the government bodies involved in forensic cases means that no report-back is made to the forensic anthropologist once the bone report has been submitted. The forensic anthropologist may never know the outcome of the inquest unless he or she is called to court to testify. The archaeological report is much more academic and, if the anthropologist is willing to do the bone description, such cases are often published in the academic literature.

2

The Lab Analysis

Forensic Pathology Services is responsible for removing bodies from the site of discovery. They slip the remains of the body into a plastic body bag or a clear-plastic police evidence bag, depending on the preservation state, and then deliver the bag to the assigned mortuary, where the forensic pathologist takes charge. That is my contact person and it is the forensic pathologist who phones or emails me with the exciting news of a new case.

The exact place that I look at the bones depends on their preservation state. I once brought a seriously smelly case into the department at the medical school, but my colleagues were so nauseated by the odour that I agreed never to do it again. Nowadays I do the dry-bone cases in the department and the 'wet'-bone cases at the Salt River mortuary down the road from the medical school.

Once the bones are in my custody, we begin a forensic anthropology inquest by looking at the remains in a specific order. At one time I was the only anthropologist responsible for the analysis of these cases in my department, but in 2009 we hired one of my newly graduated PhD students, Jacqui Friedling, and we now alternate in the job or work as a team, and one of us writes the final report.

The first task is to lay out all of the remains in anatomical position on the laboratory table. This can take some time, depending on the skill of the helpers. Jacqui or I could do the task alone, but not only would that be no fun, it would also deprive us of an excellent teaching opportunity. There are always postgraduate students around, so I generally warn everyone that a forensic case is coming in, and the students have the opportunity to do the sorting.

Laying out the skeleton on the table allows us to make a number of observations. Right away we know if we have more than one person on the table. We are also able to sort the non-human material from the human material. This is a frequent occurrence if the bones come from a disturbed archaeological context, not only because animal bone may be in direct association with the skeleton, but also because the FPS team picks up all of the bone at the discovery site because they are not sure which bones are human and which are not. This does occasionally mean that we receive bird and seal bones from the beach or old braai bones discarded from a picnic site a few metres away, but this is normally pretty obvious because of the difference in bone preservation.

Laying the skeleton out on the table also allows us to begin recording the preservation state of the bones. If the skeleton is incomplete, it is necessary to establish which bones are missing. We also have to assess whether the bones look the same and determine whether any of the bones have been exposed to different preservation conditions. Sun bleaching can tell us the position in which the bones were lying at the time of discovery even if the remains were disturbed by post-discovery events. Sometimes the bones have been moved by the person who discovered them before the police were called, a situation that often occurs when the discovery is on a construction site. At this time we also make detailed recordings of the remnants of adhering soft tissue ('biltong' in local

South African parlance) and signs of the chemical decomposition of bone from soil moisture or plant roots.

Once records of completeness and preservation have been made, we begin the second task. I like to call this the 'demographic' analysis, as it consists of identifying the sex, age and biological origin (race) of the skeleton. The investigating officer usually asks for these three things before anything else is asked about the case, yet the information is actually of limited use in making a personal identification of the individual. What it does is reduce the search categories, which to an investigating officer really means, 'What missing persons' file do I look in?' Confirming the sex of the skeleton reduces the search categories by half, and age and race estimates further diminish the number of possible people that the corpse could be.

These categories are very broad and tend to reflect the demographic structure of our population rather than individual identity. If I identify an individual as a black male of between fifty and sixty years of age, this would represent probably 100 000 South Africans. Clearly, I could not go to court and identify such an individual as 'Sipho Khumalo' based on the fact that Sipho Khumalo was a fifty- to sixty-year-old black male. I need much more specific information to make that identification. That information is gleaned during the 'biographic' analysis, which will be my third task.

We look at sex first. Common knowledge says this should be quite easy because it is obvious that we can only be male or female, but things are more complicated than that, even with living people, never mind skeletons. Each of us has four components of sex. The first, genetic sex, is determined by whether or not we carry two X-chromosomes (female) or an X- and a Y-chromosome (male). The second, anatomic sex, is what we have between our legs: a vagina or a penis, ovaries or testes. The third, physiologic sex, is whether or not we can produce viable sperm or eggs and whether or not our reproductive cycle is continuous or monthly. The last, gender role, concerns how we would like to appear in society. Do we wear men's or women's clothing; do we wish to be known as Priscilla or Peter?

Sex determination is particularly difficult when we have only bones to assess. Using DNA analysis, bones can tell us the genetic sex of the body, but the other three elements remain unknown. We can guess at anatomic sex, but only on the basis of some pelvic characteristics that link to the enlarged birth canal and the assumed presence of female sex organs.

We can also guess at physiologic sex if we look at features of maturity that develop as part of sexual dimorphism in men and women after puberty. Sexual dimorphism literally means 'two shapes for sex', and we use this in our daily lives to tell the difference between men and women. The problem is that these features are nearly all encased in fat and skin, not bone, so it is not always obvious on the skeleton.

The issue of gender confuses everything because it is based on behaviour, while the sex is based on biology. Some of our fellow citizens live a life with a different gender from that which their sex indicates.

Now that you are confused over whether you are Arthur or Martha, I will tell you what to look for on the skeleton to identify sex. Our final decision is a diagnosis based on the sum of all the features that we have examined. The first clue is body size. A very big person (over 1.8 metres tall) is likely to be a man, and a very small person (under 1.5 metres tall) is likely to be a woman. I know that this is a 'thumbsuck', but it is generally true on first impression. On average, men are about 10 to 15 per cent larger than women, something that is more obvious in communities that are well nourished than in those that are under nutritional stress. This does mean, though, that there is a huge overlap in size between men and women, which in turn means that this method of identifying sex is unreliable unless the bone specimen is very large or very small.

Clue number two is muscularity. Men are generally stronger than women, but the really important fact is that men have high levels of the sex steroid testosterone circulating in their bloodstream, and, like any steroid, testosterone enhances muscle mass in response to exercise. This means that men have larger muscles and larger scars on their bones where the muscles attach. The upper limb is a particular site of muscle-power differential.

As a practical exercise, I have asked generations of first-year medical students at UCT to try their luck at squeezing a hand dynamometer that measures muscle strength. It is a great exercise because when I average the values obtained from men and those obtained from women in the class, the men are always twice as strong. The ladies can do nothing about it, because it is a direct reflection of sexual dimorphism in muscle development in the presence of testosterone. The best places to see the difference in muscle scarring are on the clavicle (collar bone) and the humerus (upper arm bone).

Once again, though, this is not absolute. Although a few females hyper-develop their shoulder muscles, there are many males who do not show strong muscle development. In the words of Arnold Schwarzenegger, there are 'manly men' and 'girlie men'.

The best place to look for sexual features is in the pelvis, because this is the site where we can best see the anatomy of parturition – there is indeed an anatomy for delivering babies. The problem is that a baby's brain is already well developed at birth, which means that, as the head of the infant is large, the cervix of the woman must be large enough to accommodate its passage during labour. The simplest solution would be a very large birth canal, but this would conflict with two other functions of the pelvis. The pelvis needs to be narrow in order to give good support and leverage to its muscles and ligaments to ensure that the bowels and their contents stay in their proper place in the abdominal cavity. Gravity is constantly pulling our abdominal contents downward and it is these muscles and ligaments that help prevent incontinence. The pelvis also needs to be narrow because it transfers the weight from our upper body through the lumbar vertebrae, down the sacrum (the back part of the pelvis), across the pelvis and into our hips. Wider hips could result in instability while walking and running. Like most things biological, the answer is a compromise. Women do have wider birth canals and hips, but they are not wide enough to make delivering a baby a painless exercise. So the bad news for women is great news for forensic anthropologists, because it is easy to read the differences that give women the birth-canal edge.

The breadth across the woman's pubis is much greater than that of a man, and this is reflected in the width of the angle below the pubic bones. When the three parts of the pelvis are held together in anatomical position, the width of the birth canal is obvious, as is the much wider sacrum and the width of the sciatic notch, which is just below the join of the sacrum and the hip bone. These features are quite obvious and, with a bit of training and experience, it is possible to identify the sex correctly in this way at least 80 per cent of the time.

FIGURE 2: Major features of sexual dimorphism in the pelvis

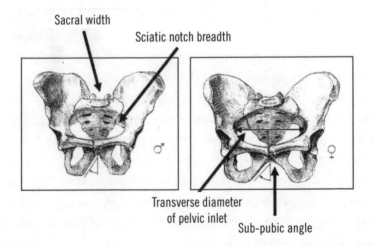

All three of the sexual features I have discussed so far are found in the skeleton below the neck, but often the forensic anthropologist receives only a skull. Fortunately for forensic anthropologists, the skull also has sexually dimorphic structures. Until puberty, it is extremely difficult to tell the difference between a male and a female cranium, but there are some secondary sexual characteristics that become obvious once puberty has been reached. These are almost all developments in the male that make the face and skull more robust. The supra-orbital region (the area above the eyes) becomes thicker in the midline and can develop quite marked projections at the eyebrows and on the outside edge of the margin of each eye.

Although no modern humans develop a real supra-orbital shelf like that of Neanderthal man, a very masculine male can have quite a dramatic projection above his eyes. All the places where the muscles of mastication touch the bone will leave stronger scars in a male, as will the muscles of the neck that support the head from the back. The big bony bump behind the ear, known as the mastoid process, is also much enlarged in men, a factor caused by neck muscle attachments and the larger sinuses that develop within the bone in men. The chin is also more developed in males than in females.

There is a long list of other features – some obvious and others less so – and a skilled anthropologist can be quite accurate about cranial sexual identity. Once again, though, the Schwarzenegger factor of 'manly men' and 'girlie men' can confound identification. But let me reassure you: there is no correlation at all between the intensity of sexually dimorphic features and the sexual identity of the person.

Now, on to age at death. Unlike sex, where there are only two options to choose from, age is a continuous variable and assigning an age is not easy. We start by dividing people into two broad age groups: those who are still within the growing period, and those who have completed growth and are on the slippery slide to old age. Unfortunately, this event doesn't have a clear dividing line. Some argue that it is marked by the cessation of growth of the long bones. This happens at around eighteen years of age, but growth can still be detected in some individuals into their early twenties. Others argue that the dividing line must be when the ends of the long bones fuse (a process that is discussed a little later). However, although nearly all of this happens by about eighteen or nineteen years of age (coinciding with the end of growth in height), there are some places where the fusion takes place in the early twenties and the midline end of the collar bone fuses only in the late twenties. Whatever the precise point of transition, there is no sign of growth after a person has reached his or her thirties. By then a new process has taken over. Slowly but surely the bones begin to show progressive changes that are linked to wear and tear, and, as one's age progresses, bony changes occur that will alter activity patterns and bone health.

FIGURE 3: Major features of sexual dimorphism in the skull

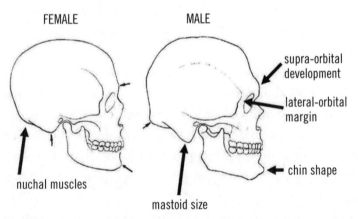

The issue of bone maturity is quite important. Bone maturity usually corresponds fairly closely to the legal definition of maturity. The question of when a person is socially mature is culture-bound, but most Western cultures tend to define it as eighteen years of age, although I know very few eighteen-year-old girls who would accept the argument that an eighteen-year-old boy is mature. Despite the culture and sex bias, the age of eighteen is frequently recorded as the age at which we take responsibility for our actions – financial, political, social and legal.

In countries where capital punishment is still practised, this age literally means the difference between life and death. Until the abolishment of capital punishment in 1994, murder in South Africa could be punished with the death sentence if the perpetrator was over the age of eighteen, but this was not a legal option if the convicted murderer was younger than eighteen at the time of the crime. This subject was exactly the situation of my very first appearance in court as an expert witness.

I was asked to appear on behalf of the defence in the murder trial of a young man in April 1987 at the High Court in Cape Town. The defence attorney, Geoffrey Wittenberg, had taken on the case pro bono and was worried that the prosecution might call for the death sentence if his young client was convicted. The case was a sad South African story. The young man on trial had been raised in dire poverty near the Namibian border. He had come to Cape Town with no education, no prospects and the belief that the streets were paved with gold. He ended up sleeping on the streets and becoming involved with a group of petty criminals who were making their living through mugging and property theft. An argument developed one evening when he sat drinking with two of his new 'friends', and, during the heat of the alcohol-fuelled debate, the young man drew a knife and stabbed one of the drinkers.

The police were keen to make an example of this case and the prosecution argued that the knifing was premeditated. Advocate Wittenberg was convinced that the young man did not plan his act, but he wanted to make sure that the death sentence was not an option if things went horribly wrong at the trial. The accused did not know his date of birth and both of his parents were dead. He thought that he was about sixteen when the murder was committed, and since he had been held in jail for nearly two years before his trial, this would have made him approximately eighteen when I became involved.

I was able to examine a hand and hip radiograph of the man and it was obvious to me that he was indeed about eighteen years old. Because this meant that he had been under eighteen years of age at the time of the crime, the death sentence was no longer an issue. My role in the trial was minimal, but it was my first experience of the court system and I learnt a great deal.

The judge agreed with Geoffrey Wittenberg that it was a spur-of-the-moment crime and that alcohol had been the aggravating factor. The sentence was lenient, but with no education and no prospects, I do not think that a very bright future for this young man lay ahead. He served his time and then disappeared from my personal radar.

Let's move away from the difficulty of determining maturity and look at the techniques that are available for estimating age. As a rule of thumb, the younger the person is, the easier it is to age them. Babies grow so fast that there is a whole sequence of bone changes that can be mapped with little difficulty. A good example is the 'soft spot' on the top of the skull, which can be felt on a living baby and is seen as a hole – known as the anterior fontanelle – in the dry bone.

During embryology, the base of the skull is preformed in cartilage, a tough but pliable material that gives support to the growing cranial nerves that pass through it. The rest of the braincase is formed by a tough membrane that covers the top of the brain but doesn't restrict brain growth. The bones of the braincase form in the membrane and grow outwards from a central point known as the primary centre of ossification. Each of the parietal bones (on the side of the skull) has one centre, as does the occipital bone (at the back), but the frontal bone has two – one on each side of the forehead. The process of ossification starts very early, when the baby is still inside the mother's womb, and by the time of the birth the bones are nearly complete.

Within a couple of months the bones touch each other and the membrane is no longer visible. The last membrane-coated hole to be covered over by the growing bone is at the junction of the two parietals and the frontals. This generally happens at around eighteen to twenty-four months, so an open hole on the skull means that the child is less than two years, while a closed hole means that he or she is older than eighteen months.

FIGURE 4: Cranial bones in a newborn infant

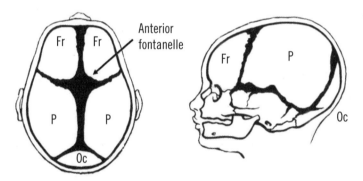

Fr: frontal   **P:** parietal   **Oc:** occipital

Even better than fontanelle closure for age estimation in the skull is the eruption and calcification of the teeth. Every dentist's office, probably in the world, will have a copy of Schour and Massler's 1941 chart of dental eruption. The first baby teeth arrive in the form of the lower central incisors at around six months. All of the baby teeth are in their sockets by about two years of age, and the first of the permanent teeth – the first molar – erupts behind the last of the baby teeth at approximately five or six years of age.

Then there is a period of 'mixed dentition', when the permanent teeth begin to erupt under the baby teeth and the child has a mix of the two sets. By nine years of age the permanent front teeth (the incisors) are fully erupted, with the second molar coming in at around twelve. All but the last molars (the wisdom teeth) are fully erupted by around the age of sixteen. It was originally thought that this process followed a clockwork schedule, but we now know that nutrition and health can interfere with the timing of eruption, if not the sequence. The third molars are often noted as erupting at around eighteen years of age, but in fact they can erupt any time between the ages of sixteen and twenty-five, and for quite a number of people they never erupt at all.

A better dental 'clock' is actually the formation of the tooth rather than its eruption. Taking a radiograph of the developing jaws shows exactly how much of the tooth crown and root has formed below the gum line. This development, or calcification, is under better genetic control than the eruption of the teeth, and it is now used to obtain a more precise age estimate. There are slight variations between world populations, and a six-month difference in the timing of eruption can occur between people with dissimilar racial origins. Vince Phillips, my colleague at the University of the Western Cape (UWC) Faculty of Dentistry explored this issue for his PhD thesis, and he has set calcification standards for South Africans of different geographic locations and origins.

There is another method of identifying age in growing children that uses not the cranial features but the bones of the post-cranial (below the neck) skeleton. Most of the long bones that make up the structure of our arms and legs begin a process of ossification after their general shape has been formed in cartilage during embryology. In the same manner as the bones of the skull vault, a primary centre of ossification begins around the middle of the shaft of the growing bone and lays down the bone itself from the middle towards both ends.

At birth, each long bone has a hard bone shaft with open ends showing the last of the cartilage. Growth takes place at the ends of the bone, with new cartilage being laid down, followed a short while later by the ossification of the bone growing outward from the shaft. This is the situation until about two or three years of age, when something very interesting happens at the ends of the bones. Deep within the cartilage a secondary centre of ossification begins to grow. This does not unite with the shaft; it develops into a little cap of bone that floats above the cartilage, getting larger at the same rate as the main shaft of the bone.

The purpose of the secondary cap, known as an 'epiphysis' (from the Latin for 'sitting on top of'), is to form a solid articular surface for each bone so that the joints are undisturbed by the growth of the bone below. The growth of the long bone happens at the junction between the epiphysis and the growing cartilage at a place called the 'metaphysis'.

Finally, at somewhere between fifteen and twenty years, depending on the bone, the ossification from the shaft of the bone catches up to the cartilage and the shaft fuses with the overlying epiphysis. No further growth in the length of the bone can occur after this, and we record the bone as 'adult'. The exact timing of the beginning of the growth of the epiphysis and the point at which it is united with the shaft differs for each joint, and a great deal of time has been spent recording this. It always happens earlier in women than in men (often by as much as two years) and there is some evidence to show that it differs in different world populations.

A few years ago I received a call from an international lawyer who was part of the Charles Taylor war crimes prosecution team in the Netherlands. Because many of the soldiers involved in the Liberian civil war were child soldiers, the request was for information on the state of growth and attainment of adulthood in African children. There are in fact almost no data on this subject, and this simple request has grown into three student projects using the low-dose digital X-ray (LODOX) scanner to look at the bones of African (and other) children. Kundi Dembetembe and Belinda Speed have both focused on the bones of the hand, while Kavita Chibba has commenced a PhD project that will examine the epiphyseal closure on the long bones of a large sample of children. Hopefully these students will give us new data for Africans.

FIGURE 5: Centres of ossification in the hand

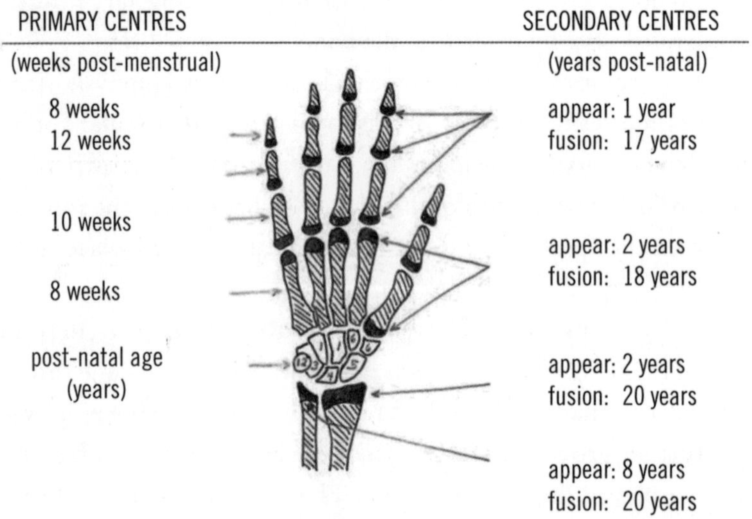

PRIMARY CENTRES	SECONDARY CENTRES
(weeks post-menstrual)	(years post-natal)
8 weeks	appear: 1 year
12 weeks	fusion: 17 years
10 weeks	
	appear: 2 years
8 weeks	fusion: 18 years
post-natal age (years)	appear: 2 years
	fusion: 20 years
	appear: 8 years
	fusion: 20 years

The textbooks give us lists of the fusion dates in long tables that I have never bothered to memorise – I figure I can look up the information when I need it. There is a general pattern of joint sequence. The first epiphyses to unite are in the wrist, while the last are at the shoulder. I learnt a mnemonic when I was student to remember the sequence: 'Every Ham Actor Knows William Shakespeare'. It stands for 'Elbow, Hip, Ankle, Knee, Wrist and Shoulder'. I know this mnemonic is very Eurocentric, but I have asked my students to come up with a new one and so far no one has come to the fore.

As an aside, these mnemonics can be very useful. When I was a student in Phillip Tobias's department in Johannesburg in the 1970s, the medical students had a great one with which to remember the eight small bones in the heel of the hand. 'Students Love To Pull Toby Tobias's Curly Hair' translated as 'Scaphoid, Lunate, Triquetrum, Pisiform, Trapezium, Trapezoid, Capitate and Hamate'.

The story of growth is over once all of the epiphyses have united with their adjacent shafts. Bones can continue to grow in width but they can never become shorter or longer. We have to turn to other features of the skeleton to identify age after this, and these are the features of degeneration rather than of growth.

Thomas Wingate Todd, working way back in the 1920s, was the first to notice a very curious fact of bone anatomy. Wherever there is a joint between bone on one side and cartilage on the other (like the place in your ribcage where the hard bone of the ribs meets the soft cartilage attaching to your sternum), the bone surface seems to change over time in a predictable pattern.

Since Todd's pioneering work, standards have been set for three anatomical locations: the pubic symphysis (in the front of the pelvis), the auricular surface of the ilium (the joint between the hip bone and the sacrum) and the sternal rib ends (usually the fourth rib-cartilage joint is used). The patterns seen in individuals of different ages have been copied in models that we have purchased for our laboratory, but they are not easy to use. It is difficult to explain the subtle differences in age categories, but once a student has grasped it, the technique works reasonably well.

There are complications, however, especially at the pubis, because of the influence of obstetric history in women, but it is generally possible to place adults into categories of about ten years. The age ranges get wider with older individuals and it is often only possible to say that a person was older than sixty at death, although the use of a new statistical technique called 'transition analysis' has helped us to be slightly more specific with the estimation of age of the very elderly. With this lack of precision, it is always best not to rely on this method alone but to try other ageing methods as well.

Teeth are a good supporting method to estimate age. We know that the form of the tooth crown is determined during growth and that, once the tooth has erupted, the shape of the crown cannot change. However, as soon as it has erupted, the tooth is exposed to wear and tear in the mouth. The chewing or 'occlusal' surface of the tooth is worn down by constant contact with food and also by the opposing crown in the opposite jaw. Wear caused by food contact we call 'abrasion', and wear caused by banging against the opposing tooth is termed 'attrition'. Tooth wear has been used as a forensic age-at-death indicator since the work of Gösta Gustafson in the 1950s.

The system is based on six observations of changing structure of the tooth with age, but Gustafson standardised his system on European dental patients. Since tooth wear is diet dependent, the system works best on modern Europeans or people with a similar lifestyle. If we assume that an unknown person had a 'Western European' diet of highly refined foods, small amounts of fibre and little grit, then Gustafson's method works really well. However, if the person had a rougher diet, then this method will overage him by a significant amount.

My colleague Vince Phillips generally uses the Gustafson system to age his forensic cases. I used to get a kick out of asking him to age Khoesan hunter-gatherer teeth for me because I knew that, if he used that system, a Khoesan individual in his late twenties would look like a forty- or fifty-year-old. There is currently no system for ageing archaeological skeletons that is as precise as Gustafson's, but Don Brothwell from the United Kingdom has set up a relative set of standards based on the exposure of dentine on the occlusal surfaces of molar teeth. This system enables us to rank individuals by relative age.

In the first half of the twentieth century it was firmly believed that the sequence of fusion of the cranial sutures was rigidly time dependent. The sutures are the edges of the bones covering the braincase that we use to age developing babies. Once the bones are complete, they do not fuse with each other because they still need to leave room for the brain to grow in later childhood. With the brain size being more or less at adult level by twelve years of age, there is no need for the bones to remain separate. However, they do not begin the process of fusion until a person has reached his or her thirties.

Earlier researchers believed that they then followed a precise sequence, but research like that of my predecessor at the University of Cape Town, Ron Singer, showed that the sequence is unreliable. We *do* know that the process tends to accelerate in middle-age and that a person with some sutural fusion is probably well past his fortieth birthday.

A similar kind of guide to older adulthood is the advent of degenerative joint disease – arthritis. Once again, it is unlikely that younger individuals will show features of arthritic change to their joints unless there is a disease process present. Normally males begin to complain about their joints from the age of about forty-five and females from about fifty.

There are two other methods of estimating age at death that warrant some discussion, although both require specialised equipment that is not always available to the investigator. I am fortunate in that my Department of Human Biology includes a division made up of biomedical engineers. Tucked away in their section of the building is a LODOX scanner that is the focus of one of their major research projects. They let me do radiographs of bones if I ask nicely, but there is a second LODOX machine at the Salt River mortuary that I can use if the engineers' LODOX scanner is unavailable.

The images from the LODOX machine clearly show the internal structure of the proximal (top) end of the long bones, another zone of age-dependent change that is particularly useful for the oldest age group. As we reach our fifties and sixties, our physiology begins to remodel the interior trabeculae (see page 234 of the glossary) of the long bone ends. These are bony struts that follow the lines of force running down the bone to give it strength. A radiograph reveals the state of this remodelling, telling us how many of the struts have been removed and how much thinner the supporting bone on the outside of the shaft has become.

By the time we are in our seventies and eighties, this process has become quite marked, and the thinning may have progressed so far that we are at risk of femoral neck fracture. Women are more at risk than men because they have wider hips and less anatomical strength in the neck of the thigh bone (remember the trade-off in the anatomy of parturition) and elderly women break their hips three times more often than men of the same age.

Last but not least is the use of microscopic bone structure for estimating age. This is the most accurate of all methods and can frequently estimate age to within five years of real age, but it requires the destruction of bone. We need to grind a cut section of long bone shaft until it is thin enough to see under a microscope. The problem is that we don't always have permission to do this. Archaeological bone is often considered to be too precious to grind up, and sometimes the cases are too socially or politically sensitive to do damage to the bone.

In terms of our 'demographic' analysis, we now have a very good idea of the person's sex and a reasonable idea of age – more accurate if the person was young at the time of death. We still need to do one more analysis to determine race, but, as this is so filled with difficulty, a new section is required to deal with it.

AN OBSESSION WITH RACE

A few years ago there was a robbery at a doctor's surgery in Claremont, a suburb of Cape Town. Two well-dressed thieves who had been posing as patients in the waiting room herded all of the staff and patients into the doctor's small surgery and relieved them of their valuables. They then removed the telephone and locked the door to ensure that there was time for a getaway. However, they missed a cellular phone that the doctor kept in one of his desk drawers, and as soon as the thieves left the doctor phoned for help.

Since the crime had happened only minutes before, the doctor rang a local talk-radio station instead of the police, and asked that word be spread that the two thieves were driving down the neighbouring Lansdowne Road in his brown BMW – the doctor even gave his licence-plate number. The radio station immediately phoned the cops and asked listeners in the area to report the whereabouts of the getaway vehicle if possible. Amazingly, there was an immediate flurry of calls to the radio station, not to provide information, but to ask what race the thieves were. Despite the fact that the make, colour and licence-plate number of the car had been broadcast, along with a brief description of the robbers as two well-dressed men, the public wanted to know their race.

Thinking back, I should not really have been surprised by the listeners' response. South Africans live in a society obsessed with race, and we are not the only ones. American society is also preoccupied with the classification of people. Both countries have a history of legislated racism and are struggling to deal with the consequences of that history.

Right in the middle of this obsession with race are the forensic anthropologists. They have the unenviable task of identifying the race of a person from skeletal information when the system that is requesting the identity of a body doesn't use the same markers to recognise race. The forensic anthropologist and the investigating officer use the same word, 'race', but have no agreement on its meaning.

In May 2007, the American Association of Physical Anthropologists held a conference for physical anthropologists in New Mexico to debate the meaning of 'race'. There was an almost immediate separation of the delegates into two camps: the 'morphologists' and the 'geneticists'.

The geneticists argued that lineage (ancestor) tracking by DNA markers clearly shows that all modern humans are derived from Africans and that the observed pattern of genetic variation does not support a simple three-group racial classification into Caucasoid, Negroid and Mongoloid.[1]

The morphologists, on the other hand, argued that worldwide geographic patterning in cranial form does produce observable regional patterns and that, although these flow into one another, there are some fairly distinct clusters. They didn't go so far as to say that the 'distinct clusters' are a good match for the three race groups, but they did suggest that statistical classification techniques used in forensic contexts have high success rates in assigning individual skulls to 'broad ancestral groups'.

The geneticists argued that 'race' simply isn't a good way to describe human variation, while the morphologists said that a person's head shape gives a pretty good idea of where his or her ancestors came from on the planet. So who is right? Does race exist, and, if it does, can people of different races be identified from the way they look?

As usual with this kind of argument, the answer is a compro-

---

1   The old names Caucasoid, Negroid and Mongoloid come from the work of Johann Friedrich Blumenbach in the early nineteenth century. Caucasoid (NOT Caucasian) refers to all of the people of Europe plus those of the Middle East and the Indian subcontinent. Negroid refers to the peoples of sub-Saharan Africa, often but not always including the Khoesan, and usually excludes the people of the Mediterranean south shore who would fall into the Caucasoid category. Mongoloid usually includes the peoples of both East Asia and the New World of the Americas. Blumenbach was not sure where to put the Australian Aborigines, so he placed them somewhere on the path to becoming Negroid. Twentieth-century racial classifications have often given the Australians their own category – Australoid.

mise. A colleague of mine in the United States refers to this as the 'any-fool-can-see' theorem. It is obvious that people from different parts of the world look different. I ask my medical students to look around at each other in class and none of them have any trouble identifying the physical features of Europe, Africa and Asia in their classmates.

But if I ask them to mentally delete the soft-tissue features – hair form, skin colour and ear shape – they agree that the task becomes harder. If I then ask them to concentrate not on the features that they assume identify race but the features of their classmates that make each individual different, then the reality of human variation becomes apparent.

It is difficult for us to make that leap because we have been trained to look for features that lump people into categories. Because we assume that black skin puts people into the Negroid category, for example, we tend to ignore the variation in skin tone that we see in the group. In southern Africa, many people who are accepted as Negroid have very pale skins, some grading into the darker skins of Caucasoid people from the Mediterranean regions.

Suddenly my students realise that all black (or white) people are not the same. I then invite them on an imaginary walk with me from Cape Town to Cairo. With us we take a 'skin reflectometer', a gadget that shines a very precise beam of light onto the skin and measures the amount of light that is reflected. Dark skin will absorb light and reflect very little of it, while pale skin will reflect a great deal of light. We are going to shine our light into the armpits of people that we meet. The reason we choose the armpit is that the skin there is not normally exposed to sunshine and therefore won't be darkened by the environmental effect of tanning.

As we walk north, skins become progressively darker until we meet people in the northern Congo, Uganda and southern Sudan, where our little gadget shows very little reflection. Then the skin colours begin to reverse and, as we travel down the Nile, there is more and more reflection. We stop in Cairo, but I tell the students that if they want to continue north on their own, they will find the most reflection on people from the north-east coast of England.

Our imaginary excursion has demonstrated two aspects of human variation that are not present in the traditional three-group racial classification. Firstly, people are tremendously variable as individuals and it is impossible to make a 'one-colour- (or shape- or size-) fits-all' definition for a race. Secondly, physical features change gradually over the globe and there are no clear dividing lines between where one race ends and the next one begins.

The geneticists agree that the three-race model isn't very clear, but they also recognise that different genetic markers (genes) are present in varying frequencies in different parts of the world. Why not use genes to identify the region people come from? Genetic data are much less ambiguous than skull shapes or skin colours. Actually, using DNA to identify race is almost pointless. There is no such thing as a 'race gene'. Each of us carries our heritage of genes, and examining parts of that genome (the complete set of genes) gives us interesting clues to our biological past, but it is not forensically valuable. The problem is that genes that are useful in identifying our ancestry do not tell us anything about our appearance.

Let's say that the analysis of semen from a rape case, for example, showed the presence of a single gene for Gaucher's disease (you have to have the pair of matching genes to start showing symptoms). Gaucher's disease is a rare inherited disorder that has its highest frequency in Ashkenazi Jews (the Jews of Eastern Europe). Does this mean that our rapist was a Jew? Of course not; it means our rapist had a distant ancestor who carried this one gene. In fact, there is a small number of 'coloured' people in Cape Town who carry the gene and are unaware of any Jewish connection at all. Perhaps if there were half a dozen suspects, then the Gaucher's gene might help identify the perpetrator, but why would you be interested in one gene when a whole genetic fingerprint from his semen sample would nail the guy with absolute certainty?

A similar situation would be the presence of an L0 mitochondrial gene: the so-called 'Bushman gene' because it is present in nearly 100 per cent of Khoesan people. However, once again this gene marks the heritage of *one* female ancestor, and all it says is that the person had a Khoesan ancestor somewhere along the line. If our rapist showed L0 in the analysis of his semen, who do we tell the police to look for? The L0 mitochrondrial haplotype is not visible on the outside, so we would have to make a jump in logic. If our man has L0 in his genome (which means he had a female Khoesan ancestor), then we might want to assume that he looks Khoesan. So we tell the police to look for a short guy with yellowish skin and tight peppercorn hair. But in reality he could look like any one of a million men in the city of Cape Town. At least half of our population has a 'mixed ancestry' and a significant portion of those might very well have a distant Khoesan ancestor. So we stop telling the police to look for a 'Bushman' and we start telling them to look for a 'coloured' person instead. We have now crossed the boundary and moved out of biology and into sociology and politics.

A 'scientific' classification of people is supposed to be based on physical features of biological origin, but the popular concept of race is actually a social classification system. It is a folk taxonomy that summarises the popular perception of racial categories agreed on by people within the society. Taxonomy is simply a system of naming, and the old three-race grouping of Caucasoid, Negroid and Mongoloid is a good example, but it was created by scientists trying to shoehorn the wide range of human variation into three manageable groups.

A folk taxonomy may have its roots in actual biological differences between people, but it really is a conflation of ethnicity and biology. Ethnicity is about culture: religion, language, family structure, socio-economic level, clothing style and psychological differences. Ethnicity is often unstable, changing with the social and political transformation of the society that has spawned it. As the definition of a folk taxonomy is a combination of biological and social factors, it is different in different parts of the world.

The category 'coloured' in South Africa, for example, is very complex but has historically referred to people of a 'mixed genetic ancestry'. It is a boundary group between 'black' and 'white', both in themselves categories with significant cultural contexts. However, in the United States, the historical use of the term 'colored' (nowadays 'African American') refers to anyone with a partial African ancestry. Historically it would include anyone with one-sixteenth African ancestry – that is to say, having had an African ancestor four generations before: a great-great-grand-mother or grandfather who was African.

In the United States, someone who could trace his roots directly to an African ethnic group such as Zulu or Sotho would be in-cluded in the 'African American' category, but not in South Africa, where such a person would be considered 'black' (coming from a traditional African people speaking a Bantu language and having an African culture).

Despite the confusion in a folk taxonomy of ethnic and biological features, however, it is the folk taxonomy that has a real impact on people's lives, especially as related to social and health inequalities. In apartheid South Africa (1950 to 1991), the folk taxonomy was made real by law, and race classification had an impact on every aspect of every citizen's life. Although legislated apartheid is long gone, its system of classification is still with us and continues to influence our lives.

The apartheid classification was intended to entrench the eco-nomic and political dominance of the white minority, and also to ensure that the white group maintained an imagined racial purity and was not 'diluted' by mixture with other races. An original system of three races ('White', 'Bantu' and 'Mixed') evolved into a four-category administrative system of 'White', 'Black', 'Coloured' and 'Indian', where 'Coloured' was intended as the catch-all category including not only those of mixed genetic ancestry, but also those who historically came as slaves from the Dutch East Indies, Ceylon (now Sri Lanka) and South China, and those of Khoesan ancestry, mixed or not.[2]

Indians, sometimes called 'Asians' in official documents, were given their own group on the basis that they were culturally distinct and had their recent roots on the Indian subcontinent. Eventually even these categories were subdivided into a myriad smaller groups defined primarily by culture. They included separate black identities for each 'homeland' and separate identities for various 'Coloured' people (Malay, Chinese and Griqua, for example).

All of this categorisation had residential, social and political implications. Special permission, for instance, was needed for a Malay person to marry an Indian even though both might be Muslim and South African born, because apartheid demanded that Indian and 'Coloured' people live in different areas. Although there were obvious ethnic differences within the white group, at least at a similar level to Malay versus Indian, white ethnic groups were never administratively separated.

The end of apartheid officially brought an end to this system of classification and, from 1991, race was no longer a category entered in the population register. However, most South Africans continue to have clear racial identities and still view others in terms of the four apartheid 'races'. There is still relatively little social or residential integration.

My colleagues at UCT, Jeremy Seekings in the Department of

2 Mrs Marike de Klerk, later to become South Africa's first lady, was quoted in 1983 as saying, 'The definition of a coloured in the population register is someone that is not black, and is not white and is also not Indian, in other words a no-person' (Maclennan, 1990: 59).

Sociology and Mohamed Adhikari in the Department of History, have independently pointed out that different groups within our folk taxonomy see each other and themselves in very different ways. Black and coloured South Africans tend to think of themselves in terms of 'culture' groups, whereas whites are inclined to perceive physical features such as paler skin to be more important. Culture for whites appears to be less of an issue than biological appearance.

Coloured people have tended to internalise a negativity about their identity as being 'neither white nor black'; nevertheless, the idea of a coloured identity separate from other groups has strengthened since the end of apartheid because of a perceived loss of privilege of coloured people to black African members of society.

So where does forensic anthropology fit into all of this? It is difficult for us to reconcile the demand from the police for an identity based on folk taxonomy with a scientific classification system that uses physical appearance of bones as the sole classifying method. Many forensic anthropologists, both in South Africa and overseas, still fail to see the difference between the two systems.

Despite our growing understanding of human variation in the post–World War II period, W.M. Krogman chose to give a very rigid nineteenth-century view of racial variation in his book *The Human Skeleton in Forensic Medicine*. His table of cranial features for each race has remained unchanged in the 1986 edition of the book by Yaşar İşcan. Krogman continued to use a stereotype of race that was already being dismantled in the other branches of physical anthropology at the time. It contains an overemphasis on Europeans, giving them three regional variants, compared to its single stereotyped description of all people of African and Asian origin, as if somehow all Negroids and Mongoloids look alike.

Knowing of the battle among anthropologists in the 1990s concerning the use of the old three-category racial system, I did a quick sampling on my bookshelf and found three books on forensic anthropology published in 1999 and 2000. To my surprise (and horror) it appears as if the three racial categories of Caucasoid, Mongoloid and Negroid are still very much alive. The worst of the three was *Forensic Anthropology 2000*, published by the National Museum of Health and Medicine and the Armed Forces Institute of Pathology in the United States. Unashamedly the book says that 'in forensic anthropology three races are considered' and then goes on to give Krogman's list of cranial features for the skull. Myriam Nafte's little book *Flesh and Bone: An Introduction to Forensic Anthropology* was better. She also cites the three-race table with a list of features, but is fairly circumspect in its use. Nafte obviously followed the race debate in the literature, as she writes:

> Whatever the classification scheme, however, the use of these racial categories is considered problematic primarily because it relies on the concept that standard racial traits are inherited in a consistent pattern and can be generalized into well-defined geographic categories.

My third reference was Karen Burns's *Forensic Anthropology Training Manual*, which is even cagier. She also provides a table of racial features, but she doesn't refer to them in the three racial categories. Rather, she classifies them as 'American Indians', 'European Whites' and 'African Blacks'.

Burns has narrowed down the big races into slightly smaller groups – an interesting try, but not entirely successful, and still problematic. She goes on to warn the analyst of the race trap and proposes that the practitioner rely on more detailed description, listing each trait and referring to the literature for exact frequencies of these traits in racial groups. Burns then suggests that the report 'allows room for interpretation and use[s] the terminology that best communicates with the people that will be reading the report'. She is at least recognising that there may be confusion between the scientific perception of race and that of the police.

This means that the forensic anthropology textbooks haven't helped at all. In 1996 two anthropologists from the University of Tennessee, Stephen Ousley and Richard Jantz, produced a computer program called FORDISC, which can be used to identify race from cranial measurements. This is a discriminant-function software package. The technique makes use of at least ten measurements on a known set of groups of reference skulls. It then combines these measurements in such a way to make the groups of reference skulls look as different from each other as possible.

If, for example, a few of the groups of people have very narrow faces with projecting noses – a feature frequently seen in people from the European continent – then it will give extra mathematical weight to the measurements that tell us about narrow, projecting noses. This will make these people appear more different from the other people on the graph than they really are in life. This is called discrimination.

The same ten measurements are then introduced for our unknown skull and the mathematics compares the new measurements to the sets of reference skulls, and places our unknown body as close as possible to the best-fitting group. The database that Ousley and Jantz used is mostly that of William White Howells, who gathered measurements on skulls in museums all over the world in the 1960s. He ended up with twenty-eight population samples, but Ousley and Jantz have augmented these reference groups by adding more skulls from their own research and from the literature, where available.

The program works reasonably well but is limited by the fact that not all world populations are represented. The discriminant function will force a skull from a different population into the nearest 'best-fit' group and this can sometimes lead to spectacular errors.

Many of the papers currently being presented at forensic anthropology conferences, especially in the United States, discuss the use of the FORDISC program and concentrate on ways to improve its statistical success in identifying Caucasoid, Negroid and Mongoloid skulls from cranial measurements. This bothers me very much, as I struggle to comprehend why an anthropologist who has studied human variation and understands the difficulty in fitting racial types to reality is still prepared to use this mathematical application based on old racial science.

The explanation for this anomaly is that it is grounded in legal practice, not science. The problem for the courts is that scientific evidence must be clear and precise to be acceptable. If the evidence is based on the skill of the observer rather than the result of a well-defined scientific methodology, then the testimony of the expert witness can be contested on the basis of its being his or her 'opinion' rather than fact.

The output of a laboratory machine or a statistical calculation is seen by the court as hard evidence unaffected by the skill of the technician. If the dot on the graph falls below the line marking the halfway point between the average values of the reference samples, then the unknown person must be from the race whose members are mathematically defined by that group average. I guess this would make sense if you are reading blood alcohol results or a specific sequence of base pairs on a strand of DNA, but it makes no sense when applied to the continuous range of highly variable cranial shapes in humans.

My colleagues in Pretoria are currently adapting FORDISC for South African use, but I am not hopeful. I have no idea how they are going to create mathematical formulae that will allow the continuous range of variation of people in Cape Town to be divided into categories. I wonder how they are going to factor in language, religion and accent – characteristics that are used to identify race in this region.

If you were hoping for a list of features that identify race, you must be pretty disappointed by now. And I still haven't divulged my answer to the police when they ask me for a racial identification. I do indeed have a technique; it is called the 'exclusion principle'. I try to imagine myself being cross-examined by the most tenacious and aggressive prosecuting attorney in the business, and I ask myself, 'What do I absolutely know for sure, and what am I guessing at?'

Rather than try to fit my unknown skull into a stereotyped average value, I try instead to suggest which group he or she is most *unlikely* to be a member of. I am often most confident about the ancestry that my unknown skeleton does *not* have. I look at the full range of variation of cranial characteristics for the likely population and I note which osteological traits are missing from my skull. I look at the dispersion graph of cranial features of my various reference samples and determine if my guy falls outside of the range of variation of any of them. Then I am quite confident about saying whom he is not, but I am very careful about saying who he is.

I tend to use expressions like 'falls within the range of' or 'cannot be excluded from'. I am also not afraid to say that I don't know. I realise that this frustrates the police, but I would rather leave them frustrated than send them on a wild goose chase if I get the category wrong.

The bottom line is that, once we have a possible identification for our unknown, we would never confirm the identification on the basis of race. The final identification is based on the distinct appearance of the individual. Visible features that mark us as individuals are *not* related to race.

And that is where we must go now – to the part of the laboratory analysis that looks at individuality, the biographic component.

THE BIOGRAPHY OF THE SKELETON

It has been a hard slog, but we now have a good idea of sex and age, and hopefully some idea of biological origin. We have completed the 'demographic' part and can now begin to concentrate on task three – the issue of individuality. We need to ascertain what this skeleton tells us about the person in life, and we try to use this information to identify him and tell the story of the events leading to his death.

The first step is to determine the stature of the individual. We have known for a long time that the length of the bones of our limbs is proportionate to our standing height. Our skeleton forms the frame for our body, and adding up the length of each contributing bone will give us 90 to 95 per cent of the total height of the person. A French physical anthropologist named Georges Fully did exactly this in the 1950s. He added up the height of the skull, the body of each vertebra from the neck to the top of the pelvis, the length of the femur and tibia, and the combined height of the bones of the heel and the ankle. He then created a 'correction factor' from cadaver data that included the average value of the thickness of the skin of the foot and scalp and the thickness of the discs in between each vertebra.

'Fully's Method', as it became known, is still the most accurate way of reconstructing the height of a person from his bones, but it is of limited use because we don't always have a complete skeleton to measure. We have to introduce an average value for any bones that are missing and this affects the reliability of the result.

The second-best way of reconstructing stature is from regression data. For generations anthropologists have measured the length of cadavers and then compared those measurements to the length of the long bones from the same individuals. This has enabled them to create mathematical formulae to predict the height of a person from the length of individual bones.

There can be errors. One fascinating fact is that a person is taller when dead than when alive. This is because when you are standing upright, there is pressure on your vertebral column that compresses the discs. The compression is greater the longer you stand – you are therefore shorter in the evening than you are in the morning. In death, the discs relax and you are taller, a factor that needs to be calculated to adjust the height reconstruction formula.

Regression formulae are not as accurate as Fully's Method, but they do give us a quick method that works well if we are certain about the sex and genetic origin of the person. We need to know sex and race because different sexes and local populations have different limb proportions in relation to their height. In South Africa we have good formulae for people of South African black and white origin from the cadaver collections, but not for people of other groupings. But is an age- and sex-free method of ascertaining height in life possible?

Some years ago, John Lundy produced just such a calculation. John was a postgraduate student with me in Johannesburg in the late 1970s but returned to his native United States to become a forensic anthropologist after finishing his PhD. It is his doctoral research data on height reconstruction of South African black people that we still use today. John and his colleagues went through the data on over 10 000 skeletons and found that there was a very strong general relationship between the femur length and height, and if you simply multiplied the maximum femur length by 3.745, then you would achieve a pretty good estimate of stature in life for anybody.

I must admit that I have given this value to several generations of forensic pathologists, but it really is a lazy man's estimate and it doesn't always work well. Although it seems moderately accurate for people of average height, it is seriously flawed for use in very tall or very short people. It is not bad as a thumbsuck, but it is not nearly as accurate as the population- and sex-specific formulae.

We also need to know the age at death because people get shorter as they grow older. The long bones never change their lengths, but the soft-tissue intervertebral discs become compressed, reducing the height of the person. Each disc is like a golf ball, with a thick outer layer of dense fibres (the annulus fibrosus) and an inner viscous, fluid-filled compressible centre (the nucleus pulposus). The disc acts as a shock absorber, and if you jolt your back, like when you walk down steps, the nucleus is compressed and the force moves sideways into the annulus on each disc. The force is at least partially dissipated by the time it reaches your lower back.

As you grow older, the annulus becomes less efficient and allows the nucleus to flatten, dropping your height. This can be quite dramatic by the time you reach your sixties or seventies – it is possible to lose as much as two centimetres of stature in old age.

As part of task three, we now start to look in detail at the structure and shape of each bone, moving up the skeleton from the feet to the head. We are searching for signs on the bone of the activity pattern of the person in life, and for any signs of health or disease on the bones. We also now need to look very carefully for anything that might tell us about the events at death. There is no checklist to work through and this part of the analysis depends heavily on the acuity of the observation of the forensic anthropologist, and his or her knowledge of what looks 'normal' on bone and what looks 'odd'.

OCCUPATIONAL, CULTURAL AND HABIT MARKERS ON BONE

Activity patterns mark bones. Nearly all of us are either right-handed or left-handed, but a few lucky individuals are ambidextrous. This shows up very early in our development and is linked to the development state of the brain. If we carefully measure the length of our arm bones and compare the length of the bones of the right and left arms, it becomes apparent that our arms are different lengths. This is the result of overusing the dominant arm during the growing period. Bone is alive and responds to extra forces by growing longer when you are a child or thicker once you are an adult. Tennis players and baseball pitchers have notoriously longer dominant arms, and it would be an interesting experiment to try out on cricketers. I predict similar results. The pliability of bones during growth, and to a lesser extent once growth has stopped, gives us a great deal of opportunity to read the activity patterns of the person whose skeleton we are now examining. There are three clues that we look for: 1) signs of increased bone lengths or enlarged muscular attachment sites; 2) increased or decreased strength of the bone itself; and 3) changes in the articular structure, suggesting that the joints could be placed in abnormal postural positions.

A very long list of signs of occupational activity has been recorded on the skeleton. I have a number of papers from the literature in my files that detail special cases ranging from Viking boatmen to medieval tailors. All of them link particular features on the bones with evidence of activity in life, so what we need to do in each case is to look for patterns that catch our eye.

A good example is one of the archaeological skeletons from the historic cemetery of Cobern Street in Cape Town. We were working our way through each of the excavated skeletons in the same way that we would do a forensic case, and we noticed some rather odd things on one skeleton in particular. The shoulders, especially the clavicles, were strongly developed, and there was a curvature to the spine. The bones of the legs were all there, but the muscle markings were not as strong as on the upper limb bones. We were seeing the signs of someone who had habitually used crutches.

Two of my students have studied particular bony signs of activity on people here in South Africa. Virginia Sanders booked time on a computed tomography (CT) scanner at a Cape Town hospital to look at the elbow and upper arm of a number of sportsmen. She chose three sets of people: weightlifters, rock climbers and medical students, and compared the size of the muscle attachment sites she could see on the reconstructed CT bone image to the strength of the upper arm bone in cross section. She was also able to measure the muscular power of each individual in the sports science laboratory, so she had exact figures for strength.

Since the muscles involved were mainly the biceps and triceps (muscles that give power to the flexing and extending of the elbow), she expected to see the weightlifters at the top, followed by the rock climbers and then the less physical medical students, but she was in for a surprise. From the size of the muscle scars, the weightlifters were obvious. There was no question that muscle mass, muscle strength and the size of the muscle attachment sites were linked. But in the bone-strength analysis the rock climbers came out way on top.

The key was in the nature of the exercise. The weightlifters elevated very heavy weights but only for short periods of time. As their muscle mass increased they responded by increasing the amount of weight being lifted. It was an ever-increasing exercise regime that was limited only by the maximum strength of the muscles. The rock climbers, on the other hand, lifted much lighter weights (their own body mass) but kept it up for hours at a time. Their muscles did not hypertrophy (overdevelop), but the constant stress on the bones caused the internal structure of the bone to strengthen.

The medical students had weaker bones and muscles than both of the sporting groups. Virginia was seeing exactly what we see in forensic cases. Heavy build-up of bone at the muscle attachment sites in the upper limb and shoulder suggests heavy labour, but smaller, well-delineated muscle scars with increased bone strength suggest better tone rather than strength, indicating that a person engaged in physical activity but did not necessarily use great muscle strength in that activity.

A couple of years after Virginia completed her excellent master's project on biomechanical strength in bone, I became interested in the presence of squatting facets on long bones in archaeological samples. Squatting is a common resting posture among people who do not habitually use chairs. It is defined as sitting in a position where your buttocks touch your heels, and it is virtually impossible to do unless you squat throughout childhood and continue into adulthood. The laxity in the joints means that any child under the age of two can do it with ease, but as a person ages the joints limit the extreme flexion that is required to squat. To assume a full squat, you need to bend (hyperflex) your hip, knee and ankle, and this shows up in extended joint surfaces called 'facets'. If you are an adult 'squatter' then we will see signs of that hyperflexion at each of these joints. Nhlanhla Dlamini was working on a master's project that focused on skeletons from archeological Iron Age contexts at the time, and I asked her to look for the signs of squatting on skeletons from other sites as well. Nhlanhla assembled a set of cadaver skeletons: a series from the eighteenth-century Cape Town cemetery at Cobern Street, and a set of Later Stone Age forager skeletons from the collections at UCT and the Iziko Museum. She also had her own data from the Iron Age skeletons she had been observing for her thesis.

She discovered very interesting facts: not one of the modern people in the cadaver collection had been squatters and only one of the twenty-one skeletons from Cobern Street had squatting facets. But the situation among the prehistoric Iron Age people and the Later Stone Age foragers was very different, with over half of the skeletons indicating squatting habits. Needless to say, we do not often see squatting facets on forensic cases, but their presence may give us a clue to a person's origin. Someone from an urban context in South Africa is unlikely to use squatting as a rest posture, but there are still places in rural Africa where squatting is the norm.

Another environmentally induced sign on the skeleton is arthritis. Depending on the clinical classification, the textbooks on orthopaedics list eight or more types of arthritis. Each one affects the joints and causes change, from minor lipping around the edges of the joint to the complete loss of articular cartilage, as well as destruction and sometimes fusion of the joint. Most are pathologies such as rheumatoid arthritis or ankylosing spondylitis, but one category, degenerative joint disease (DJD), is potentially useful in forensics.

This is the normal form of arthritis that affects all of us if we live to old age, but the joints that are affected are often determined by our activity pattern rather than simply by our age. It has been noted for some time that hip-joint arthritis (and subsequent surgical replacement of the joint) is much more frequent in highly techno-logically developed countries because it is linked to a reduction in activity and long periods in a sitting posture. Perhaps we should call it the desk-jockey disease. On the other hand, that annoyingly healthy neighbour who jogs ten kilometres every morning prob-ably won't suffer from hip-joint arthritis in his sixties, but there is a pretty good chance that his knees will pack up at about that time.

Unfortunately, most of these correlations of occupation and ana-tomical location of arthritic change are visible statistically in groups of people but are much harder to predict in a single person. Being a jogger doesn't mean your knees *will* give out, but if you develop arthritis in old age it will probably start in your knees. Most import-ant, from the forensic point of view, is that arthritis is nearly always painful, so if the forensic scientist can document the location of arth-ritic damage, then it's a good bet that in life the person complained about pain in that joint. That could be very useful in securing a possible identification.

Everything I have mentioned so far was not planned by the individual but resulted from his occupation or habit. However, sometimes behaviours determined by fashion or tradition can mark us in more than psychological ways. I chuckle every year in class when I ask how many young women in the group wear high-heeled shoes. I argue that this is a fashion trick dreamt up by men to make women's legs look longer and, although it does look kind of sexy (at least in my humble male opinion), there is a major price to be paid.

Under normal walking conditions, pressure comes first on the heel. It then moves along the outside edge of the foot, onto the ball of the foot and finally onto the great toe as you 'push off' into the next step. High-heeled shoes destroy this phenomenon by forcing the first contact with the ground to be directly in the midline on the ball of the foot. This is all wrong, makes balance difficult and forces the woman to give a boy-ogling wiggle to her hips while she finds the right position. She must then push off into the next step from the middle of her foot, so her great toe is forced towards the middle of her foot and her small toes dig in to balance her.

This is definitely bad for posture but it's good for young men and for forensic anthropologists, who can see the malformation of the toes in the bones and can use this information as an identification clue. Fortunately this malformation doesn't have to be permanent: given enough time, the foot posture will correct itself as a woman stops wearing high-heeled shoes. But other marks of fashion are permanent. My favourite is the 'Cape Flats Smile'.

I hadn't been in Cape Town for very long when I had the opportunity to meet a professor (now long retired) in the Department of Oral Pathology at the University of Stellenbosch. We were discussing an interesting dental condition on an archaeological specimen and we ended up talking about dental anthropology in general. I mentioned that I was fascinated by the people around Cape Town who didn't have their four upper incisors (making a big gap in their smiles). The professor knowingly smiled and told me that it was a sexual thing that 'coloured' girls did so that they could pleasure their partner, and that the pressure of the penis on the roof of the mouth also changed the shape of their palates. Local Capetonians even had a name for it – the 'Passion Gap'.

I couldn't believe that a learned professor in a clinical field could believe such patently obvious nonsense. Not only was the business of the changed palatal shape simply impossible to generate without hours of sustained pressure (the mind boggles), but I had seen many more men with their four upper incisors removed than I had women. Either homosexuality was a lot more common in the Cape than I had been led to believe, or the professor's racist views so coloured his vision that he was willing to believe anything that matched his preconceptions.

The comments I had heard encouraged me to research the subject. I asked an undergraduate science student, Carolyn Davies, to do a pilot study. She interviewed sixty men and sixty women who had removed their teeth and asked them each for their reason for doing so. It was a preliminary study and there were some design faults in the questionnaire that made the outcome unreliable, but the general results indicated that peer pressure, either from gangs and/or from friends, was the driving force behind the practice.

As it was only a pilot study, Carolyn's work did not provide any idea of the frequency of the practice nor did it show the profile of people who removed their front teeth. That had to wait for the master's thesis of Jacqui Friedling a decade later. Jacqui's work was top class and we have produced two scholarly publications from it. Jacqui and I designed a project that would look at a set of adjoining neighbourhoods in the northern suburbs of Cape Town. She planned to interview a random sample of people without basing her selection on whether or not they had removed teeth.

In the end, Jacqui interviewed over 2 000 people, all of whom lived in one part of Cape Town. The interviewees were from different races, included men and women, and ranged from sixteen to ninety years of age. She found that the practice of dental modification (a term she prefers to my use of the word 'mutilation') is the result of peer pressure in low socio-economic groups in Cape Town. Despite the socio-sexual racist belief expressed by the erstwhile Stellenbosch dental professor, the practice was found to happen in all races, slightly more often in men (44.8 per cent) than in women (37.9 per cent), but overwhelmingly in poor communities.

The average age at which teeth removal occurred was 17.9 years for girls and 16.8 years for boys. When Jacqui compared family income with the practice, its frequency dropped to very low levels in higher income groups and among better educated people. When the data were gathered in 2002, the frequency was 73.6 per cent of individuals whose family income was below R2000 per month, but only 9 per cent of individuals where the family income was more than R5000.

The stated reason for removal was, as mentioned, peer pressure. Simply put, in the lower socio-economic areas of the northern suburbs of Cape Town it was 'cool' for teenagers to have no front teeth. We had disproved the socio-sexual theory – blown it right out of the water, in fact – and had developed a really interesting forensic tool. We now knew that if we had an unknown individual whose front teeth had been removed, he or she was very likely to have come from one of the poor areas of town.

Since then I have used every opportunity to urge people to change the name given to the practice. The 'Passion Gap', although catchy, is simply wrong, and I have been pushing the 'Cape Flats Smile' as an alternative.

We have looked at signs of occupation, habit and fashion that can be detected on the skeleton, but we also need to consider medical intervention. In a sense, this is as much cultural as it is scientific. Although we frequently consider medical treatment to be something we must do to improve our health, the choice of intervention is often cultural and its presence or absence is frequently determined by income rather than health need.

Obvious signs, like the amputation of a limb or finger, are clinically necessary and are visually obvious in life. Other interventions that are not always visible, like dental work, are income dependent. The most common dental treatment in poor communities is extraction – if a tooth hurts, pull it out. When money is available, however, we start to see fillings of various substances, root-canal work, dental bridging and tooth implants.

All of these are clues to identity, especially if there are dental records with which to compare the teeth of a skeleton.

One of the more interesting medical practices is that of trephination. It occurs in archaeological populations all over the world and, in general, involves the cutting of a small hole or disc out of the skull bones. It sounds crazy, but the belief is that the hole enables spirits to leave the head.

On a technical note, the cutting must be very precise because if the dura mater, the outer membrane covering the brain, is cut, then the patient is doomed. The cause of death will be infection of the brain lining and it will be quick. This is interesting to observe in archaeological cases, but has little importance in forensics, except that there are several modern surgical techniques that require burrowing through the bones of the skull, and we sometimes do see these.

Our team at UCT examined the remains of a young man brutally murdered with a panga in Grassy Park. His remains had been found in a shallow grave. He had probably been buried a year or two before the discovery. When we examined the skull we found a very clear hole in the back of the right parietal bone with a small tube passing through it. This is known as a ventricular shunt and it indicated that he had been suffering from raised internal pressure of the cerebrospinal fluid. He had had pressure on the brain and it was clear that his operation had been carried out in a hospital. Sadly, despite this knowledge and a facial reconstruction published in the newspapers, the young man has still not been identified.

YOU ARE WHAT YOU EAT: DIET AND TOOTH DECAY

Teeth are my favourite part of the skeleton to analyse. They are nearly always present in the sample, no matter how badly preserved the skeleton. Their formation is under tight genetic control so I can see signs of genetic individuality in each specimen, but even more important is that, unlike bone, teeth can never change shape once completely formed. Bone is like plastic and will change shape as a result of biomechanical pressure, disease process or simple ageing. Teeth, on the other hand, are locked into their final shape while forming below the gum line and anything that happens to them after eruption is caused only by environmental damage in the mouth.

The mouth is the interface zone between the carefully controlled biochemical environment of the body and the dangerous world outside. The digestion process begins the moment food is put into the mouth, with the teeth breaking the food into smaller, more manageable chunks and the saliva providing the environment for chemical digestion to begin.

Different foods trigger different changes in the chemical balance in the mouth and the hardness of the food has a direct impact on how the teeth are worn down. Not everything that is put into the mouth is food: many people chew things out of habit and some even use their teeth as tools to do delicate jobs like holding needles while sewing. The teeth are also susceptible to trauma, either accidental, like a hockey stick in the mouth, or intentional, such as the removal of teeth to enhance a Cape Flats Smile.

From a forensic perspective, dental health is really useful in identifying where a person comes from and what kind of life they lived before their demise. Confronted with a set of teeth, hopefully still in their sockets, we look for three kinds of information: wear on the teeth from chewing; the frequency and location of cavities (called 'caries' in technical jargon); and teeth that were lost before death from disease.

We already know much about occlusal tooth wear and we use this as an ageing method. As long as a diet is 'Western' and contains similar amounts of soft foods, then wear follows a fairly consistent progression with age. A set of teeth that looks as if it has been filed down flat on an individual that otherwise doesn't look very old is a dead give-away that the skeleton is not modern;

it is probably a prehistoric hunter-gatherer. In terms of individuality, the particular pattern of wear is of greater interest than the general wear state.

A person who favours one side of the mouth over the other when chewing will end up with different wear levels on each side. Others may compensate for lost teeth at the back of the jaw by chewing with their front teeth. We might even recognise a 'bruxist' from his teeth. Bruxism is the nervous habit of clenching one's teeth and grinding them either consciously or during sleep. Because bruxism is caused by attrition (direct contact between the tooth crowns) it tends to be either in the front of the mouth or at the back, and sometimes has an impact on the temporomandibular joint (TMJ) between the jaws as well.

Constant grinding of the teeth can generate muscular pain and TMJ arthritis over time. Often such a person visits the doctor complaining about headaches rather than dental problems.

And, of course, there are pipe-smokers. I used to smoke a pipe in my early twenties because I thought it looked cool and maple-flavoured tobacco was tasty. Pipe-smokers are generally people of habit who almost always clench the pipe in their teeth in exactly the same position day after day. That isn't a problem these days, as modern pipes have ebonite mouthpieces – this hard, plastic-like material doesn't damage the teeth – but until the early twentieth century the pipe of choice was the clay pipe, and its rounded contour and abrasive substance could deeply erode the tooth surface. The pipes may have been different in historic times, but the pipe-smokers were not. Their rigid choice of pipe position means that we can see the polished channel that crosses the tooth row where the old-style pipe was held. If planed flat teeth are a dead give-away of prehistoric hunter-gatherers, then the round contour channels of pipe-smokers' wear is a dead give-away of eighteenth- and nineteenth-century origin for the skeleton.

Strangely, there is an interesting side effect of smoking. Tobacco smoke helps to protect teeth from cavities. I am not advocating smoking for dental health – given the choice between tooth decay and lung cancer I would most definitely opt for tooth decay. Tobacco smoke triggers a biochemical change in the mouth that changes the pH (acid-base level) of the saliva, which inhibits tooth decay but promotes the development of 'calculus' or tartar.

The delicate balance between acidic pH and basic pH in the mouth is important. Our tooth-enamel surfaces are covered by a 'bio-film' that contains bacteria. These bacteria are necessary to commence the process of digestion as we chew. When we begin to chew, the bacteria start to break down the starches into sugars and the biochemical environment shifts to acid. For the hour or so after we have eaten, our mouths are acidic and the enamel of our teeth is at risk of the chemical erosion that can produce a cavity. This is why dentists recommend that we brush our teeth after every meal so that we remove the sugars and allow the saliva to return to neutral.

The very worst thing we can do to our teeth is to eat high-sugar or high-starch foods at constant short-term intervals during the day, as this means that our mouths do not have the chance to shift out of 'acid' mode, promoting cavities. Diets with soft milled foods (like maize meal) only make matters worse because, without regular cleaning, the sticky food becomes trapped between the teeth and creates pockets of high-acid environment around the roots and between the teeth.

The only things that will save the teeth in that situation are regular brushing and eliminating snacks between meals. A mouth full of cavities tells us a great deal about the diet and the dental hygiene of our skeleton. Tobacco smoke, on the other hand, slows down the activity of the bacteria. The mouth goes from an acidic pH to a basic pH. This is great for teeth, but the saliva is rich in calcium, which is now deposited along the pathway by which saliva moves around the mouth. Tartar builds up at the roots of the lower incisors beneath the tongue and all along the roots of the molars. Although cavities are inhibited, the build-up of tartar starts to inflame the gums, and periodontitis, the infection of the tissues around the teeth, sets in.

We now have two situations that cause loss of teeth before death (antemortem tooth loss). If periodontitis sets in, the gum retreats, exposing the roots of the teeth. Pockets of infection called abscesses can develop between the tooth roots. Dental caries erode the outer enamel and then eat into the softer dentine. A large cavity may have only a small entry hole through the enamel but it will have caused lots of damage inside the tooth. Once the erosion has reached the inner pulp of the tooth, bacteria from the mouth can move right into the heart of the tooth and cause infection that produces an abscess right at the tip of the tooth root. This 'apical' abscess can grow within the bone of the jaw and cause much pain and misery. Either way, periodontitis or dental caries result in our losing teeth if we don't sort out the problem.

The pattern of tooth loss is what we look for forensically. Missing front teeth without any other sign of dental problems is a certain sign that the teeth have been removed for purposes other than dental health. We can usually tell the difference between a person who has had his front teeth knocked out and one who has had the dentist remove them because it looks 'cool'.

Extraction pulls directly on the tooth and there is no fracture of the bony socket. Knocking the tooth out, however, causes fractures along the inside of the socket margins and we can see signs of healing there. If our victim came from a poor community, then we are likely to see a pattern in antemortem tooth loss, as the badly affected teeth either fall out on their own or have been extracted. If our victim had access to more sophisticated dental care, we should see a pattern in caries from the fillings in the teeth.

In a Western diet, the first tooth to become diseased is often the first permanent molar. This tooth erupts at age five or six years and therefore it is the tooth in the mouth that has been exposed the longest to the rigours of diet and disease.

In a hunter-gatherer, the tooth usually affected first is the last molar – the wisdom tooth that erupts at the end of the person's teenage years. The hunter-gatherer's diet is low on sugars and starches and therefore episodes of strong acid environment are rarer in the mouth, and the diet is also rich in rough foods with high fibre content.

The mechanical action of chewing fibrous foods, like celery, cleans the teeth, but the one tooth that is hard to clean by chewing is the third molar because it is at the back of the mouth.

STRESS AND THE SKELETON

Stress is exactly what you think it is. It is the worry that you haven't learnt enough to pass the end-of-year exam, or the anxiety about the bill you haven't paid, or the thought that the wrong political party (in your opinion) is going to win the local elections. Psychologists tell us that we need some stress to lead normal lives as challenges keep us focused and give us direction. However, too much stress is unhealthy, especially if the stress is constant. The problem is psychological, but the symptoms can be physical as a person's immune system starts to lose its efficiency. A highly stressed person seems to catch all the bugs that are doing the rounds and appears always to be sick.

The diseases that a stressed person picks up are seldom specific and are often relatively minor. The stressed patient turns up at the doctor's surgery complaining of an inability to sleep, tiredness, recurrent colds, headaches and depression. Clearly, none of these complaints is going to leave marks on bone, and certainly none is likely to be fatal.

Stress on the skeleton is visible in two forms: in the record of disruptions of growth in childhood, and in the general state of health of the bone in the adult. We routinely radiograph the ends of the long bones in all of the skeletons we examine and we look for a small opaque line in the X-ray just on the shaft side of the metaphysis (the old growth plate) of the bone. These are known as 'Harris lines' and tell us that growth stopped for a short while and started up again.

The ossification process that we use to track age at death was mentioned earlier. There is a race between the laying down of new cartilage to lengthen the bone and the process of ossification that hardens the cartilage and turns it into bone. When a child becomes ill, the cartilage stops growing while the body marshals its resources to combat the disease.

The ossification process continues, although the cartilage has stopped growing and, if the sickness lasts a week or two, the ossification will catch up and reach the metaphysis. When the child begins to feel better, the growth of the cartilage begins again but the ossification stalls to give the cartilage a head start. The result is a thin band of bone where the ossification laid down an extra layer of bone salts while it waited for the cartilage to jump ahead.

The exact position of the line in the shaft tells us when the growth arrest occurred. Lines closer to the mid-point of the shaft would have been formed at a younger age than those near to the end of the bone. The Harris lines are all laid down in childhood, but sometimes they are resorbed and reformed during adulthood. The presence of a Harris line indicates a growth stoppage, but its absence does not necessarily mean there were no growth arrests during childhood. Not so for the lines of hypoplasia in the teeth.

Bones are always reforming and restructuring in response to biomechanical and health dictates, but the tooth crowns are formed once during childhood and are never remodelled. The enamel is laid down in a series of crystals called 'enamel prisms', and when a childhood disease hits, the process of enamel production is stopped in the same way that bones halt their growth.

The process of tooth-crown formation starts again when the crisis is over, but there is a discontinuity where the process halted, and we see this as a line of growth arrest on the surface of the enamel. These are enamel hypoplastic lines and they will never remodel once the crown is complete. They are a permanent record of growth stoppage and their position on the crown of the tooth tells us how old the child was when he or she experienced the health emergency. Counting Harris lines and enamel hypoplasias tells us not only the age but also the frequency at which a person had health problems during childhood. In adulthood we are interested in the state of health of the person just before his or her demise and, once again, there are two features that we look for to give us a clue.

One is periosteal infection on the surfaces of the long bones. In life, every bone in our body is covered by a membrane called a periosteum (literally meaning 'around the bone'). The surface of the bone below the periosteum is very much alive, and there are cells that constantly lay down new bone and eat away old bone. This is the mechanism by which bone grows in thickness and we retain this ability to thicken and reshape the surface of our bones throughout adulthood.

This dynamic anatomical location is very susceptible to low-grade infection. Often the periosteum becomes inflamed and lays down little lines of new bone growth in response to a mild systemic illness. No specific disease causes this; it is instead a response to the general health condition of the body – that is to say, stress!

A second sign of stress is found on the roof of the eye sockets in the skull. The bone of the cranium (including the roof of the eye sockets) is made up of an inner and outer layer of bone (called a 'table') with spongy bone (the 'diploë') in between. In a sense it looks like an Aero chocolate bar in cross section, with the solid inner and outer tables held together by a thick diploë packed with air bubbles and thin bands of bone. In life the diploë is filled with red bone marrow, which is responsible for the production of new red blood cells.

One of the symptoms of stress is iron deficiency anaemia. The lack of iron inhibits the transfer of oxygen in the blood and the body suffers. The patient complains of tiredness and inability to function. The body's response to anaemia is to intensify the manufacture of red blood cells, and the red bone marrow begins to thicken. In the skull, the thickening of the diploë happens at the expense of the inner and outer tables of bone.

FIGURE 6: The impact of stress on bone

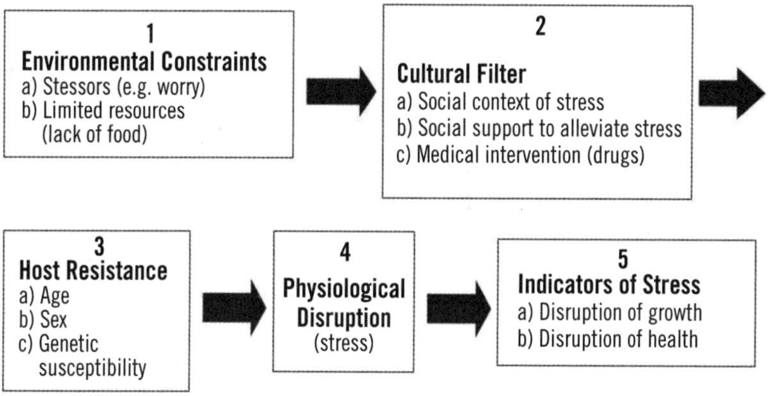

1
Environmental Constraints
a) Stressors (e.g. worry)
b) Limited resources
(lack of food)

2
Cultural Filter
a) Social context of stress
b) Social support to alleviate stress
c) Medical intervention (drugs)

3
Host Resistance
a) Age
b) Sex
c) Genetic
susceptibility

4
Physiological Disruption
(stress)

5
Indicators of Stress
a) Disruption of growth
b) Disruption of health

Adapted from Cohen & Armelagos, 1984

When the anaemias are life-threatening clinical disorders like sickle-cell anaemia or thalassemia, there may be patches of small holes over the outer tables of the parietal and frontal bones, but when the anaemia is mild, the only place where the expanding red marrow may be visible is on the inner table of the thin orbital plate above the eye. We call this 'cribra orbitalia' when the holes are visible, and it is a sure sign that something is wrong physiologically.

The cribra may be active at death or they may have healed, indicating that the crisis had passed and at least that part of the body was healthy at the time of death. Not everyone is in agreement about the exact cause of cribra orbitalia, but most skeletal biologists agree that the cause is iron deficiency even if they are unable to determine the reason for the anaemia.

VIOLENCE, DISEASE AND THE CAUSE OF DEATH

A forensic pathologist has an advantage over a forensic anthropologist in identifying disease and the cause of death because disease is a physiological process involving cells and cellular function. To diagnose a disorder definitively, a whole body and a battery of histological and biochemical tests are needed. The poor forensic anthropologist never has that kind of detailed information.

In general, diseases that affect bone are referred to as 'non-specific' in the sense that they don't leave very distinct markings that we can match to the records of diseases known in life by clinicians. Diagnosis in forensic anthropology is based on the appearance of the bone alone, and any diagnosis we make is interpretive. We also only see a small part of the pathological whole. The vast majority of diseases that have fatal outcomes kill humans because our physiology shuts down, not our anatomy. With all of the missing information held in the soft tissues that are long gone by the time the forensic anthropologist sees the case, the odds are tiny of getting a diagnosis so exact that it will tell us the cause of death.

So usually we cannot comment on the exact cause of death – instead, we concentrate on signs of disease that tell us something special about the person in the years before his death, or, if we are incredibly lucky, about the events that led up to his death.

There are a few diseases that leave unmistakeable calling cards on bone. One of these is tuberculosis (TB). This disease is an old scourge of humankind, but we haven't had it forever. It first appeared around 7 000 or 8 000 years ago and we almost certainly caught it from cattle. Animal diseases that have spread to humans are known as 'zoonoses' and TB must be the nastiest of all. It requires large groups of people living in close proximity to sustain itself (think of cattle herds) and is an airborne disease spread when an infected person coughs or sneezes around other people.

In its pneumatic form, TB is highly contagious and produces symptoms of chest pain, coughing and bloody phlegm. About 5 per cent of TB cases move from being a lung disease to a systemic form of bone disease. The tuberculosis bacilli attack the bone tissue and cause it to erode – called 'lytic' damage in technical jargon. The damage can be anywhere on the skeleton, but TB has two favourite bony sites: the hip and the bodies of the middle thoracic (chest) vertebrae.

It doesn't look like degenerative joint disease when it strikes the hip because the damage is all in the ball-shaped head of the thigh bone, with almost no damage to the joint surface. When TB develops in the vertebrae (which it does in nearly half of all bony TB cases), the effects are dramatic. The TB bacilli attack the rich red bone marrow in the middle of the vertebral body and eat it away. Eventually the vertebra collapses, a tell-tale sign of TB in skeletal biology and known to clinicians as 'Pott's disease'.

In life the TB sufferer's chest is shortened and he or she develops a classic hunchback appearance. Forensically, TB is important because it is exceptionally common in South Africa, especially in the Western Cape. Although the final cause of death is likely to be something like pneumonia, an individual with advanced bony TB would have been in extremely poor health for a long period before death.

There are some other diseases that mark bone, but few are so diagnostic that we can identify them as easily as TB. Some, such as syphilis or leprosy, do indeed leave distinct marks on the skeleton, but in modern times there are drug treatments that stop the disease before it gets to the bony stage. Syphilis is no longer a threat to life (although it still marks the bearer as being less than fastidious in his or her choice of sexual partner).

Most bone diseases show up as infection sites that tell us about the state of the disease at that moment but don't give us a clue to its origin.

Cancer, for example, is visible as metastasised tumours, but only once the disease has reached its late stage. We can certainly say that the cause of death was cancer, but we cannot identify the kind of cancer responsible for the death. There are rare situations when soft tissue turns to bone and we gain a little bit more insight into the disease process, but, in order to see this, the skeleton has to be carefully excavated and if the state pathologists have simply 'collected' the bones, then we may miss it.

My students and I excavated such a rare case in a late prehistoric Khoekhoen grave in the Northern Cape in the late 1980s. We had located a late seventeenth- or early eighteenth-century grave along the Orange River as part of my research into the peoples of the Northern Cape and we excavated the skeleton of a woman of between fifty and sixty years old from the grave. As we carefully exposed the region of her abdomen we discovered two bilaterally placed masses of unformed bone in the exact anatomical position of her kidneys. Once back in Cape Town, I called in an expert to help me with this.

Allen Rodgers of the Department of Chemistry at UCT analysed the bony material and confirmed that it was of biological origin and related to the kidney, but it wasn't from typical kidney stones. We took the specimens to our contacts in the clinical nephrology department, who told us that they had never seen anything quite like this, but that it was definitely a form of infection related to the kidneys. We were never able to work out the exact cause of these masses of unformed bone, but it was obvious that the poor woman had suffered from severe kidney disease that must have been the cause of death. The severity of the renal disease must have made her very ill for some months before death and it's likely that she required a great deal of care during her illness.

The evidence for cause of death is strongest when we deal with the evidence of violence and trauma on the skeleton. This provides the opportunity for forensic anthropologists to be absolutely precise in diagnoses because the evidence comes directly from damage to the bone itself.

Of utmost importance is our ability to differentiate between antemortem fractures (those that occur long before death), perimortem fractures (around the time of death) and postmortem fractures (long after death). We use our knowledge of the biology and physics of bone to sort out the three categories. Fractures that happen some time before death will always show signs of healing. Breaking a bone is a very serious incident but the healing process begins immediately. The fracture site becomes swollen with extra blood and within a few days the body begins to lay down new bone over the break site. This new bone is unstructured and serves as glue to hold the broken parts together. The new layer of bone forms a thick callous over the break site and holds its position for a few months while the broken edges knit.

Once the break has healed properly, the body begins to resorb the callous, a process that takes from six months to six years. In the case of perimortem fractures, the body has not had a chance to begin the healing process and the fractured edges of the bone are still sharp. From the bone alone it is impossible to differentiate between a fracture that happened a couple of days before death and one that happened at death or a couple of days after death.

Postmortem fractures are only visible once decomposition has removed the soft-tissue internal structure of the bone. Half of the structure of a bone in life is made up of living cells and collagen fibres that not only give the bone its capability to adapt to forces and diseases, but also give it its strength by directing forces along pathways in the bone where the hard calcium structure is strongest.

Most of these cells and fibres decompose within a year or two after death and, with their loss, the bone becomes brittle and breaks in a very different pattern from living bone. Having divided off the ante- and postmortem fractures, we examine the bone for clues about the perimortem events.

If our forensic case was the victim of a knife attack, the clue that would give it away would be the presence of a 'sharp-edge injury' on the bone. Fatal injuries caused by a knife are usually deeply penetrating wounds. It certainly is possible to stab someone in the chest without touching bone, but it doesn't happen often. The knife would have to pass through the intercostal space (between the ribs) sideways in order to avoid nicking the ribs.

What usually happens is that the knife blade catches the sternum (breast bone) or scrapes against a rib or two, and the sharp-edge injuries can be seen. Sometimes the weapon isn't a small knife, but a large chopping weapon such as a panga. These wounds differ from each other because a long cutting edge leaves a long slash mark on the bone.

In the Grassy Park case mentioned earlier in relation to the ventricular shunt, the telltale signs of panga damage were visible on the victim's head and arms. He had been slashed at least twice across the back of the head (one of the blows causing a major radiating cranial fracture that could have led to death), but he had tried to defend himself before this and he had blocked four successive panga strikes with his left arm.

Not all sharp-edge wounds are related to the fatal injury, as similar kinds of marks can be made during the process of dismemberment of a corpse. Using a saw means that you can quite easily cut your victim into 'storable' pieces, but the cut marks will be very distinctive and it is even possible to identify the kind of saw and its origin. Using a knife to cut up a body means that one has to pay attention to the anatomy because humans are big animals and don't separate into pieces easily. Knife marks from dismemberment, though, look very different from knife marks intended to kill. We can usually see signs of cutting around the joint edges where the tough tendons have been severed, and the cut marks tend to follow the contour of the bone.

Blunt-force trauma, either from an accident or from intentional violence, is quite different in appearance from sharp-edge injuries. The factor here is not the sharpness of the blade or the angle of attack, but the amount of energy involved in the trauma. Sometimes it is hard to tell the difference between fractures sustained when someone falls and fractures created by a weapon. The similarity is that the force radiates from the original point of impact.

One of my master's students, Laché Rossouw, recently completed a project on a series of human skeletons collected from a thirty-five-metre-deep sinkhole in northern Namibia. A radiocarbon date indicated that the remains were about a thousand years old. We wanted to establish how these dozen or so people had ended up in the hole. The only way in was a straight drop, and Laché's analysis of the bones indicated that most, if not all of these people, had taken the direct route down. We were keen to find out whether they had been dead or alive when they'd fallen in.

Laché was not able to determine the cause of death conclusively but there were several sets of fractures that indicated blunt-contact trauma, and none of the fractures was antemortem by more than a few days at most. This mystery will have to remain unsolved, but whether they were clobbered and pushed or only pushed suggests that man's inhumanity to man has a long history.

The ultimate trauma is caused by gunshot wounds. As a rule of thumb, the bullet entry wound in bone is small compared to the exit wound, but there are many complications. The size and the speed of the projectile are important. A gun generates a great deal of energy, and if this has not been dissipated by distance, all of that energy damages the bone when the bullet hits it. The entry wound will be roughly the size of the projectile, but if it was a large-calibre bullet fired from a powerful weapon, there will be radiating cracks as the energy from the bullet was transferred to the bone.

Very careful notes have to be made of all the bone damage. We have to assess whether the bullet struck the bone directly or ricocheted off something before it struck. If the bullet can be located, we try to establish whether its size matches the damage caused to the skeleton. This could be a clue that indicates how far away the gun was when it was fired.

All in all, evidence about the cause of death will rarely be so clear that we can make an absolute decision about how the person died. The task of the forensic anthropologist is therefore to gather information as circumstantial evidence to establish the cause of death.

DNA

Part of the *CSI* effect is the misguided belief that DNA testing can solve all forensic problems. This is a myth.

Thanks to Craig Venter's wonderful invention of the Polymerase Chain Reaction (PCR) machine, it is now possible to generate DNA data on an industrial scale. Our police laboratories are way behind many European and North American laboratories, but we are getting there, and our capacity to analyse DNA in criminal investigations is growing. Any biological material that contains DNA can be analysed because of the PCR machine: it amplifies a small snippet of DNA from a very specific region of the whole genome and replicates enough of it for easy laboratory analysis.

Contrary to popular belief, the whole DNA sequence of a person is not analysed. That would be a huge job and is, in fact, unnecessary. Only a small piece of DNA is needed because it is so complex that no one, except an identical twin, has the same sequence of base pairs. What DNA analysis does, therefore, is to confirm identification. Different pieces from one body can be compared to find out if all of the pieces come from the same person: we can compare bodily evidence like skin flakes, hair, semen or blood to match against a possible subject (victim or suspect), and we can compare bone or tissue from an unknown person to those who are closely related to him or her. It is impossible to find a name from a piece of DNA without having someone to compare it to.

The use of DNA to make an exact match between, say, blood at a crime scene and the victim found elsewhere is known as a 'DNA fingerprint'. The idea is that, like our fingerprints, the sequence of base pairs in our DNA is absolutely unique and quite different from anyone else's sequence. The geneticists have already identified parts of the human genome that are highly variable, and therefore only a small section of anyone's DNA has to be replicated to find a unique pattern. Matching a bone sample against an individual for whom we already have the DNA fingerprint is therefore relatively easy.

It becomes much more difficult when we don't have a reference sample and we need to compare the DNA of the unknown person with that of his or her possible close relatives. Since we inherit our mitochondrial DNA from our mothers and our Y-chromosome DNA from our fathers, we should easily be able to exclude our unknown body if he or she is unrelated to the purported family members. The DNA identification system works best where there is some form of database of DNA samples to compare our unknown to.

Television programmes make it look incredibly easy to obtain a DNA result, but the reality, especially when it comes to bone, is much more difficult. The longer a person has been dead and decomposed, the more difficult it is to extract DNA. The bone must never have been exposed to heat, nor can it have been soaked in acidic or basic fluids. The sample for analysis must be carefully drawn from deep within the bone because contamination from skin flakes, or even the sweaty fingerprints of anyone who has handled the bone after discovery, can easily occur. A separate laboratory is also needed for the bone analysis. Even with all of these precautions, the failure rate is extremely high. They don't tell you that on television.

I have a great relationship with the geneticists in South Africa who work on DNA identification, and that means I don't normally do the DNA work. This makes me very happy because I am a bone man, first and foremost.

MAKING FACES

Way back in the early 1980s I read a book called *Gorky Park* by
Martin Cruz Smith. It is a great story about an under-resourced
Moscow police inspector, Arkady Renko, who is trying to solve the
murder of three people whose bodies have been found in Moscow's
Gorky Park.

Each person's face has been neatly skinned and their fingers removed. The story is set in the days before DNA identification and
there is no way to identify the bodies, so Arkady enlists the help of
Professor Andreev of the Russian Institute of Ethnology to recreate
the features of one of the bodies. By this stage Inspector Renko has
an idea of whom she might be, but he needs the reconstruction
to confirm his suspicions. Let me quote the words from the book
when Arkady sees the resurrected face for the first time:

> Valerya Davidova, murdered in Gorky Park, was alive again.
> Her eyes sparkled, blood coursed through her cheeks, her lips
> were red and parted with anxiety, she was about to speak.
> What seems incredible was that this apparently living head had
> no body: its neck balanced on a potter's wheel.

Wow! This is such a powerful passage. The good professor had
not only replaced her face, but in a sense he had brought her back
to life. I loved the book and the film that followed, but the passage
about the facial reconstruction particularly stuck in my mind, and
I determined to find out more.

It transpired that Smith's Professor Andreev was based on a real
person, Professor M.M. Gerasimov (1907–1970) of the Laboratory
for Plastic Reconstruction at the USSR Institute of Ethnography
in Leningrad. His forte was not forensics, but the reconstruction
of people from Russia's past. His most famous reconstructions were
of Ivan the Terrible and Tamerlane. He did on occasion help the
police to find a face, but it is obvious from his autobiography *The*

Face Finder, published in 1971, that it was the historical figures that intrigued him most.

My research alerted me to others aside from Gerasimov who were experts at facial reconstruction. Two names in particular came up: Clyde Snow and Betty Gatliff of Oklahoma City in the United States. Unlike Gerasimov, Snow and Gatliff frequently worked on police cases and by 1980 their reputation was such that the unknown dead were brought to them from all over North America. I actually first came across these two Americans in an article in the *Toronto Star* in September 1980 about an unknown body from Alberta.

The victim had been tortured, shot and deposited in an old septic tank, and he was hardly in a fit state for human company by the time the Royal Canadian Mounted Police found him. The newspaper article outlined the procedure that Snow and Gatliff used to reconstruct his face and illustrated a final version of the reconstruction, but then gave me some information that was conveniently ignored in *Gorky Park*.

By 1980, Snow and Gatliff had worked on sixty skulls, of which two-thirds had been identified, but only between 10 per cent and 20 per cent of the identifications were the direct result of the reconstructions. In other words, even though it was possible to put a face back on a skull, there was only one chance in five that it was the *right* face.

So is facial reconstruction real science or is it simply a fancy technique suited only to the realm of fiction? We need to consider who carries out these reconstructions and what their reason is for doing so.

Facial reconstruction is a last-ditch attempt at identification. It is only done when there are absolutely no leads in the identification of a person and there is no hope of any leads. There are various ways to identify an individual and these methods are ranked in order of difficulty.

First, clothes and personal effects are examined. If these aren't available, then comparison of the unknown's teeth and injuries with dental or hospital records is an excellent method, but, of course, there must be some idea at that point of whom the person might be. The third option is a photo superimposition of the skull onto a photograph of somebody who is suspected to be the missing person.

Only then would a DNA test be carried out to confirm an identity, but, once again, this is a technique that needs at least a guess as to whom the missing person might be. As I said earlier, it is of no use to look at the 'DNA fingerprint' of a person unless there is someone to compare it to. If none of the above is successful, then a facial reconstruction becomes an option.

Take the case of DR 758/95, a young woman found in a shallow grave in the back garden of a house in Crawford, Cape Town. The neighbour had bought the property as an open field in 1991 and he was as surprised as the police when he found the skeleton while clearing the overgrown weeds at the plot's edge in 1995. The skeleton was estimated to have been there for six years or so and was that of a woman in her early twenties. All of the soft tissue was gone, but she wore a summer dress and still had a bangle on her arm.

Without an identity, the police had no clues. A facial reconstruction was done and the image was published in the Afrikaans and English newspapers and was shown on the television programme *Crime Stop*. The Cape Town newspapers didn't reach most of the countryside, and no one responded to the newspaper publicity, but the television programme was viewed widely by South Africans of all communities and it received a hit.

Early in August 1995, the investigating officer received a phone call from a woman who said that the picture looked like her friend who had gone missing in 1989. Through this caller the police contacted the missing woman's family, who lived in the small village of Twee Rivieren on the border of Botswana, some 700 kilometres from Cape Town.

Twenty-three-year-old Rabeka Cloete had come to the big city to work in 1986. Although she had found a job as a domestic helper in the suburb of Oranjezicht, things had not gone well. She had been raped by three men in 1989 and she'd filed charges against them. The men had threatened her, and shortly afterwards she'd disappeared. Her parents were not in contact with her and no one reported her missing until the reconstruction of her face was broadcast on television.

The picture was not an exact representation of the woman's face, but it was close enough to trigger a response, and both her parents and her sister-in-law testified that the reconstruction matched Rabeka's face. The alleged rapists could not be linked to the finding of her body six years after her death, and the conclusion of the inquest was that no one could be identified as being responsible for her death. To this day the case remains unsolved.

The fact that we don't often succeed is not important. The principle is that we reconstruct cases only where there is *no* hope of identification, so if we get only one identification out of five, that is better than none.

What isn't visible in a reconstruction is the amount of time and effort that goes into creating it. Generally, at least two people are involved: a forensic anthropologist and an artist. Which of the two is more important is difficult to say. Clyde Snow was the forensic anthropologist of the American pair, but the reconstruction was created by Betty Gatliff, based on guidelines provided by Snow. The skill of the anthropologist enhances the accuracy of the reconstruction, but the skill of the artist is responsible for the lifelike appearance of the reconstruction.

The experts in facial reconstruction in South Africa are few and far between, and I am lucky enough to have worked with three of them. I first met Bill Aulsebrook when I was a student in Johannesburg in the late 1970s. He was a dentist with an interesting and distinctive work ethic. He firmly believed that working three full days a week was adequate for his financial needs and any employment beyond that simply filled the coffers of the tax man. As a result, he had plenty of spare time in which to indulge in his favourite hobby – pottery making. He was a superb craftsman whose pots verged on sculptures.

Eventually he took a more academic route and relocated to the Oral and Dental Hospital in Durban, which was then attached to the University of Durban-Westville, now the University of KwaZulu-Natal. There he combined his dental anatomical knowledge with his artistry and began working on facial reconstructions for reconstructive surgery and for the police forensic identifications. One distinctive feature of Bill's reconstructions is that he often produced three from the same skull, each with a different facial fatness, as this is something that cannot be identified from the bone alone.

In Cape Town I have been extremely fortunate to have inherited a pair of collaborators, Vince Phillips and Susan Rosendorff. Vince is Professor of Oral Pathology at the University of the Western Cape, and Susan is a recognised artist living in Oranjezicht in Cape Town. The two of them have been working together since the 1990s, and they were responsible for the reconstruction of the Crawford case mentioned above. They have done several police cases since then, but I have been mostly involved with them on the reconstruction of five archaeological specimens from Cobern Street in Cape Town.

Cobern Street is the focus of later discussion, but at this point I need to introduce it as an eighteenth-century cemetery that we excavated in 1994 and 1995. Although there were hard scientific methods used to identify the origin and life history of these long-dead people, I was determined to 'bring them back to life', Arkady Renko–style, and I asked Vince and Susan to reconstruct five well-preserved skulls from the site. The resulting heads are so lifelike that one of the students eventually asked me to move them from the shelf in my outer office, where the postgraduate students sat, because the five watching faces were making him nervous. Now *that* is lifelike.

Now we know 'why' and 'who', but I haven't yet described 'how'. What exactly is the process of reconstruction and how do we know which aspects of it are accurate and which are not?

A facial reconstruction always starts with all of the bones of the body if they are available. We need some very basic information about the person, for example the sex and approximate age at death. We need to establish whether they have any distinguishing features that made them very recognisable in life. Perhaps he or she had a broken nose or a flattened cheek bone. We also need to find out whether the face was bilaterally symmetrical – many of us do not have exact mirror images of left and right in our features. In addition, there could be signs of disease that affected facial appearance.

All of this information is fed to the artist as the reconstruction takes shape. One controversial aspect is the identification of the race of the individual. Racial identity will impact on many of the surface features, including skin colour, hair form, ear shape and eye colour. None of these features can be identified directly from the underlying bone structure. It is not the confidence in identifying race that is the issue; it is the assumption that everyone within that race has similar features that causes the crisis.

By the time the preliminary work is done, we already know quite a bit about the person and can make some sound assumptions about features we aren't able to see from the bone, but the bulk of the job is still to come. At this stage we need to begin physically putting 'flesh' on the bone. Many artists like to use modelling clay or plasticine, but placing this directly onto the bone surface can cause a great deal of damage to the skull, especially if the bone preservation is not good

The best practice is to make a plaster cast of the skull. The detail need not be perfect, as long as the surface features of the cast are a true reflection of the surface features of the bone.

There are two ways in which we can start laying down the 'flesh'. The master, Gerasimov, used his skill as an anatomist to determine precisely the size and shape of each facial muscle and then to re-create the original anatomy on the skull. This method, sometimes called 'Gerasimov's method' or the 'Russian method' is extremely difficult and requires a great depth of anatomical knowledge, but it is potentially extremely accurate because it is based on exact anatomy rather than average features.

The alternative is what I call the 'American method', which uses mean values for tissue thickness at set points on the skull. It is rather fun to see a reconstruction in progress using this approach because a forest of plugs of different lengths project porcupine-fashion out of the skull, representing the tissue depth at each location. In fact, both methods need to use some tissue-thickness estimation because, no matter how well you understand the anatomy, the underlying bony structures give no clue to the thickness of the skin and fat and connective tissue above it.

The artist now begins to lay down strips of clay equalling the depths of skin and muscle over the whole of the face, but he or she still needs to deal with the eyes, nose, lips and ears, none of which have preservation clues on the bone. Once again we need to return to the averaged values obtained from studies of cadavers and living people. Placing the eyeball in exactly the right position in the socket is tricky because, contrary to belief, it isn't right in the middle. The data tell us that it is slightly off centre, towards the outside, and a little bit above the midline of the eye socket.

Clues to the shape of the nose come from the opening of the nasal passage in the front of the skull and from a small projection below the nasal opening called the 'sub-nasal spine'. The spine is the seat of the nasal cartilage that wiggles back and forth when the soft-tissue part of the nose is pinched. A wide aperture gives us

A puzzled constable ponders the origins of the human skull, full of holes and covered in candle wax, which was found on a traffic sign in Claremont on Monday 28 February 1994

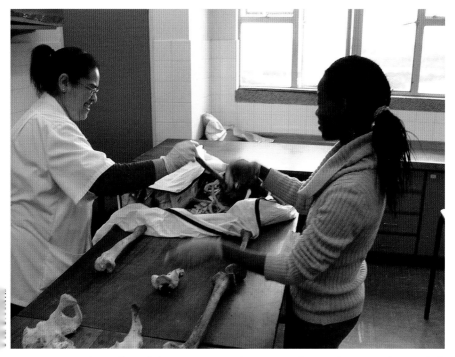

Dr Jacqui Friedling of the Department of Human Biology and Dr Itumeleng Molefe of the Department of Forensic Medicine laying out a bone case for analysis

Four gentlemen from the Kalahari in full squatting posture discuss the future of ostrich eggs

A group of friends from the Cape Flats outside Cape Town give the photographer a welcoming smile

Exposure of the calcified left-side kidney mass in a late prehistoric skeleton from Omdraai 1 along the Orange River near Augrabies Falls in the Northern Cape, South Africa

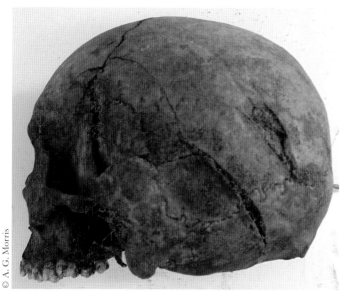

Wounds caused by the sharp edge of a panga (similar to a machete) can be seen on the skull of the young man discovered in Grassy Park, Cape Town

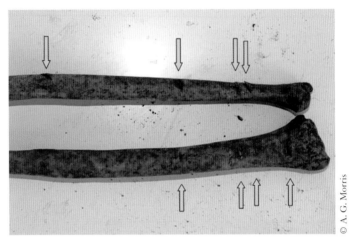

Defence wounds inflicted by a panga on the left arm of the same victim.
The arrows indicate four separate chop marks crossing the back of his arm

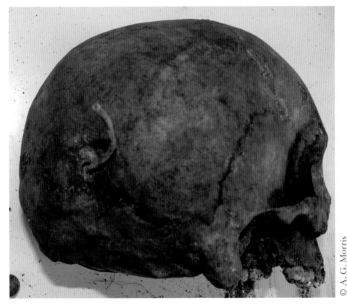

The skull seen from the other side, showing the burr hole and
outlet tube for a ventricular shunt

Rebuilt face may yield clues

CRIME REPORTER

A UNIVERSITY of Stellenbosch oral pathologist has made a reconstruction of the face of a woman whose remains were found in Crawford in March — and police believe it may help solve the mystery of her death.

The remains of the woman, believed to be about 23 years old when she died about six years ago, were found in a shallow grave in a Camberwell Road garden.

Police believe she may have been murdered, but have few clues about her fate.

Professor Vince Phillips has reconstructed the woman's facial features with the help of an artist.

He said yesterday that the work had taken about four weeks and that the model of the "mixed race" woman was not necessarily accurate, but it was hoped it would help someone to recognise her.

The woman was wearing a brown-and-white skirt when she died.

Anyone who may be able to assist the police in their investigation is asked to contact Sergeant Colin Hayward at 696-4800.

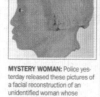

MYSTERY WOMAN: Police yesterday released these pictures of a facial reconstruction of an unidentified woman whose remains were discovered in a Crawford garden earlier this year. Detectives investigating the case believe the woman was murdered about six years ago.

A newspaper article comparing the facial reconstruction of the young woman from Crawford with a photograph of the victim provided by her mother

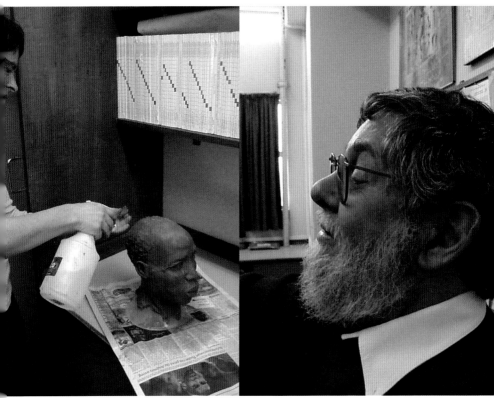

The artist Susan Rosendorff, a facial reconstruction expert (left);
Forensic dentist and facial reconstruction expert Vince Phillips (right)

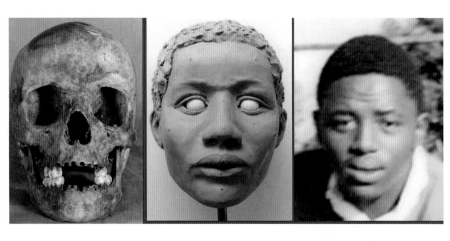

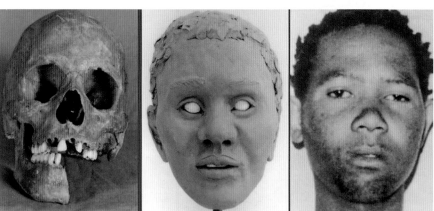

© V M Phillips

The results of the Phillips/Rosendorff collaboration. Reconstruction of the faces of two boys recovered from shallow burials in the dunes at Port St Johns in 1995

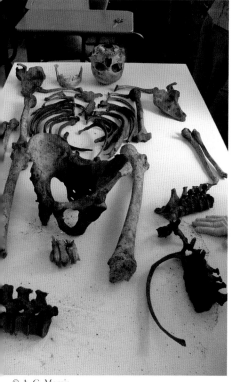

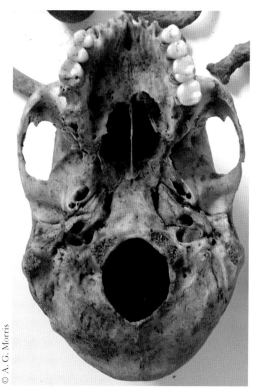

Case 2288/2008 from Muizenberg: specimen laid out for analysis

Case 2288/2008 from Muizenberg: the base of the skull shows damage to the back of the palate caused by animals that had chewed on the remains. Note the enlarged size of the opening of the spinal cord

The old man from Atlantis: The police off-road vehicle used to reach the site on the power-line cut between Melkbosstrand and Atlantis

The old man from Atlantis: Dr Len Lerer and the author examining the remains as they were found

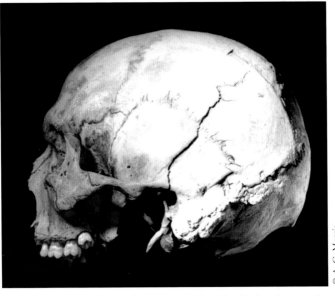

Case 2859/1996: breakage of the front teeth and radiating fracture from the base of the skull are consistent with a fall from a great height

The mass stranding of spiny rock lobsters (*Janus ialandii*) at Elands Bay, 1997, showing the prolificacy of these scavengers along the West Coast of South Africa

wide soft-tissue nostrils, and a projecting sub-nasal spine tells us both the extent of projection of the nose and its direction.

Ultimately we have to guess the exact position of the lips and the ears because the underlying bone structure gives us no clues. Here is where issues of racial identity become critical. The thickness of lips or projection of ears is entirely based on our perception of these as racial features, and if that perception is wrong or stereotyped, then the reconstruction will be flawed.

Finally, the artist needs to sculpt the skin and hair. If we were brutally honest about the reconstruction, our model would be bald and unsmiling with perfectly smooth skin, and, in all likelihood, completely unrecognisable. The artist must now make some completely unscientific choices. Does the woman have long hair or short hair? What colour should we paint the skin? Is she an English rose or a Mediterranean olive?

Since we know the age at death from the anthropological assessment, should we put little crow's feet around the eyes of our fifty-year-old woman or an upwardly creeping hairline for our middle-aged man? Should our model stare blankly into the distance or should we give her a *Mona Lisa* smile?

With each and every one of these minor adjustments, and with our reliance on average values, we lose some accuracy in relation to the original facial appearance. The broad features of the face may be correct, but not necessarily the detail. Some forensic researchers worry so much about these errors that they have stopped calling the whole process a 'facial reconstruction' and instead have started to use the less precise term 'facial approximation'. The artist cannot produce a photograph of the missing person, only a likeness to what they may have appeared like in life.

Is it possible to measure the accuracy of these reconstructions? I don't even know if we should try. Remember, the object is not to make a perfect reconstruction of the face, but to trigger recognition from the public so that other lines of investigation can be followed.

A CASE REPORT – MUIZENBERG

Each and every forensic anthropology case that we deal with is different, and we have no idea what is coming in until we unzip the bag in the laboratory. Part of the fun is working on the case with other people – both the students and the pathologists – and every case is a learning experience for all of us.

In Chapter 3 of this book we look at a number of these cases, but here follows a typical forensic case as it arrived in the Department of Human Biology.

Steven Afonzo is one of the registrars training at UCT to become a forensic pathologist. He has the standard medical degree (MBChB) in South Africa, which he earned at the University of Cape Town, so I taught him as an undergraduate, but now he is under the gentle care of Lorna Martin, who will guide him through the post-graduate training programme in forensic pathology.

Steven sent me an email in mid-October 2008 asking if I would have time in the next week or so to look at a nearly complete skeleton that had been found in an open field near Muizenberg on the False Bay coast of Cape Town. This is pretty typical for a bone case. With no immediate sign of identity, and no information suggesting a crime, the pathologists frequently put the case aside until the rush of the more important postmortems is over.

Steven and I agreed on a day and he met me with box in hand at the appointed hour outside my office. I had forewarned my students about the case as I like to give them the opportunity to learn first hand. We always do our work as a team and the students identify as much as they can by themselves, with my guidance.

The skeleton came in a sealed plastic bag identified with the number WC-11-2288-2008, indicating that this would be the 2 288th postmortem of 2008 for the Salt River mortuary. Steven cut the bag open and the room rapidly filled with the faint odour of decay. The bones were damp and there were small scraps of soft tissue still adhering to the inside of the skull, but skeletonisation was nearly complete and the faint bad odour was an annoyance rather than a hindrance.

The police report indicated that the bones had been found in an open field under a bush, and that the body was associated with a City of Cape Town yellow workman's jacket and some other clothes. The location stated on the form was 'Baden Powell Drive', a road that crosses uninhabited and overgrown sand dunes following the coast of False Bay between the 'coloured' suburb of Mitchells Plain and the 'African' suburb of Khayelitsha. No question that this case was forensic and relatively fresh.

The students started the process of analysis by laying out the skeleton in anatomical position on the main table top. This immediately told us that not all of the bones were present. The lower leg bones (both tibiae, the left fibula and both kneecaps) were not in the bag, yet, surprisingly, one of the bones of the lower leg (the right fibula) was present.

Even more surprising was that both feet were more or less complete, despite the fact that most of the lower leg bones were missing. Steven solved this small mystery by telling us that the feet had still been in their shoes when the police had found the body, so the foot bones had been protected. Several vertebrae were also missing. One lumbar vertebra was gone from the small of the back, along with four of the neck vertebrae, including the first two (the atlas-axis pair).

How could the bones of the neck, back and lower legs go missing? This was easy to solve, as there were clues all over the skeleton. The base of the skull, lower jaw, lower arm bones, pelvis and knee joints all showed signs of animal chewing. The bone damage was not done at the time of death, as it was generally the ends of the bones or prominent ridges that were damaged. The chewing must have been on bones exposed after the flesh had mostly rotted away. The animal could not have been large, as the damage was limited at most sites. The back of the palate was chewed, along with the bottoms of the mastoids (the bump behind the ear) and the top of the left eye socket.

A big animal would have done much more damage than that, but another bigger animal may have been involved with the loss of the legs. The ends of the thigh bones were badly chewed and the kneecaps and all but one of the bones of the lower leg were gone. Something must have pulled the shoes with the feet from the decomposed body and dragged the bigger bones away. My vote would go to a dog as the bigger culprit, but the little guy could have been a mongoose or a similar-sized animal.

Once we had an idea of how complete our skeleton was, we needed to determine when the person had died. Decomposition was so far advanced that it was unlikely that the person had been dead for less than six months. The skeleton had been in the field throughout the Cape Town winter – a cool and wet period, but one in which decay would have progressed steadily. Could it have been there for years?

Probably not, as the odour of decay and the fresh nature of the bone were consistent with a period of less than a year since death. The time of death, therefore, was somewhere between six months and a year, but the smell of decay suggested that perhaps the time was closer to six months than a year.

The next question was about age and sex. The sex was easy. All of the classic signs of masculinity were there. The pelvis was complete, although the crest of the hip bone was chewed, and this is by far the most diagnostic set of bones for sex identification. The angle formed by the bars of bone below the pubis was acute and the blades of the hip bones were high and rounded. All the signs on the bone pointed to a male sex. At this stage I reminded the students *not* to use the word 'gender' when they mean 'sex'. Gender is about behaviour, and we have no idea if this person thought of himself as male or female. We do know, though, that his anatomy was clearly male.

The age, however, gave us more trouble. The general features suggested someone older than fifty years at death. Tooth wear was moderate – a sign of middle age in people with a modern agricultural food diet – and the ends of the ribs were strongly cupped where the bone overlapped with the junction of the cartilage on the front of the ribcage.

But there were some features that normally occur only in the very old. The pelvis was fused as a single bone. For the vast majority of us, the pelvis is made up of the right and left hip bones, which are joined at the back by the sacrum. The bones stay separate throughout life and move gently when we walk to help distribute the stress of our upper body weight as the forces pass down through the pelvis to our lower limbs. It is extremely rare for the three bones to unite, and this usually only happens in the very elderly.

The abnormal fusion was also present in the vertebral column. The synovial (freely mobile) joints connecting the ribs at the mid-chest level were heavily lipped and the rib was fused to the vertebra on the left side. The cartilage connecting the first ribs to the top of the sternum had been completely transformed into bone and was attached to the upper part of the sternum.

All of this was confusing. How could he have been in his fifties yet show signs of having lived into his nineties? When things like this don't make sense, it is time to think about pathology. We discussed this at length and agreed that an age at death of between fifty and sixty was most likely, but that something was terribly wrong with the man's skeleton. He must have been stiff and not terribly mobile in life. But this did not seem to be the degenerative arthritis of old age, rather a progressive stiffness of joints that had relatively little mobility anyway. It was a form of arthritis, but one of unknown cause.

Our man's body build was robust and the large collar bones marked out his broad shoulders. The muscle scars on the bones of his upper limbs were all well delineated, giving us an idea of his muscular strength. We measured his left thigh bone, and its length of 44.8 centimetres allowed us to calculate his height in life to be around 1.68 metres. The fact that he had lived into his sixth decade told us that he probably didn't stand as tall as that. After the age of thirty, as mentioned earlier, we all begin to lose height as the discs between our vertebrae lose their resilience and compress. He might have only stood about 1.6 metres tall in the last few years before his death. He was strong and well built, but of only medium height.

In South Africa, 'race' is still an important part of any forensic report. I have always agonised over how to deal with this question, as the apartheid race-categories of 'white', 'Indian', 'coloured' and 'black' are still recorded by the police and recognised by most of the general public.

The problem is that 'racial' identity is often confused with 'ethnic' identity, and people frequently self-identify with a group based on language, religion or culture, irrespective of their biological background. But the police crime records are all neatly categorised into the famous four South African categories, and I needed to put this guy somewhere where it made sense in the system.

In the end I used the exclusion principle. I could see no features that indicated a genetic origin in Europe or Asia and none that obviously matched a Khoesan 'Bushman' origin. The skull anatomically fitted into the broad African range of variation seen in southern African Bantu-speaking groups, and since he didn't have any of the features often seen in white or coloured South Africans, I slotted him into the South African Negro group.

All of this gave us what we like to call the 'demographic' aspects of identification. We could now guess at his biological origins, his age and his sex, but we needed some 'biographic' clues that could lead to our learning his specific identity. In fact, we already had a couple of hints because we could estimate his height and general body build. There were no signs of events that occurred at around the time of death – no bone fractures, no cut marks and no gunshot wounds.

However, there was an interesting pathology that told us something about the man's life. We still didn't understand why he was showing the abnormal bone fusion, but when we looked at the base of his skull, something was definitely wrong. The biggest hole on the bottom of skull, the foramen magnum, is the place where the spinal cord leaves the brain and travels down along the vertebral column. This guy's foramen magnum was way too large and all of the bone surrounding it was thin and delicate. The neurosurgeons know this well and have given it the name 'Chiari Malformation'.

In about 30 per cent of these cases the malformation is totally without symptoms, and, if our guy was one of these cases, he did not know that anything was wrong and spent his life in blissful ignorance of a very serious clinical problem at the top of his neck. In the majority of cases, though, the person would have suffered potentially awful problems.

The Chiari Malformation allows the basal part of the brain to slide down through the foramen, which causes pressure on the brainstem and nearby areas. If the cerebellum starts to slip down, there could be problems with walking and the person could develop spastic movements. If the brainstem slips and becomes compressed, then there could be problems with sensory perception, and groups of muscles could become weak and even paralysed. At the very least, a sufferer might complain of headaches and pain at the back of his neck.

The whole examination process took about an hour, but I spent more time than that writing up the official account. The guts of the report said that the person from Muizenberg was a South African Negro male of between fifty and sixty years at death. He had been dead for at least six months, but probably less than a year.

The man was well built and about 1.6 metres tall at death. He had a number of physical complaints that his friends and companions might have known about. He was stiff when he walked and had persistent pain in the middle of his back. He may have also been unsteady when he walked. He may have had headaches and possibly had problems with the sense of touch. All of the information about animal scavenging wouldn't help the police find an identity, but it was interesting and we included it in the report.

The completed report concluded our job, and everything passed on to the investigating officer. We also recommended that a facial reconstruction be done in this case. Perhaps if we could have put a reasonable approximation of a face back on this man, it might have sparked someone to give us a name that the investigating officer could check.

No facial reconstruction was done in this case and after two years of storage the skeleton was cremated and the ashes destroyed. A small sample of bone was kept for future DNA analysis if required, so if a lead does develop some time in the future, then there is still a chance that we could find an identity.

3

Murder and Mayhem

In 1997, Maryna Steyn and her team at the University of Pretoria published a review of the cases they had seen in their anatomy department from 1993 to 1995. These were the early days of forensic anthropology in South Africa, and relatively few skeletonised cases were being passed on for anthropological analysis – most skeletal cases were handled only by district surgeons or forensic pathologists.

One of the issues that Maryna addressed in the paper was the failure of the police to provide feedback on the cases on which she and her team had had the opportunity to work. The paper analysed the thirty-two cases they had seen (almost one case a month) and provided some interesting data. Sixty per cent of the cases were male. Many of the female cases were bodies discarded by serial killers, and some of these were therefore linked. Two individuals were white and twenty-eight were black. Only a few of the cases were children, one of which was a dismembered child from a muti murder. Six of the thirty-two cases (just under 20 per cent) showed signs of violence on the bones.

For the twenty-seven individuals who were unknown, the South

African Police (SAP) had arranged for facial reconstructions or sketches, but to Maryna's knowledge, only three – a shade over 10 per cent – had been identified by the date of publication. She ended her paper rather prophetically by emphasising the large number of unidentified skeletons being found and the need for forensic anthropologists to be involved in the investigations:

> Formal recognition, in South Africa, of forensic anthropologists as members of the team involved in the analysis of decomposed remains, is still a long way off, but the problems faced are of such magnitude that everything possible should be done to improve the situation (Steyn, Meiring & Nienaber, 1997: 25).

A decade later I set about gathering all of the case reports for our department at the University of Cape Town. Times had changed significantly in ten years, although reports back from the police were still almost non-existent. Forensic anthropologists were being recognised as specialists in their own right in South Africa, and the University of Pretoria's group was restructuring itself as a separate unit known as Forensic Anthropology Research Centre (FARC). I had been a great deal less systematic in Cape Town and had been collating case reports only since the mid-nineties. Prior to that I had simply given an oral report to the pathologist responsible for compiling the written report. My notes were in a mess and I needed help, which came in the form of young Laura Brummer, a second-year medical student who chose to help me order my records as her special studies module.

Laura was able to find records for 104 cases from between 1980 and 2008, with most of the cases being from the previous ten to twelve years. We both knew that the list was not complete, but at least it was large enough for us to do some statistical analysis on the sample. We were particularly interested in comparing the Cape Town data with those of Pretoria.

One immediately visible difference was that 29 per cent of the cases seen in Cape Town actually came from archaeological rather than forensic contexts. All of these 'heritage' cases were recorded initially as police investigations. The reports on the skeletons went to the state pathologists but the skeletons were retained at UCT. It was unclear if Pretoria simply wasn't getting archaeological cases or if the researchers there were not including them in forensic samples.

Before 1999 there was no requirement to report archaeological cases to the heritage organisations, and archaeological cases taken to the University of Pretoria may have been accessioned to their collection without a report being written.

Other than the archaeological cases, the experiences of Pretoria and Cape Town were similar. Sixty-nine per cent of our forensic skeletons were male, 82 per cent were adult and 26 per cent showed signs of violence.

The success rate in identifying unknown individuals was as bad in Cape Town as it was in Pretoria, with only 8.5 per cent of the unknown skeletons in Cape Town successfully identified. Also, receiving feedback from the police in Cape Town was just as difficult as getting feedback from the police in Pretoria.

The dry statistics, however, tell only part of the story. Laura's analysis of the Cape Town data was excellent and it demonstrated to us the need to keep clear and detailed records. The records that we had for each case detailed the circumstances of discovery along with the record of analysis, and it is these details that give us a feel for the real value of the forensic anthropology investigation.

VIOLENT ENDINGS

A telephone call from the state pathologist is not the only way that I am requested to help sort out a question about bone. Sometimes the police contact me directly, especially if an investigation is already under way and the police and prosecutors need more information.

I do not advertise as a forensic anthropologist, and, in all the years I have been doing skeleton reports, I have only once charged for my services. So finding me is a matter of word of mouth among the police, pathologists and lawyers, and I am always happy to assess the bones while they wait. I see these cases as another education opportunity and the policemen seem to enjoy the informal lessons.

One of these casual assessments occurred when the police and prosecutor brought several bags of burnt bone fragments to me in May 1992. The question they asked was simple enough: 'Are the bones in the bags human?' My identification, they said, would have an impact on the investigation and the subsequent court case.

The sample consisted of three small bags of badly burnt bone pieces, along with charcoal, some burnt metal and other bits and pieces.

We carefully emptied the contents of each bag onto separate sorting trays and I began the finicky job of dividing the bone from the other material. Then I very carefully separated out the bone fragments that could be identified. The pieces were small and showed different burning temperatures. Bone that burns at between 300 °C and 400 °C tends to have blackened areas where the carbon has been incompletely oxidised. Bone burnt at above 400 °C is white and chalky in appearance and is highly fragmented. Burning bones at more than 500 °C makes them 'calcined' and they take on the appearance of burnished pottery. The bones in the first bag were burnt at varying temperatures, but most of them seemed to have been burnt at temperatures of about 400 °C.

The bones were all broken up but there were some identifiable bits – a tooth here, a vertebral arch there, a finger bone mixed in with the charcoal. Every identifiable piece was human. I repeated the process for the other two bags and found similar results. There was no duplication between the bags – each bag had different anatomical bits, and it was entirely possible that only one person was represented by the remains in all three bags.

The prosecutor then outlined the story for me. A man was living with his wife in a squatter camp near St Albans outside of Port Elizabeth in the Eastern Cape. He was well known to the police in the area because every time he got drunk, he beat up his wife. She had repeatedly complained to the police, who had regularly calmed him down, but no social workers were involved and the wife refused to press charges. The drinking and the beatings continued.

One Saturday evening the fellow got drunk once again, and this time his beating was more ferocious than usual. He passed out in an alcoholic stupor, and when he came to, he found his wife dead on the floor of their house. Certainly this was not the most clear-headed fellow on the planet. He decided to burn the body and to tell all and sundry that his wife had left him. Behind his shack was a garbage-filled deep hole that he quickly cleaned out and filled with the body, an old mattress and a pile of wood, topped with a good dollop of petrol. He lit the fire and he kept it burning all day by adding more wood and whatever else he could find that would burn.

Several people asked after his wife, and he told them that she had finally become fed up with his drinking and had left him. His brother-in-law was suspicious, as he had seen him dragging heavy 'things' out of the house early that morning to place on the fire. It was he who rang the police late the following day. The police arrived at the house twenty-four hours later to find the fire burnt out and the ash from the hole removed and dumped in three separate locations in the bush beyond the squatter camp. The prosecutor told me that the police had questioned the man, who had confessed to killing his wife accidentally and disposing of her body.

The court case was now well advanced, but the man had changed his mind and recanted the confession. He now said that his wife had indeed left him after one of the usual Saturday-night beatings, and that he had simply been burning rubbish the following day.

The issue of the body had become important to the case, and the police had made the effort to find the three locations and to dig up a sample of the ash from each for analysis.

My observations and subsequent testimony confirmed that there was a body in the ash and that it was almost certainly female.

The bone fragments told me that it was likely that, despite the three locations, only one body was present, and that the damage to the bone was consistent with damage caused by burning for over eight to ten hours at temperatures in the range of 400 °C. My testimony did not confirm that the remains were of the man's wife, but this evidence and the man's first confession were enough for the court to confirm guilt. He was not convicted of murder because the court felt that he had not planned the murder and that it was 'accidental'.

A less formal approach by the police was demonstrated at the end of November 1993, when they hand-delivered to me three cranial fragments in a bag. A minibus taxi had been taken for a roadworthiness test. The mechanic found under the van three fragments of bone, some gooey material that he thought could be brain tissue, and matted hair stuck in the suspension of the vehicle. The mechanic phoned the police, but the driver disavowed any knowledge of the bits discovered in his vehicle's undercarriage.

I had a close look at the bone fragments and could show that they fitted perfectly onto the left side of a human skull as part of the parietal and temporal bones above the ear. They hadn't brought the hair and rather smelly supposed brain tissue, so I could make no comment about that. The bone fragments were dry, but there was some membrane attached to the outside of the bone that may have been muscle-attachment fascia.

Could this be animal bone? The curvature was the shape of a large brain, too big for a baboon but too gradually curved to be that of a larger animal. The general anatomical structure was most consistent with a human. I guessed that it was a male because the muscle markings were strong, but I couldn't be sure. The detective involved was uncertain of his next step.

Technically, it was not illegal to drive around with human brain tissue stuck under your front axle. It did suggest, though, that the driver had been somewhat tardy in reporting that he had run over a person's head and left smashed bits adhering to the vehicle. It sounded like a crime to me, but there was no reported accident and the rest of the body was nowhere to be found. With no body, no report of a vehicle accident involving such serious damage and no admission of guilt, the police gave up.

I rather hope that perhaps I was wrong and that the skull fragments and brain tissue indicated the demise of a baboon. If this had happened more recently, it certainly would have been a good case in which to run DNA tests for species identification, but back in 1993 the case simply remained a mystery.

FIGURE 7: Location of cranial fragments found in vehicle suspension (*bone fragments highlighted in grey*)

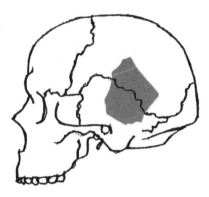

There are other times when the police don't seem willing to pursue an investigation even when there is a body and a crime seems certain. In February 1996 I was asked to go to the Department of Forensic Medicine at UCT to examine four skulls that had been brought in by the Eastern Cape police. Decomposition was not quite complete, so it was better to look at the skulls in the forensic medicine laboratory rather than in one of the teaching rooms in the anatomy department. Annie Katzenberg of the University of Calgary in Canada was visiting me that day, so I suggested that she come along to give her opinion. I don't think Annie had had much opportunity in Canada to deal with the kinds of forensic cases we were seeing on a regular basis.

In the laboratory were two pairs of skulls that had been found about two weeks apart in July and August 1995. They had come from shallow graves in the sand dunes at the mouth of the Umzimvubu River near Port St Johns in the Transkei. The four bodies had been whole, but the police had sent only the skulls. We estimated that the bodies had been there for between one and three years.

All four individuals were young black men ranging in age from around fourteen or fifteen to the early twenties. One individual had an obvious bullet wound entering the skull behind the left ear and exiting at the base of the skull. The wound would have been fatal. There were no signs of violence on any of the other three, but of course we had only the heads to examine.

The police seemed disinterested in the bullet wound, and it transpired that they already had a good idea who the four might be – all they wanted was a verification of identity. I completed my report and the skulls were passed on to Vince Phillips and Susan Rosendorff for facial reconstructions. I recommended that the rest of the remains be exhumed for examination, but there was no response nor any further interest from the local police in the Transkei. Facial reconstructions from each skull were done and they were close enough to allow the families to confirm their identities. The bodies were turned over to the families for burial. No perpetrator was identified and the investigation simply stopped.

Some understanding of South African politics is needed to comprehend the police response. The young men had most probably died some time during 1992 or 1993 when the Transkei was an 'independent homeland', before our first national democratic election on 27 April 1994. Transkei had been launched as a nation in 1976 with the support of the South African government, and it was ruled by the brothers Kaiser and George Matanzima until 1987. As long as the money kept rolling in from Pretoria, the Matanzimas remained friends of apartheid South Africa and the liberation movements were kept out of the Transkei.

But the level of corruption and nepotism was so high that eventually the Matanzimas were overthrown by their own defence force. The new government in the Transkei began to welcome the African National Congress (ANC) and the Pan Africanist Congress (PAC). By the early 1990s, it was obvious that the end of the apartheid government was near and that the Transkei would be re-incorporated into South Africa. Friction began to develop between the ANC and the PAC over who would be dominant in the vast and populous land of the Xhosa.

The four skulls were part of the outcome of that rivalry. The young men had all been PAC supporters, while the local police were strongly pro-ANC in the last days of the independent Transkei. It is very likely that a police hit squad was responsible for their deaths.

At other times the police have been much more diligent. It is a rare occurrence for me to be called out to a crime scene, but that is exactly what happened on 25 March 1995 in the Cape Town suburb of Steenberg. For the previous decade, the poor suburbs in the south of the city had been in the terror grip of a serial killer known as the 'Station Strangler'. This man had strangled and sodomised over twenty boys and, finally, at the beginning of 1995, someone had been arrested for the crimes.

Norman Afzal Simons was eventually convicted of the murder of one boy, but the judge concluded in his summation that there was prima facie evidence that he had killed at least six others and that it was likely that he was responsible for the deaths of fifteen more. Simons' trademark was that he lured the boys into the bush on vacant land near a train station under the pretext of helping him to carry something. He then killed the children, leaving their bodies lying face down in the veld or in a shallow grave, with their hands tied behind their backs and their pants pulled down to their ankles.

We were confronted in Steenberg with a complete skeleton lying face down with the arms and hands under the chest. The hands were dug slightly into the sandy soil and the bones that were more deeply buried still had some adhering desiccated soft tissue. Clothing was lying next to the skeleton, but the undergarments were still on the body, pulled down to the middle of the bones of the lower leg. The skeleton was lying on some twigs and plant stems that had been burnt in the recent past, but the bones had no signs of burning.

The local police told us that the area had been burnt by a veld fire the previous September or October, so we knew that this boy had been killed shortly after that, perhaps in October or November 1994. His age at death was between fifteen and seventeen years. The bones, although defleshed, still had a greasy feel and an unpleasant odour. This made absolute sense for a body that had been exposed at surface during the Cape summer for a period of four to six months.

The cause of death could not be determined, but we found a peri-mortem depressed fracture on the back of the skull and surmised that it was quite possible that the boy had been killed by a blow to the back of the head.

This could have been another Station Strangler murder, as Simons was still active when this boy died. Of concern was that a 'copycat' murderer was out there.

Within a few days, however, the police managed to get an identi-fication and some details about the victim's death. The boy's name was Theo Groenewald. He was fifteen years old at the time of his death and had been missing since 21 November 1994. Theo had been killed by another youth who had stabbed him with a sharp object and then struck him on the back of the head with an electric drill. His body had been placed in the veld to look like a Station Strangler victim so that the police would be misdirected in their investigation.

So many of the skeletonised cases in which we are involved result in no court case and no punishment for the perpetrator, but the following case did end up in court, and there was closure.

Elizabeth Martiens died on 14 April 2007 at just over eleven years old. She had been abducted by a farmer in the Karoo and sexually molested (although the latter was never confirmed), and her body had been placed in an old water tank on a farm in the desert region. It remained there for nearly four months before it was discovered. The farmer, Pieter Botes, who had previous convictions of indecent assault of children under the age of sixteen, was convicted of Elizabeth's murder in 2009.

I was called in when the investigation was already well advanced. The child's remains had been brought to the mortuary in Cape Town so that the bones could be radiographed on the newly installed LODOX machine at the state mortuary. By this stage Botes had already admitted to killing Elizabeth, but he argued that her death had been accidental – supposedly she had fallen off the back of a bakkie. He said he had disposed of the body in the water tank because he was afraid he would be accused of murder.

Our task was to examine the bones to see if there was any sign of injury consistent with a fall from a moving vehicle. There was none. I wrote this in a letter to the state pathologist, Mariette Hurst, but the court decided that I needed to make that statement at the trial.

I don't often go to court because my reports are generally part of the background information for the state pathologist. In this case there seemed to be only two things I could tell the court: I could confirm the girl's age at death and I could state that there were no broken bones. It seemed to me a great waste of resources, as I had to be flown to the nearest airport at George on the southern Cape coast and then fetched from the airport for the one-hour drive north to the town of Oudtshoorn, where the court was sitting – simply to confirm what I had written in the report.

Once in court, I realised that my testimony was more useful than that. I was asked the usual questions about my qualifications, and when I had seen the remains and under what conditions, but then the judge and his assessors asked me a series of questions designed to clarify other issues of concern rather than have me simply repeat what I had already said.

They quickly accepted my account of the girl's age and lack of bone breakage, but then gave me a series of crime scene photographs that I had not seen before. These were the photographs of the body as it had appeared on discovery in the water tank. The court wanted to understand how the small body would have decomposed and how long it would have taken to get down to bone. They also noted that some rags had been placed over the body and that these had been burnt. They wondered how it was possible for a fire to burn the rags without touching the bones.

I did not argue one view or the other; I simply provided information on how to interpret the evidence. The rags were charred but not thoroughly burnt, and I explained that this indicated that the fire had not reached a temperature high enough to damage the bone. I also explained the process of decomposition and especially the role of insects and moisture, or lack thereof.

My testimony lasted about three-quarters of an hour. I had lunch afterwards with the prosecutor and the investigating officer, who told me that the judge was being extremely thorough because this case had attracted a large amount of public scrutiny. The victim was poor and coloured, while the perpetrator was white and advantaged. The judge wanted the case to be heard 'by the book' because there was potential for it to take on racial overtones. In the end, Botes was convicted of abduction and murder. There were no extenuating circumstances.

HUNTING FOR IDENTITY

South Africa has far too many invisible people. During the apartheid years people who did not have the correct documentation to live in the area of their choice would do everything they could to avoid officialdom. Thousands of people moved from the 'homelands' to the urban areas to seek work. To be picked up by the police meant immediate expulsion to the homelands, so hiding from the police became a necessary and common life skill.

Our citizens became more visible after the rise of the 'New South Africa' in 1994. Gaining the vote meant obtaining an identity document in order to vote. Having an address in the city, even if it is a shack number in a squatter camp, is no longer a criminal offence. But since the advent of our freedom, hundreds of thousands of new migrants have crossed our borders from countries to the north. A very large percentage of these people do not have residence permits, and now it is they who find it necessary to hide from the authorities. Where before our unknown bodies came from the rural 'homelands' within South Africa, our new unknowns come from Zimbabwe, Malawi, Mozambique, Namibia, Angola and, more recently, the Congo, Rwanda and Somalia. The odds of our identifying one of these people if he or she ends up as a skeletonised case in a shallow grave are virtually zero.

The other group of invisible people is the destitute. The move to the cities has accelerated since the end of apartheid, and not everyone who has come to Cape Town and other cities has found the streets lined with gold. The poorest of the poor in South Africa do not necessarily live in the burgeoning squatter camps that surround our cities. Although their lives are filled with social problems and poverty blunts their access to the things that most of us consider bare necessities, the poor in the urban squalor of these makeshift cities make as much of life as they can. To be poor and live in a shack is not shameful, and the vast majority lives in the hope that our post-apartheid government will slowly improve their lot.

But there is another group of people that is way past hope. Capetonians often call them 'bergies', an Afrikaans word meaning 'people who sleep on the mountain'. These homeless people take shelter where they can, sometimes in doorways or disused buildings, and often in the bush that grows on the mountain slopes just above the houses of the fairest Cape. Many have lost all direction and find solace solely in the embrace of alcohol. This is either in the form of cheap wine for those who have managed to beg or work for the money necessary to purchase it, or it is in the form of the cheapest of all highs, the 'Blue Train'.

There are two meanings for the 'Blue Train' in South Africa. One of them, the luxurious train that travels between Pretoria and the Cape, rivals the *Orient Express* in its service and lavishness. The other is at the opposite end of the social spectrum and refers to drinking blue-dyed methylated spirits. The ethyl alcohol that is the active ingredient in alcoholic beverages is a poison that we can tolerate reasonably well, as the side effect is merely drunkenness. Methyl alcohol is a similar poison that also produces drunkenness, but it has additional and ultimately fatal side effects. The blue dye is a clue that not only will this compound make you sick, but, given time, it will kill you in a most unpleasant manner. The instructions on the bottle warn us to use this product to clean paint brushes and oil off the floor, and not to drink it. Although it is widely known that swallowing methylated spirits will make you sick, blind and dead, good-quality ethyl alcohol is expensive, and for the very poorest of people the chance to buy a bottle of almost pure alcohol for just a few rands is a chance they may sometimes take to dull the pain of life.

Typically, a hiker on the lower slopes of the mountain will report to the police that he or she has found a skeleton. The police can generally work out what has happened from the context of the discovery. The 'crime' scene reveals a home-made shelter of cardboard and plastic. Garbage in the form of old plastic bags and bottles surrounds the site and inside the shelter lie the bones of a person still wearing the ragged clothes that he or she last wore. No name tags, no identification documents, no council bills. This was a person who barely had an identity in life, and has no identity in death.

This is a worst-case scenario for the investigating officer. Sometimes other homeless people may know the person's identity, but if the person had chosen an isolated place to build the shelter, there is almost no hope of making an identification, and it is only the forensic anthropologist who can help. This is where the 'signs of individualisation' or 'osteobiography' become important. We need to identify features of the person that were distinctive. These could trigger those who knew him or her to make a connection. It would help if the person were very tall, for example, or had a missing limb. The best of all, however, is a facial feature that no one can mistake.

Death register number 211/90 was found under bushes just up the hill from the houses on Devil's Peak, Cape Town. Her body had been in the scraps of her shelter for months; when the police were finally told about her, she was only bones with fragments of dried flesh still attached in places. She was perhaps in her fifties when she died and had the genetic make-up of thousands of her fellow Capetonians, showing roots from at least two, probably three, continents. She was of average height and average body build, showed no obvious signs of disease, and nothing indicated a violent death.

There were a few signs of osteoarthritis on the bones of her back, and she had lost all of her teeth long before death. She had probably died in her sleep after years of substance abuse and poverty. Perhaps she had been on the Blue Train, as the site was littered with the usual collection of rubbish, including empty plastic bottles.

But the bones of her face were distinctive. She had broken her nose and jaw some time long before death, and although the bones had healed, her face was distorted. Her lower jaw was pushed sharply to the left, and there were other fractures up the left side of her face resulting in a nose that was also pushed to one side. Her face must have been absolutely unmistakeable with its toothless smile and signs of past violence.

This case came up before we began to liaise with Vince Phillips on facial reconstructions, but we asked our medical illustrator in the UCT Department of Anatomy to try her hand at drawing a face that we could send to the police. Her efforts worked very well and I am certain that she captured a good likeness, but sadly the police could find no one who recognised the woman. I am still uncertain about the success of facial reconstructions from bone, and I am not sure if the problem was our picture or if the police simply didn't ask someone who happened to have known the sad woman. She is still unidentified.

FIGURE 8: Facial reconstruction of DR 211/90

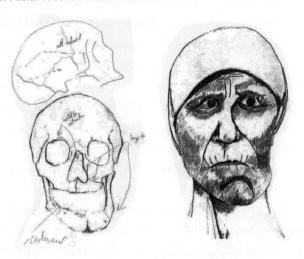

Drawing by Elise Fuller

You don't have to be a homeless bergie to disappear in South Africa. For many, the disruption of society caused by apartheid meant that family links were broken and people who lost contact are no longer traceable. This was, and probably still is, especially true for the elderly.

One of the very first forensic cases in which I became involved was that of an old man from Atlantis whose bones were found in the power-line cut between Melkbosstrand and Atlantis on the northern edge of the Cape Town urban belt. So-called coloured people didn't have a 'homeland' to which they could be exiled, so the apartheid social engineers created an entire suburb in the sand-dune scrub about forty kilometres north of Cape Town in the 1970s.

The government plan was to grant massive subsidies to industries that moved from the city to this area in the hope that the coloured working-class people would follow. At first a number of companies took the incentive, but even with the subsidy it was not economically viable to be so far out of town, and the companies began to fail. By the 1980s, the new town of Atlantis had one of the highest unemployment rates in the province and it remains a centre of poverty, drug abuse and social misery today.

Eskom power-line maintenance workers were clearing the brush below the towers in 1989 when they came across a complete skeleton in the shade of some overgrown vegetation. Len Lerer was the state pathologist assigned to the case and he asked me if I wanted to visit the site with him. We met the police at Melkbosstrand and were taken in a police vehicle to the body.

The bones were clean and white and had been there for some years. The clothes, although mostly rotted, were still present, and while collecting the bones we found a plastic medicine packet in the pocket. The name had faded and was illegible, but the prescription line was still clear. The tablets had been issued by Groote Schuur Hospital five years before and were for a drug used to control congestive heart failure. The man, in his early sixties, had been walking along the power line but he had obviously felt ill and lain down to wait out his heart palpitations. As he lay there his heart must have finally given in, and he died under a bush far from his home. A sad way to go, but it is made even sadder by the fact that no one reported him missing to the authorities.

Other people who are not necessarily poor go to secluded areas to end it all, and one of the favourite places for this is Table Mountain. I have now seen two or three cases of skeletons retrieved from the bottom of the cliff face, especially on the Camps Bay side of the mountain. Typically, these are of young men, and the bones show signs of violent trauma caused by a fall. There are often multiple fractures created by repeated violent impact with the ground as the body bounced from rock ledge to rock ledge on its way down 300 metres of mountainside.

Women seem to prefer a gentler way to go. In October 1994, Vince Phillips and I were called out to the top of Table Mountain to examine a skeleton found by a Dutch tourist who had walked no more than fifty metres off the main pathway to get better reception on his portable radio. He had found the remains of Rheta Barnard, who had chosen the top of Table Mountain to end her life.

Six years previously, she had taken the cable car up to the summit and walked to a private place where she could see the beautiful view from the top of the mountain. There she carefully placed her shoes and her handbag beside her, took a lethal dose of sleeping tablets and lay down to die. Her parents later said that this troubled young woman had always loved the mountain and, although they would never understand why she chose to take her own life, it was under-standable to them why she had selected the location she had.

All of these cases were found on dry land and I was lucky enough in several of the investigations to be able to go out to the site at the time of discovery. But there is no crime scene when a body washes up on the beach.

I have recently become very interested in marine cases because I discovered that I had been under the misapprehension that decomposition in cold water is slower than on land. I am pretty sure that the error of my assumption is part of my Canadian upbringing.

Way back in 1969 I had the chance to work over the summer as a park naturalist on the shores of Lake Superior. This was wild country where bears, wolves and moose were commonly found. The countryside is absolutely stunning and the waters of the lake are exceptionally cold. Lake Superior is so large that the middle never freezes in winter, and, conversely, it doesn't warm up in summer. The locals told me at the time that people who drown in the lake often sink and take years to decompose. I was hardly in a position to confirm this bit of folk science, but it stuck in my mind when I saw cases of decomposed bodies washing up on the Cape coast. I assumed that decomposition that would take months on land would take years in the water.

During 2010 I was called to look at two cases of completely decomposed bodies that had washed ashore, one on the West Coast and the other on the South Coast. They had in common that their bones were picked absolutely clean. The bones were still greasy to the touch and didn't smell good at all. Based on my misassumption, I thought that these people had died at least a year or two previously, but Linda Liebenberg of UCT forensic medicine sent me an article that described the speed of decomposition of some case studies in cold water.

It turns out that the speed of decomposition in cold water can be very fast if there are appropriate flesh-eating critters on the sea bed. I am still following this up, but I am hopeful that we will be able to identify the unknown person from the Cape West Coast and I should have my answer then. We do indeed have the right scavenger on our coast, although those who enjoy a good lobster dinner may not appreciate this fact, as our best scavenger by far is the Cape spiny rock lobster (*Jasus ialandii*), known to all around these parts as 'crayfish'. They can have very dense populations despite high fishing pressure.

This has been demonstrated several times when mass die-offs occur on our coast due to oxygen-sapping red tides. A red tide is a massive bloom of plankton that drifts close to shore. The decomposing plankton uses all of the available oxygen in the shallow water and the crayfish begin to suffocate. In a desperate attempt to gasp for oxygen, the crayfish crawl out of the ocean, which gives us a view of their numbers.

In a stranding at Elands Bay in 1997 it was estimated that there were over 1 200 tons of shellfish. This was followed five years later by another stranding in the same area, when an estimated 1 000 tons of crayfish were stranded. That is a vast number of carrion eaters, and explains how a body could be rendered down to nice smooth bone in a relatively short time.

Although I have mentioned only the two local wash-ups of human remains in 2010, there are quite a number of these cases. The state pathologists see many more cases that are not decomposed, but they generally only notify me if the body is more or less down to bone. I now have records of several single human bones that have washed up, presumably after the body has been cleaned by scavengers, and I have even had one case of a human skull found in the bottom of a fishing trawler's net five kilometres offshore. It looks like bodies need to sink to the bottom, however, to completely decompose. Floaters are much less pleasant and generally turn up on the beach long before the job of decomposition is complete.

Deon Knobel, the head of Forensic Pathology at UCT in the 1990s, asked me to help him with a floater that came ashore on the False Bay coast. A human torso in an advanced state of decomposition had washed up on Muizenberg beach, and Deon said that there was little to go on except the bone exposed in the remnants. He was in no rush but did want to get the report done as soon as was reasonable.

Now I have no problem in dealing with dry bone, but I am not good with the odour of decay if it is any more than a background smell. The thought of working with someone who had been float-ing in False Bay for so long that the forensic pathologists couldn't write a report on it was clearly not going to be fun. Despite that, I made the appointment to meet Deon at the Salt River mortuary on Monday morning.

The weekend had been a busy one for me, and on Sunday I was starting to feel a bit 'off'. I didn't sleep well on Sunday night and woke early in the morning knowing that I should be feeling better. I had a cup of tea and a light breakfast. I arrived at the mortuary at around 8.30, but the pathologists had been hard at work for at least an hour and a half by then. It was a busy Monday morning, as the weekend murder crop in the Cape was higher than usual. A taxi war had broken out on Saturday and there were at least eight people on the slabs being postmortemed.

Taxi wars are a distinctly South African phenomenon effectively triggered by apartheid planners but now part of everyday life. When the apartheid planners began putting their black citizens in separate townships on the margins of white cities, they intended to solve the problem of moving vast numbers of people into the cities for work by using the railway network. But the people developed their own transport system by means of twelve-seater 'minibus taxis' that pick up customers in the townships and deposit them along a wide range of routes into the city and neighbouring town-ships. South Africans love to hate the inconsiderate drivers of these vehicles, who drive by their own rules and stop wherever they choose to pick up and drop off passengers, but in fact they provide an efficient service for millions of people. The problem is their success. There is great competition between routes and taxi associ-ations, and this frequently ends in gunfire.

That Saturday morning, a killer hired by one of the taxi bosses opened fire with an automatic weapon on passengers getting into a vehicle from a rival taxi association, and eight people who started their Saturday morning with nothing more ordinary than a desire to go to work, visit friends or go shopping, never made it to the afternoon.

As I walked into the main room of the mortuary, Deon called me over to look at what he was doing. Most of these poor people had died of multiple gunshot wounds, and Deon and his team were busy tracking entry and exit wounds and their trajectories. He insisted that I look over his shoulder at the dissections, and he was excited about showing me one wound after another. I watched for fifteen minutes but I could feel my self-control, and possibly my breakfast, slipping away. Finally I reminded Deon of the reason for my visit to the mortuary and he reluctantly broke away from his grisly task.

He led me out of the mortuary and into a back alley, where a single body trolley, covered by a thick sheet, had been placed well away from the building. When we approached the trolley Deon pulled back the covering to reveal something almost unidentifiable. Only the lower part of the trunk down to the knee was present. No organs remained – only muscle tissue with bones projecting out here and there. The smell struck me as I looked at this mess, and without a further word to Deon, I ran back up the alley and began gagging against the wall. I don't think I ever wrote the final report for him.

Not all remains that I evaluate are human. Sometimes a seal flipper that has washed up on the beach in an advanced stage of decomposition is mistaken for a human hand. Several of the American osteology texts for forensic anthropology include a detailed diagram of the hand bones of the bear. This is because the skeletonised paw of a bear and a human hand are broadly similar in size and look surprisingly similar to the untrained eye. Needless to say, bears are not prevalent in Africa, but we do have the occasional forensic case that involves animal rather than human bone. The police, however, require us to confirm the identity as non-human even if they already have a good idea that the bone is animal. Their maxim is rather to be safe than sorry.

Most often I see the remains of the good old South African braai. Being a non-denominational osteologist, I actually enjoy sorting through the animal bone and identifying not only the species but also the butcher's cut. Food remains on an archaeological site are always interesting, and my background includes analysing animal bone from butcheries in historic sites. Some of my police and forensic pathology visitors have chuckled when I've shown them not human bones but the midline cut for lamb chops and the long lumbar spines in the T-bone steaks. No crime here, simply a place to dump the ash from the fire and bone remnants from prime beef and lamb.

Sometimes the animal bone is associated with archaeological skeletons that have come in from accidental discoveries, which have been routed to the Department of Human Biology by the police or forensic pathologists. Sadly, we are seldom called to the site of discovery, and the bones are sometimes delivered to me in a black bag if the police haven't opened an inquest document or in an official evidence bag if the police are unsure of the antiquity of the bones. In these cases the animal bone may very well be a clue to identifying the origin of the person.

Later Stone Age graves along the coast in South Africa were often interred in vast shell middens that accumulated from shell-fish gathering on the rocky coastline over generations. A few of these prehistoric garbage dumps are huge, especially on the West Coast between 3 000 and 4 000 years ago. The archaeologists call these sites 'mega-middens'. The deposits are jam-packed with shells, animal bone, stone tools and the occasional burial.

When these graves are disturbed accidentally, the haphazard collection of bones from the site usually includes some of the asso-ciated material. The bones are not from domestic animals, and the presence of bones of small buck such as duiker and steenbok, along with bones of shorebirds, tortoises and sometimes a seal or two, can mark this as the grave of a Later Stone Age individual.

My favourite animal bone job came to me in May 2004, when I was visited by the Directorate of Special Operations (DSO). The South African DSO was modelled on the American Federal Bureau of Investigation (FBI) by our first democratic government. Its job was to tackle organised crime. The unit fell under the Department of Justice so that investigation and prosecution could be performed under the same command, and it also allowed the DSO to be separated from the South African Police Service (SAPS), then (and still) struggling to rid itself of incompetence and corruption.

Although the unit was officially called the Directorate of Special Operations, everyone in South Africa knew it as the 'Scorpions'. For many of us in South Africa, the demise of the Scorpions in November 2008 was a great loss for policing in the country. They were good at their job, but when they started to investigate the politicians in the ruling ANC, a parliamentary process to dissolve the unit was launched. Only the ANC voted for the Scorpions' dissolution, but since the party held the majority in parliament, it meant the end of the unit.

In the first half of 2004 the Scorpions were investigating a case of organised crime in abalone smuggling on the southern Cape coast. Poaching of these increasingly rare shellfish is very lucrative, as the dried meat sells for astronomical prices in the Far East. The same people who orchestrated the poaching were also heavily involved in the drug trade – they were the real target of the Scorpions. However, as so often happens, the thieves fell out. Two of the people being watched by the Scorpions simply disappeared. As the investigation continued, the Scorpions received information that the two had been killed, dismembered and dumped in the channel between Gansbaai and Dyer Island, about 150 kilometres east of Cape Town.

The plan from the murderer's point of view was a good one. Dyer Island is the home of several thousand South African fur seals and, because of this, the channel between the island and the mainland supports the largest population of great white sharks in the country. There is active ecotourism in the channel in the form of cage diving, where eager tourists pay large sums of money to be submerged in the water in a cage for a close-up view of sharks. The great whites are attracted to the boats by chum (fish oil poured into the water) and bait packs containing kilograms of meat. The sharks are well accustomed to their handouts. It seemed obvious to the murderers that nicely portioned sections of human would quickly be disposed of by the hungry sharks.

The Scorpions took a gamble. Great white sharks are messy feeders. They bite off huge chunks of meat but there are always scraps that are missed, which sink to the bottom of the ocean. The Scorpions hired a ski-boat and dredged the channel exactly where their informants said the bodies had been dumped. To their great delight, the dredges brought up plenty of bone.

My job was to sift through the contents of eight evidence bags of bone that they brought to me. The first bag contained three skull fragments and bones from the fore and hind leg of a juvenile seal. The second bag was mildly more interesting, as it contained the remains of several seals, some adult and some juvenile, along with a large fish bone. Bag three held seal and sea bird. The rest of the bags didn't vary at all. They contained seals of all ages, but nary the sign of a human.

Senior Special Investigator Prinsloo was unimpressed and slightly embarrassed, but he was doing his job as thoroughly as he could and, in the end, he had to accept that not all lines of evidence give results, and sometimes the budget is blown with no positive outcome.

4

Muti Murders

It was a horrible discovery. On 29 September 1994, a pair of hands and the forearms of a child were found on a refuse dump in the Boys Town squatter camp outside Langa in Cape Town. The arms had been severed with a large knife and the left ring finger was missing – amputated at around the time of death. Less than a week later the police arrested a sangoma – a southern African traditional doctor – on information received from people in the community.

When they searched the sangoma's shack they discovered the base of a human skull in the ashes of a fire on the floor, five pieces of dried human skin, a portion of scalp, a mandible with ten deciduous teeth and a small piece of skull vault. Elsewhere in the shack they found a green T-shirt wrapped around another piece of scalp with an ear attached, a section of the spinal column from the neck, and two pouches – one containing decomposing brain tissue and the other decomposing fat.

Shortly afterwards the police arrested the sangoma's eighteen-year-old assistant and, in due course, the two of them pointed out a metal trunk dumped at the side of a nearby freeway. In the trunk were the rest of the remains of a five-year-old boy.

My colleague Vince Phillips was called in at this stage to help identify the body. The arms and head were missing and the external genitalia had been cut off.

Subsequent DNA analysis confirmed that the arms on the dump, the body in the metal box and the pieces at the shack were all from the same child. The finger, the genitalia and most of the head were never recovered.

The newspapers reported the grisly finds and the people of Cape Town were incensed. This kind of murder involving a child and the harvesting of body parts had not occurred in Cape Town in recent memory, if at all.

The sangoma never made it to trial. He had a long record of mental instability, with psychotic episodes for which he had been treated at the local mental hospital, and the court had him committed to an institution under the Mental Health Care Act. His accomplice was tried, but there was not enough evidence to convict him, so he was released. The local Langa community, however, made him pay the ultimate price: he was necklaced with a tyre; it was placed over his head and shoulders and set alight with petrol.

Nearly six years after the Langa case in Cape Town, the police approached Maryna Steyn in Pretoria to examine three pots that had been recovered from a sangoma's house in the city. They had arrested a car thief, and under interrogation he had admitted to abducting a young man during a hijacking and delivering him, possibly still alive, to a sangoma in the township. During their search for the missing victim, the police had found the three suspicious pots in the sangoma's house. There was, however, no sign of the missing man. They consulted Maryna because they wanted an expert opinion on the substance of the pots.

Maryna and her colleagues carefully laid out the three pots (now labelled Objects A, B and C) in the laboratory and examined both the pots themselves and their contents. Two of the pots were intact (A and C), but the police had broken open the middle pot.

Object A turned out to be a plant gourd and, although decorated with beads and bird claws, there was nothing sinister about the pot itself.

But the same could not be said about its contents. Inside the pot was a thick, foul-smelling fluid that contained a human tongue cut out with the hyoid bone of the throat still attached. The pot also contained several hand bones, some bone fragments, the first two neck vertebrae and parts of the bony eye sockets of a skull. All of the bones were human.

Object B also contained a thick fluid with a large number of inclusions. Besides two unspent rifle shells, some coins from various southern African countries and some animal bone, there were six human teeth, six human hand bones and several bone fragments, all human. The pot itself was a human skull that had been carefully trimmed of all its protuberances and then coated with some kind of epoxy resin.

The third pot, Object C, was the largest. It was similar in construction and contents to Object B. The outside of the pot was richly decorated with beads and other items. Inside Object C was more of the foul-smelling liquid and many other contents, including bones. Much of the bone was fragmentary but most of it was identifiable as human, and it included many different body parts. The pot itself was another skull, once again coated with epoxy resin.

Maryna and her colleagues carefully cleaned out the two skull pots and chipped away the epoxy resin. In both cases the faces had been broken away and only the braincase remained. Any protruding structures had been sliced off to make the skull functional as a pot. The skull of Object B was that of a young person, perhaps in her late teens. Maryna couldn't confirm the sex as female, but decided that in the light of its small size and delicate features it was most likely female. The skull that made up Object C was larger, slightly older (perhaps late teens or early twenties) and almost certainly male. The bone was fresh, with some soft tissue still attached.

The bone found inside all three pots was harder to deal with because it was, for the most part, broken up. Careful analysis of the pieces showed that the bones came from no more than two people and the fragments suggested that one of the people was larger and slightly older, while the other was smaller and younger. The implication was that all of the bone fragments belonged to the same two people represented by the skulls.

Maryna's analysis also looked at the shape of the two braincases in comparison to her database of skulls in the collection of the anatomy department at the University of Pretoria. The measurements of the skull from Object B fell within the range of variation of the South African Negro individuals in her sample, but the skull from Object C was different and was a better fit for her comparative sample of Caucasoid (European) origin.

By now you know that racial analysis does not thrill me, but in this case it turned out to be extremely valuable. This is certainly a case where 'racial identification' reduced the search categories in order to help with individual identification. With virtually no useful identifying features on the butchered skulls, the fact that one of the skulls was from someone of Caucasoid origin suggested that Object C might very well be the missing hijacking victim. This was indeed confirmed through DNA analysis. Sadly, no DNA comparisons were suggested for the young black woman whose skull formed the container of Object B.

The two cases outlined above were clearly both solved with the help of forensic anthropologists. The car hijackers told the police that they had gone to the sangoma to ask for charms to make them bullet proof and to put the police off their scent. The sangoma in Cape Town was not lucid enough to account for his actions, but it transpired that the victim was his nephew and that a family feud had existed between branches of the family for more than ten years. In both the Cape Town and Pretoria cases the object of the murders was to harvest human tissue to make medicine or, to use the isiZulu term, *umuti* – muti, as it is commonly known. Are these hideous cases simply aberrations that occur from time to time, or is this something that happens more often than we care to admit? Is this a part of life (and death) in southern Africa?

In order to understand the logic behind the traditional belief in potions, which leads to brutal murder to obtain body parts, we need to look at the social beliefs of the population as a whole.

WITCHES, SANGOMAS AND THE AFRICAN APPROACH TO THE SPIRIT WORLD

African belief systems are not inherently violent, nor are they bloodthirsty. The central concern is about the 'big questions' of life: Who are we? Why are we here? What happens when we die? In that sense, the African world view is not terribly dissimilar from that of any other people, and although there are some unique approaches to answering these questions, there are parallels else-where in both geography and time.

What happens when we die? Do we simply cease to exist, or is there something else out there that allows us to live on after our demise? Each of the major religions asks the same question and then tries to provide an answer. Religious philosophy consistently denies the absolute nature of death by proclaiming it as a new beginning. We leave one world and journey to the next. Effectively we are negating the finality of death with the promise of a new life that is, we hope, better than the one we have just left.

The Judeo-Christian view is based on the Greek idea of salvation, while the great religions of the Indian subcontinent have chosen reincarnation as their form of 'new beginning'. Old Testament Jewish beliefs had no real concept of life after death and souls were said to go to a timeless place that was neither heaven nor hell. The Hellenistic Greeks passed on the idea of a last judgement (when the just will be rewarded and the unjust punished) to the Jews during their colonial expansion into the Middle East. Jewish response to Greek oppression not only triggered the Maccabean wars, but also resulted in the first discussion of resurrection. A Messiah would come who could return the dead to life and found a new kingdom alongside God, presumably without the presence of the damnable Greeks.

For Jews, the resurrection would occur in the distant future, but not so for the Christians, a Jewish sect that became prominent in the Roman world. For Christians, salvation was immediate and personal and it came with a very clear division between good and bad – heaven and hell. When Islam began to take shape in the 600s CE, it adopted the idea of salvation along with a powerful image of good and evil.

Far to the east, Hindu and Buddhist believers chose a denial of death that did not involve a divine judgement in the same way. Their belief in reincarnation made salvation automatic, but whether or not the new life would be better than the old one depended entirely on a person's actions while they were alive. For much of the rest of the world, including Africa, eastern Asia, Australia and the Americas, the choice of death denial was 'transcendence'.

In the Western view, the physical world of people, animals and buildings is entirely separate from the spiritual world. Heaven and hell (if we believe in them), along with ghosts, souls, and all of the other flotsam and jetsam of the spirit world, are out there in another plane of existence. We may fervently believe that the souls of our much-loved deceased parents are watching us, but we cannot feel them, hear them or see them. We have the chance to interact with them only when we die.

The physical and the spiritual worlds are not separate in the African beliefs. The living and the dead are part of a continuum. You may become a spirit, or, more properly, an 'ancestor', when you die, but you haven't changed worlds; you have simply transformed from one form of being into another. You are still with the living both physically and socially. What this means is that the definition of the community includes the ancestors, and you and I are in constant contact with them in our daily lives. They can influence us and we can influence them.

This is the key to understanding African religion. Ritual controls our relationship with the ancestors and ensures social continuity. The independent spirits that are banished to a faraway place in the Judeo-Christian vision are everywhere in Africa. Ancestors, ghosts and animal spirits exist side by side with the living, and communication between them and us is constant. The integration of the physical with the spiritual world in traditional African belief systems is used to explain evil, illness and misfortune. All of us have two characters: one that is right, moral, good and healthy; and a second that is wrong, immoral, bad and unhealthy. They exist in equilibrium. Sickness and misfortune are signs that the balance has been upset and that good is being overwhelmed by evil. We need to identify the cause of the imbalance and restore the good side with protective magic, including medicine.

Missing from this world view is the concept of chance when it comes to serious ailments or significant bad luck. All death and misfortune are believed to be caused by something or someone in the physical part of the world or among the ancestors in the interconnected spiritual one. Treatment of any major illness or correction of any misfortune must involve both treating the physical symptoms of the illness and finding the cause of the imbalance. Medicines can be curative in the sense of treating an ailment, but, much more importantly, they can be preventative. Through the use of magic, medicines can provide protection from both illness and misfortune.

Typically, in modern South Africa, a person uses both Western and traditional medicines. The medical doctor who treats the illness can demonstrate good scientific principles for how the sickness can be cured, but he or she is incapable of explaining *why* the person got sick in the first place. Why does one person get sick but not another?

The closest translation of sangoma in English is 'witch doctor', but the name is inappropriate and doesn't describe the role or importance of this person in society. The sangoma (most often a woman, although occasionally a man) is an expert at divination, and it is she who can speak to the ancestors to determine the exact cause of the illness. Medicine to the traditional doctor does not just treat the illness; it also treats the cause of the imbalance, especially if it is caused by a witch. Witchcraft in traditional African belief is very real. A witch is a person who is in league with the evil spirits and is inherently malevolent.

The sangoma works for the good of the community and is most certainly not a witch. Her importance derives from the fact that she has the power to interpret the causes of misfortune and can tell if it has befallen as a result of an insult to the ancestors (a failure to perform the proper ritual) or a witch or sorcerer. Her power comes from these links with the ancestors. The most important role of the sangoma is divination, and it is her job not only to identify the cause of the misfortune, but to choose the appropriate ritual or medicine to cure the problem.

The sangoma is not the only person who can make medicines. The traditional doctor who more closely fits the English term 'doctor' is the *inyanga*. Most *inyangas* are men. Their gift from the ancestors is not divination, but the ability to make medicinal herbs to cure illness.

Perhaps we should consider the *inyanga* to be the Western equivalent of the pharmacist, as people come to him to obtain medicines to deal with specific health or misfortune problems. The *inyanga* may prescribe, but he does not divine. In modern times, especially in the urban centres of South Africa, the use of the terms *inyanga* and sangoma is becoming blurred, but the roles of the *inyanga* and the sangoma in understanding illness remain separate. Both divination and prescription are required in order to treat the patient properly.

All of this digression into religion is important so that we may understand the context of muti murders. As I mentioned earlier, in the African world view the dead are not separated from the living. We all live in one community and a request to the ancestors for help in solving problems is not unreasonable. Also not unreasonable is the belief that a witch is out there manipulating your life and causing your misfortune.

The sangoma has a special place in this context because she is the ritual expert who not only is able to identify the cause of the problem, but can also prescribe the right medicine and ritual to fix it. The medicine can be restorative as part of a ritual to appease the ancestors or it can be preventative – protecting against misfortune in the community or smoothing the pathway for an individual's future actions.

The use of human tissue in medicines is part of the preventative pharmacopoeia of some of the sangomas. The precise parts and the method of the preparation of the medicine is the preserve of the sangoma. Animal and plant materials are the most frequent ingredients of traditional medicines, but since humans have more power than animals, it is obvious that medicines made with human parts will be more powerful when special muti is required. The sangoma is not usually involved in the killing of the victim; her job is restricted to the preparation and administration of the muti. Sometimes the murder of the victim is called a 'ritual murder', but this term is incorrect because the ritual is all in the preparation of the medicine, not in the act of murder.

Now that we have an idea of the reason for muti murders, we need to ask who the victims are, and how often and where these murders occur.

VICTIMS AND PERPETRATORS

Medicine murders are not a new phenomenon in southern Africa. We have oral history and archival records going back to the 1860s noting these murders among the Ndebele, Pedi, Swazi, Tswana, Venda and Zulu peoples. I don't yet have proof of how far back in time this practice goes, but I suspect that it could be about 1 500 years or more.

In 1989 I was asked by Len van Schalkwyk of the KwaZulu Monuments Council to analyse the human skeletal remains from a site called Wosi in the Thukela Basin of central KwaZulu-Natal. The site is one of several dating from 700 to 800 CE and its occupiers were among the first of the Iron Age people to settle in the region. Two skeletons were the sad remains of a four- and a seven-year-old who had died of the normal range of causes that affected young children in pre-industrial societies, but some bits and pieces of human bones were also found in the ash middens on the margins of the village.

These garbage dumps were integral parts of the settlement and were not simply places to dispose of refuse. The largest amount of waste was the ash from the fire places of the village. This could have been dumped far away in the fields of sorghum and millet, but the midden was located much closer to the settlement: it was generally placed right in front of the main entrance to the settlement. Anyone coming into the hamlet (including the cows that would be brought in every night to the safety of the central cattle kraal) would have to walk through the ash, raising a fine dust that functioned as a very effective tick remover, annoying the blood-sucking parasites so that they released their grip and dropped off.

The excavators at Wosi had found several human foot bones, a neck vertebra of a child and a femur of a newborn baby in two middens a short distance away from the main midden, which contained the two child burials.

As I looked at the bones I realised that only one person was represented by the foot bones. The two bones that came from the excavation in Grid VI fitted together perfectly, and the single bone from excavation in Grid III – although it didn't articulate with the other two – was a perfect match in size and shape. Despite the bones' similarity and the likelihood that they were from the same person, the middens in Grids III and VI were 250 metres apart. If they were the same person, then it was almost inconceivable that the bones had 'drifted' apart. Could this have been human muti placed at the entrance of the hamlet to protect it from the evils of the world?

Unfortunately, I could not be sure. The skeletons of high-status individuals in Iron Age sites are most frequently found in the central cattle kraal or under the walls of houses, but occasionally the skeleton of a woman or child is found in the ash heaps. The two child burials at Wosi fitted this pattern.

FIGURE 9: Diagram of the isolated foot bones from Wosi with original notation from the laboratory analysis

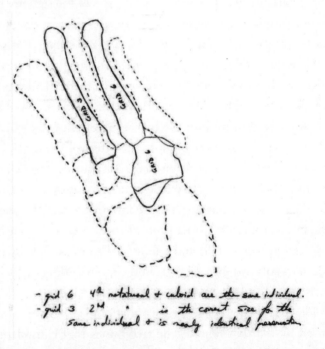

Bones do become disassociated from burials. Over the years I have seen many single bones in Later Stone Age cave sites where digging by animals or humans has moved bones from one place to another. Sometimes I even find a truncated skeleton, but there are usually signs of disturbance to indicate that the burial was once whole. Envisioning this kind of bone movement over 250 metres in the open space of an Iron Age archaeological site is much harder.

With some help from Ina Plug of the then Transvaal Museum in Pretoria, I compiled a list of as many Iron Age archaeological sites as I could where isolated human bones had been recovered along with the faunal remains. Specialists like Ina create detailed lists of animal bone and use this information to reconstruct the diet and activities of the people who hunted or kept animals. They are diligent workers and if they find even a scrap of human bone, they list it as part of their sample. They rarely comment on the discovery in their discussions. The underlying assumption is that the presence of human bone fragments is accidental and the bone must have 'drifted' in from a nearby burial even if the burial was not found during the excavation.

The data from Ina told me that isolated human bones in Iron Age sites were surprisingly common, but few were really suspicious. A minimum of five humans, for example, was found in the faunal sample from K2 at Bambandyanalo near the Zimbabwean border, but all five humans were represented by teeth only. Clearly, dumping teeth (permanent and deciduous) is something that could happen in a garbage midden or ash field without our becoming concerned.

Another frequent discovery (at seventeen out of forty sites surveyed) were finger bones. We do know that digits were amputated in the past as part of rite-of-passage ceremonies. The social anthropologists tell us that women sometimes had the little finger of one of their hands removed as a mark of widowhood.

Again it is not unreasonable to assume that the detached digits would be dumped in the ash midden, but the idea of amputated fingers simply being discarded is worrisome in the light of the traditional African belief in the power of body parts.

However, Ina's list of isolated human remains also included some bones that simply could not be 'removed' without seriously inconveniencing the owner. How do you remove a collar bone, or a thigh bone, or a neck vertebra without killing the patient? There are only two possible explanations: the bones were from disturbed burials; or the bones were intentionally placed in the special locations around the village as part of muti beliefs.

At Kamakwe, an eighteenth-century Iron Age site north of the Magaliesburg, the archaeologists Revil Mason and Trevor Jones recovered a pair of thigh bones that had been cut through on their upper ends. This could be no accident and is almost certainly not the sign of death in battle. This is dismemberment, clear and simple, and is a smoking gun as a sign of murder.

The best evidence for ancient muti murder comes from the Early Iron Age site of Broederstroom in the North West Province of South Africa, and from the Late Iron Age site of Greefswald in Limpopo Province. In both locations heads in pots have been found.

Broederstroom in the Magalies valley west of Pretoria was excavated by Revil Mason in the 1970s. This was one of the first Early Iron Age sites to be identified in South Africa and it blew apart the old apartheid education model of the peopling of South Africa. Apartheid education taught that both Europeans and Bantu-speaking South Africans were new arrivals, the former having moved east from the Western Cape and the latter having come down from beyond the Limpopo River, the current northern border between South Africa and Zimbabwe.

The two had met, our history books told us, for the first time at the Great Fish River in the Eastern Cape in the 1770s. Before then the implication was that South Africa was 'empty' (ignoring the San hunters and the Khoe herders) and that the white settlers had as much right as black 'natives' to take the land for themselves. Mason's site was hard evidence that Iron Age farmers were settled in the Pretoria area by 500 CE, over a thousand years before the Europeans set foot in the Cape.

Mason found several burials at Broederstroom, but the most disturbing discoveries of human remains were the two pot burials located in the residential area about halfway between two huts. Burial 24/73 Ko was a large pot containing the upper jaw of an adult and the lower jaw of a child of between eight and ten years of age. There were no other bones in the pot, but an arm bone was found just outside of it.

Burial 24/73 Azzt had the dentition and lower face of a twelve-year-old child inside an upside-down buried pottery jar. In his 1986 discussion of the site, Mason does not mention muti murder but instead tries to explain the mysterious pot burials as being a part of an elaborate burial described by the missionary linguist A.T. Bryant in his 1929 book *Olden Times in Zululand and Natal*.

Bryant wrote that the body of a senior person in Zulu society was buried in a sitting position, leaving the head above ground. The head was covered by an inverted pot and, after decomposition, the skull was removed and buried close to the deceased's hut. No other writer describing Zulu society has ever seen or heard of the practice described by Bryant, and it is entirely possible that Bryant was a victim of the social anthropologist's curse – accepting without question a story that has been provided by an informant with a great sense of humour and a deadpan delivery style.

Leaving a burial with the head covered by a pot would be unwise in an environment where hyaenas (and domestic dogs) were present, unless they were prepared to mount a twenty-four-hour guard for several months until decomposition was complete. Even if Bryant's description were accurate, the pot burials from Broederstroom don't fit his depiction. These are not the burials of senior men and they are not within the floor plan of a hut. Most importantly, both pots contained the remains of children.

Greefswald is the farm in the Limpopo Province that contains two of the most important archaeological sites in southern Africa and is now a United Nations Educational, Scientific and Cultural Organisation (UNESCO) World Heritage Site. Within the boundaries of the farm is the hill fort of Mapungubwe, which overlooks the Limpopo River and was occupied around 1000 CE by a society that shows all the hallmarks of advanced civilisation. Fantastically rich gold burials were found on the top of Mapungubwe Hill, indicating that it was a royal residence of a people who traded ivory, gold and other metals throughout the region.

About two kilometres away is a second hill called Bambandyanalo. No royal settlement was found there, but on the slopes of Bambandyanalo was a large town called K2 by its excavators. This town reached its zenith about 250 years later. Excavators in the 1970s found a skull and two mandibles, all from different individuals, in the cattle kraals at K2. They suspected that this could be a sign of ritual, but could not exclude the possibility that the bones were dispersed from the cemetery, which was not very far away.

This is the same site at which teeth from five individuals were found in the ash heaps. A short distance downhill from K2 is the midden debris site called K1 by the first excavators in the 1930s. Buried in the lee of a rock overhang near K1 was a Late Iron Age pot containing a skull, mandible and the first three cervical vertebrae of a single individual. It is not a disturbed grave but the intentional burial of only a head. The dating of the pot indicates that it was from several hundred years after the end of the K2 town and would be best linked to the ancestors of the Venda people living in the area.

Although Broederstroom and Greefswald K1 are different in context and archaeological associations, they share an ideology that was present for over a thousand years.

The colonial governments in southern Africa introduced various witchcraft Acts aimed at stamping out both the practice of witchcraft and of muti murders, but the Acts were failures because there was little understanding of the social relationships and belief systems underpinning the practices. What the colonial law did give us is a detailed record of court cases, especially in Lesotho. Colin Murray (an anthropologist) and Peter Sanders (a historian) have produced a tome called *Medicine Murder in Colonial Lesotho* that details 210 cases between 1895 and 1966.

In Sesotho, muti murders were known as *liretlo*, literally meaning 'the cutting of the flesh'. Oral history, summarised in the court records, suggests that the practice was present in pre-colonial times, but there was a distinct spike in the 1940s and 1950s, with more than a dozen cases a year. The people of Lesotho acknowledged that medicine made with human parts had historical roots and that such medicines were requested by the chiefs to protect the village against witchcraft, to provide protection for men in war and to protect boys at the initiation schools, but the spike in the mid-twentieth century was something entirely different. Instead of benefitting the people as a whole, the murders were now occurring to advance the causes of the chiefs.

Murray and Sanders feel that the colonial government was partly to blame because it introduced laws in 1938 and 1946 that took power away from the chiefs and turned them into administrators of the colonial government rather than chiefs representing the people. The lesser chiefs and headmen were particularly disenfranchised, and the spike in murders was a direct output of rivalries between chiefs.

In 129 court cases in these two decades, the motivation for murder was to obtain medicine to strengthen the chieftainship or to prevent another chief from gaining a place in the hierarchy. The sangomas suggested the ingredients for the new medicine, the chiefs gave the order, and the advisors and confidants of the chief carried out the action. Murray and Sanders called it a 'competitive contagion', and it involved the highest chiefs in the land.

The Lesotho court cases provide a full account of the details. The instigator was nearly always a chief, but he had accomplices to carry out the murder. Killing was intentionally a group effort and the average number of perpetrators in a single murder was eight. The people cooperated out of a combination of loyalty, duty and fear. The average MoSotho depended on the goodwill and favour of the chief. It was the chief who represented the traditions of the past and who held the key to the welfare of the entire community.

There was no consistency with regard to the victim. Traditionally, muti was gathered from the bodies of enemies killed in war – strong and brave men from other clans. In colonial Lesotho, only 65 per cent of the victims were male, while 20 per cent were elderly and less than 10 per cent were under the age of seventeen. The youngest victim was newborn and the oldest was a woman of ninety. The victims had in common that they did not have any great standing in the community. All sorts of different body parts were removed, but there was a preference for blood, bowels and generative organs. Most shocking was that the medicine was considered to be strongest if the body parts were removed while the victim was still alive.

No real pattern appeared in the location of the body disposal. However, importantly, the body was left where there might be a delay in discovery or where the authorities might assume that the person had died of other causes. A decomposed body would hide the evidence of flesh removal, and the presence of the body in water or at the base of a cliff might make it appear as if the cause of death was accidental.

The work of Murray and Sanders focused only on the colonial period, but the authors do suggest that the muti murders in Lesotho have not yet stopped. The court records of independent Lesotho are incomplete, but they do list twenty medicine murders in 1968, the highest number since 1948. The courts stopped reporting muti murders separately after 1970 and since then they have been lumped together with more 'normal' murders.

Murray and Sanders estimate that, as of the late 1980s and early 1990s, the number may be as high as two or three a month. They argue that the cause remains political uncertainty. Political uncertainty has also been stated as the cause of the muti murder spikes in Swaziland in the 1970s and in Venda in the 1980s. There were over thirty murders in the 1970s in Swaziland. Of eight published cases that came before the courts, all of the victims were women – four elderly people and four young girls. Scholars suggest that the trigger was in the anti-democratic pronouncements by the king, but, as with post-independent Lesotho, the records in Swaziland are incomplete and it is difficult to be sure.

The Venda crisis in 1988 had similar overtones to the Lesotho crises of the 1950s. One of the figures who was implicated (but with no evidence to convict) was Alfred Alidzulwi (A.A.) Tshivhase. As the Venda Minister of Justice, Prisons and the Public Service Commission, he was in the perfect position to ensure that no proper investigation of muti murders was ever conducted. Although the public record indicated only four medicine murders in the three months between April and June 1988, public opinion at the time suggested that as many as fifteen had occurred. No investigation was carried out.

Tshivhase, like the chiefs of Lesotho, denied any involvement in the muti murders right up until his resignation at the end of August that year. The upsurge in murders in Venda in the late 1980s was almost certainly due to the political structure of the new independent homeland. The apartheid creation of the Republic of Venda (1979 to 1994) required a compliant political structure that did not question Pretoria's apartheid policy and prevented the liberation movements from gaining a foothold. Where chiefs had to listen to the views of the people in the traditional system, the ministers in the apartheid vassal state were at the top of the heap, and they chose to dispense the largesse of the money from Pretoria for their own benefit. Corruption and nepotism were the order of the day and muti murders were a way of ensuring that your luck and influence were better than someone else's.

The data from Lesotho, Swaziland and Venda all suggest that medicine murders, chiefs and politics are interrelated, but the above-mentioned two cases from Cape Town and Pretoria are different. No chiefs were involved in either case. Something has definitely changed in the past two decades and the situation in the urban areas may be very different from that in old rural homelands and independent states.

In their book, Murray and Sanders note that, in the latest period of their data, the early 1960s, a few shopkeepers and café owners who had no connection to the chiefdoms were instigators of muti murders. Some were Christians while others professed a traditional religion. The three pathologists who published the report that I summarised at the beginning of this chapter on the death of the child in Langa, Cape Town, have suggested that the instigators of modern muti murders may be the sangomas themselves. In the past the sangoma was a member of the community supported by the chief, but in recent times the practice of divination has become a small business.

The sangomas and *inyangas* frequently advertise their potions and abilities in flyers at train stations and bus stops. The clients are everyday people who need some kind of help. Somewhere out there, however, are a few sangomas who are willing to prescribe human muti, and there are customers who will buy it.

I have been scouring the newspapers with an eagle eye over the years to see how often they report these cases. Senior Superintendent Gerard Labuschagne, who was head of the SAPS Investigative Psychology Unit, told the *Cape Times* on 18 January 2005 that he estimated between seventy and 100 muti killings occurred a year in South Africa.

The newspapers report several cases each year: the most recent one was published as I was writing this chapter. On 7 February 2011, the *Cape Times* reported the death of a seventy-four-year-old woman from Limpopo Province who was murdered in her home and who had had body parts removed. The cases are no longer confined to the lands of traditional rural rulers; they are just as likely to occur in urban Johannesburg as they are in rural Mpumalanga.

FIGURE 10: Advertising flyer handed out at Wynberg train station, Cape Town, 5 March 2011. Note the mix of physical, mental, sexual and social remedies available

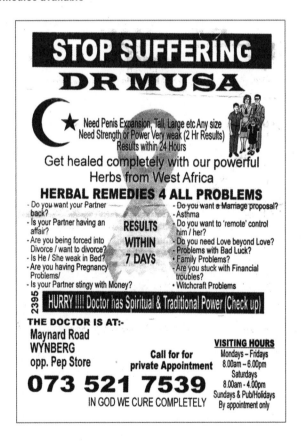

Again, perhaps the greatest horror of all is that the medicine is still felt to be powerful only if the body parts are removed when the victim is still alive. Murray and Sanders describe a case in 1950

where the victim had his tongue cut out and was completely scalped. Then, still alive, he was taken in a wheelbarrow to the next village, where further flesh was removed from his buttocks before he died.

On 6 July 1992, the *Cape Times* reported that a Soweto mother was called in to Baragwanath Hospital in Johannesburg to identify her two-year-old son. He was minus his penis, testicles and thumbs, and there had been an attempt to remove his eyes. The severely injured child had been left in the bush near Mofolo Park in Soweto. The newspaper report said the mother was in shock and the doctors were deciding on whether or not to perform a sex-change operation so that the child could be raised as a girl.

I know that I will be unpopular if I suggest that in historic times these horrific murders were thought to be performed for the greater good of the community. But even a detached scholar couldn't possibly make that argument today.

The good news is that the general community in South Africa is starting to reject the idea of muti murders. Even twenty years ago there would have been a tendency to refuse to cooperate with the police in the investigation of these crimes, but the evidence suggests that communities now feel that these incidents are aberrations, and a community's anger sometimes results in mob justice, as in the case of the sangoma's assistant in Cape Town.

When I began to write this chapter I was concerned that I might end up painting all African peoples in a bad light because of the activities of a few. Even with my anthropological eye it is patently obvious to me that belief in the power of muti is wrong. What people believe, however, never has anything to do with reality. Sadly, we don't go through our lives using logic and observation to interpret the world around us. We believe what we are told by authority and we follow the rules of tradition because our society tells us it is the right thing to do. When it comes to things spiritual, humans all over the world lose their ability for critical thought and follow tradition blindly.

During 2003 I was contacted by one of the Freemasons in Cape Town to ask if I would be prepared to take possession of some human bones that had been kept in the local lodges. His request was the outcome of police action in Pretoria, where a Freemason lodge had been warned that it was illegal under the Human Tissue Act (previously the Anatomy Act) for anyone who is not a qualified medical practitioner to keep human bones.

I agreed and, soon afterwards, delivered to my office were ten large boxes and bags containing the remains of nineteen individuals from eight Freemason lodges in the Western Cape. What were the Freemasons doing with all of these bones? Some of the bones were articulated as complete skeletons, some were skulls only and a few were loose bones from other parts of the body. Some bones were painted and others had been mounted as a display.

I asked Tasneem Salie, one of the UCT honours students in 2005, to do a complete analysis of the skeletons and to find some background information that would answer my question of why the Freemasons kept bones in their lodges. Tasneem discovered that the bones were symbols of death but were also used to remind lodge members that death should not be feared. How did they get their message across? Through ritual, of course!

Since 2003 the Freemasons have replaced their symbols with plastic models. They seem to work just as well.

You might chuckle over the Freemasons' dilemma, but keeping bones as relics is just as common in the Catholic Church, and the relics are more than mere symbols – they are very powerful. The bones of the saints are not there as ritual props. People pray to their deceased owners to intervene in their lives: to bring them happiness, to guide them in future choices and to cure illness.

Sound familiar? True believers do not require a scientist to verify the veracity of their prayers. Belief does not require evidence. Richard Dawkins, writing in his 2009 book on evolution, included an appendix on what he called the 'history deniers'. These are people who still believe in the creation of the world by God in six days despite the presence of an immense body of evidence to show that evolution has shaped life on earth for millions upon millions of years.

Perhaps our Western religious beliefs could force us to accept that evolution was divinely orchestrated, but it is impossible to ignore the evidence that life has had a long history on the planet. Forty per cent of Americans and a similar number of British people, however, reject the idea of evolution and insist on a six-day creation. Evidence be damned; we will believe what we want to believe, and that is that! So why is the belief in spirits and ancestors out of line?

It isn't. In my opinion it is mistaken, but millions of our fellow citizens accept it as a reality and, as long as they do, there will be a tiny minority who believe that a murder for muti is something that will help them. Expect more of these murders in the future. One reason is that people will use any method they can to better their own futures. A second reason is that people are very slow to change their beliefs and practices. The old ways are never removed; they are simply incorporated into the new situation. The end of muti murders will come only when people's mindsets change completely, and I doubt that that will happen soon.

5

The TRC and the
Victims of Political Violence

No one had ever tried anything like this before. By an Act of
Parliament in 1995, the South African government created a Truth
and Reconciliation Commission (TRC) to probe the past and to
offer amnesty to individuals who had committed crimes against
humanity during the apartheid era. This was not to be another
Nuremberg: the object would be to uncover crimes committed
against humanity on both sides of the political divide.

Other countries had offered blanket amnesties to political organisations to avoid civil war, but the amnesties of the TRC would be
on an individual basis. All that was required for the granting of
amnesty would be a full and truthful recounting of the past. The
government expected the whole process to take about eighteen
months. The victims' stories in fact took three years to unfold,
and there were so many requests for amnesty that the Amnesty
Committee of the TRC received an extension until May 2001 to
complete its work.

The TRC was a very public experience. For weeks on end we
saw television pictures of specially trained TRC staff comforting
people who told harrowing stories of death and destitution while

Archbishop Desmond Tutu sobbed in sympathy. We saw Captain Jeffrey Benzien of the Cape Town security police demonstrate how a wet bag could be drawn over the head of a prisoner to smother him into giving information, and we heard of Eugene de Kock's attempt at body disposal using explosives. We listened with mixed feelings as amnesty was granted to dubious individuals like Benzien, but the object of the whole exercise was national reconciliation, so we accepted the committee's decisions. De Kock, among some notorious others, did not receive absolution and is currently serving a long jail sentence.

The TRC process was severely criticised at the time. Many argued that reconciliation could not be achieved by opening wounds from the past, but these were not wounds. They were festering sites of infection that needed to be lanced before they could heal. The testimony highlighted events that had happened only ten to twenty years previously, but had been hidden from public knowledge by the system. One particular name in the ongoing testimony caught my attention because I had played a small role in the original court case. In 1987, I had been approached by Advocate Michael Donen to help him with an age estimation of his client. The client was Michael Lucas, a young man accused of murder in a crime with political overtones in the township of Bongolethu outside of Oudtshoorn in the Little Karoo.

The story told to me was that, on 15 April 1986, Michael Lucas and two others had decided to burn a bus as part of an anti-apartheid protest in the township. As they were trying to set the bus on fire, a car carrying two bus inspectors approached them. Only Lucas was armed and, when he pointed his firearm at the two inspectors, they tried to drive away. Lucas fired at them anyway, and one of the inspectors, Willem Blaauw, was killed.

There was never much doubt that Lucas was responsible, but the trial was really about the motivation of the three protestors. Donen argued that their planned act was part of a broader rise against the government because of the desperately poor conditions in the township, and that Michael Lucas had only fired his gun out of frustration. It had not been his intention to kill the man. The prosecution argued that the consequences of firing the gun were obvious. They asked why, if this were only a symbolic demonstration, Lucas had aimed directly at Blaauw.

The trial was not going well for Lucas and there was a strong likelihood that the judge would invoke the death penalty if Lucas were found guilty. The only thing that could save his life at this stage was if he had been under the age of eighteen years when he committed the crime. South African law at the time, as discussed earlier, was clear – a crime committed by a minor could not result in a sentence of death.

I did not actually meet Michael Lucas. Advocate Donen had his client's hand and hip joints radiographed at my request, and my task was simply to assess his bone age at the start of the trial. Lucas claimed that he was seventeen in mid-1986, so I had to confirm that he was eighteen at the time of the trial. There was no birth certificate, so my estimation would make the difference between life and death.

I had some bad news for Advocate Donen. My estimation suggested that Lucas was now, at the time of the trial, about twenty years old. The fusion sites of the bone ends in the wrist were complete, and the crest of the hip, along with the cap or epiphysis on the end of the thigh bone, was completely fused to the rest of the structure. We had a long talk about this and Advocate Donen suggested that we introduce the concept of 'statistical error' to the judge in order to suggest that it was still possible that Lucas had been below the age of eighteen at the time of the killing.

The fusion of the epiphyses of the bones of the wrist and the hip is usually complete by approximately eighteen years, but this is not absolute. Some individuals fuse earlier, while some fuse later. Statistically, there was about a 20 per cent chance that Lucas was actually under eighteen at the time of the attempted bus hijacking, but then again there was also a 20 per cent chance that he was over twenty-two years old now. The error works both ways. This follows the classic bell curve, with the bulk of age assessments falling near the group average, and a long tail on either side of the curve showing late maturers on one end and early maturers on the other.

I eloquently argued this in court. The bone-ageing technique indicated that Lucas was most likely twenty years old now, but that there was a small chance that he was only eighteen. I argued well and the judge accepted the argument. A week later I read in the newspaper that the prosecution had found a Catholic priest who had baptised Michael Lucas in 1965, making him twenty-two years old at the time of the trial. My argument had been correct theoretically, but I had used the wrong tail of the curve and he was actually *older* than I had estimated.

I had tried to help the defence with my testimony, but it hadn't worked. Michael Donen asked me to submit a bill for my time. In the past I had been paid the official state rate for those subpoenaed as an expert witness, but the amount was nominal – less than R50 plus expenses to compensate for a day of testimony. I was on a lecturer's salary, so any extra income was really useful. My real concern was that I was not keen to claim money from the trial if the funds for the defence had come from the poor community of Bongolethu. I asked Michael Donen who was paying for the case and he was very evasive. It became obvious to me that the funds were from sources outside South Africa and were being routed through the liberation movements. Since these movements were illegal, Donen could not say anything, but he assured me that the money was not coming from the poor people of Bongolethu township. I did in the end make a claim for a modest R200, as it had taken me the best part of three days to examine the radiographs, consult the lawyers and attend the court case.

My testimony was close to the end of the trial, and within a couple of weeks of my presentation the judge made the final decision. Michael Lucas was found guilty of killing Willem Blaauw, and he was sentenced to death. He was also sentenced to seven years for public violence and two years for 'malicious injury to property for trying to set a bus alight'.

It was obvious that he had been involved in political action and that he had not set out to shoot someone. The judgment recognised this with the sentence for public violence, yet he was convicted of murder. In the end Michael Lucas was hanged by the neck until dead. His name is now inscribed on the wall of remembrance at the Apartheid Museum in Johannesburg, and the TRC process has helped his family to come to terms with his death.

There was no need for me to testify about Michael Lucas for the TRC, but I was contacted by a lawyer during the hearings who asked me to look at some bone fragments that concerned another of the TRC cases. He and a senior policeman from Pretoria visited my office with a small plastic bag of bone. They needed to know whether the bones were human.

In the bag were tiny fragments of long bones that would normally go into my 'unidentifiable' pile in a laboratory analysis. I couldn't be absolutely sure and told them that in this case, DNA identification to the species level would be the best option. Only after I had given them my uncertain answer did they tell me about the case. In fact, the bones were purported to be the last mortal remains of a police informant killed on the farm Vlakplaas. Eugene de Kock himself had pointed out to the investigators the location where his men had repeatedly blown up a body to destroy it.

Captain Eugene de Kock was the commander between 1989 and 1993 of the South African Police counter-insurgency unit based at the farm Vlakplaas near Pretoria. This was the heart of one of the most notorious police murder units and its members were responsible for dozens of political assassinations. De Kock was personally involved in the killing of about seventy people during his ten years in the police force. He was arrested one week after the first democratic election in April 1994, and tried, convicted and sentenced to 212 years in prison.

The small bag of bones was not part of De Kock's trial, but was instead part of the evidence being considered in his application to the TRC for forgiveness. Each security branch operation had its own methods of body disposal – burning, secret burial, dumping in crocodile-infested rivers – but the group at Vlakplaas had decided to try to dispose of bodies by using explosives. At one of the TRC hearings, Chappies Klopper, an underling of De Kock, told of using five or six explosions to obliterate the corpse of Sweet Sambo, a suspect who had died under interrogation.

Klopper's testimony detailed how, after each blast, they collected the shattered fragments of flesh and bone to make a new pile to be blown up again. Klopper said, '[W]e picked up pieces until our hands were full.' I guess this gruesome method worked to a point. Without DNA-matching it was impossible to confirm the species of the bone fragments, let alone obtain an identity of the victim.

The TRC not only heard evidence, but also started a small programme of exhumations when the testimony identified the location of a missing person. The committee requested the excavation of the graves of three Umkhonto we Sizwe (MK) operatives in 1996 and then requested a further two excavations of women activists the following year in central KwaZulu-Natal.

In one of the cases, the formal identification of the remains became an issue because the police testimony was incomplete. This was South Africa's first attempt to make use of DNA typing from bone, but it was a failure. The TRC finally accepted an identification of the missing woman based on the superimposition of an identity-document photograph on the skull by local and overseas forensic experts.

About fifty exhumations were carried out by the TRC team before the end of its original mandate in 1998, but the committee was not happy with the process and made a number of observations. They noticed that some of the excavations were badly done and had not been carried out by qualified people, and that in some cases there were no photographic records of the process. No physical anthropology report (referred to as a 'postmortem report') was produced for several exhumations because of a desire to return the bones to the family as quickly as possible.

The commissioners were clearly worried that shoddy excavation and analysis might result in the loss of information about the events at death and the possibility that the wrong skeleton was being excavated. In one Johannesburg case, the appointed excavation team excavated fifteen graves in order to find the remains of two activists. In an audit of their own reports, the commission noted that nearly 40 per cent of the exhumations were inadequately performed and that corroboration of the identity in 20 per cent of the cases was a serious problem. The assistance of two members of the Argentine Forensic Anthropology Team (EAAF) was sought to examine the skeletons from the cluster of fifteen graves and they were able to confirm which of the fifteen bodies were those of the two activists.

Upon the completion of its mandate, the TRC made some recommendations in its final report. First and foremost they proposed that a new task team be commissioned to continue the search for the missing from the apartheid era. In their view, the TRC was incomplete as long as not all of the events of the past decades had been uncovered. By its own reckoning, the TRC had already produced testimony identifying 477 combatants missing between 1960 and 1994.

Finding the bodies would not be enough. The TRC recommended that not only should the new task team excavate the skeletons, but it should facilitate the reburial and reconciliation process. This would not simply be a forensic exercise – it needed also to be an exercise in human rights.

A formal request was made to President Thabo Mbeki in April

2003 to found a task team under the National Prosecuting Authority. He agreed, and the following year Madeleine Fullard was appointed head of a small group of researchers in the newly formed Priority Crimes Litigation Unit (PCLU), which would take up where the TRC had left off.

The PCLU quickly established the Missing Persons Task Team, but almost immediately it discovered that it did not have the resources to carry out the task it had been assigned. Not only was it short on budget, but the task of finding the graves involved months of searching before excavations could begin. It also needed forensic anthropologists to help with the work, and they were in short supply. In an exploratory move, Madeleine contacted the Department of Anatomy at the University of Pretoria and asked how much it would cost to have them excavate these grave sites.

Maryna Steyn and her team provide a full-service excavation that includes a historic archival search for information, a formal archaeological excavation, skeletal biology work-up and a final written report, and she thought that this was what Madeleine was requesting. Such a service takes days of person-hours and, to make it economically viable, the cost is several thousand rand per case. On the basis of this costing Madeleine realised that her budget was hopelessly inadequate so, as an alternative, she used her NPA contacts to meet up with the Argentine team that had helped with the first TRC cases. She was thrilled to hear that they were willing to help at the cost of travel and accommodation.

The first of the new Missing Persons Task Team excavations happened in the full glare of the media, and several newspapers commented on the need to import the EAAF because of the lack of forensic anthropology expertise in South Africa. This was the first time I had heard of the MPTT and I was furious that anyone would assume that there were no forensic anthropologists in South Africa. The country didn't have many, but we were represented in Johannesburg, Pretoria and Cape Town. I threw all my toys out of the cot and demanded to know why Madeleine was employing foreigners from South America when locals were skilled and available. Madeleine immediately recognised the fracas she had caused and, in a superb display of diplomacy, she quickly organised a meeting in Pretoria and invited all of us to attend. Introductions were made and confusions ironed out. Madeleine would not have a problem getting forensic anthropologists on board again. Students from all three centres would now be part of the regular excavation and analysis crews.

The full-time employees of the MPTT are still few in number, but, as Madeleine's budget has increased, she has been able to bring both anthropologists and archival researchers onto her payroll. She still draws on students from UCT, Pretoria and Wits to help with fieldwork and provides financial and organisational support for building skills capacity among the students. Most importantly, the link with the EAAF has proven to be especially important in introducing a human rights culture into the team.

The Missing Persons Task Team has had six busy years. The job of finding the missing starts with the testimony of the TRC, but a great deal of additional information needs to be gathered as well. Postmortems were performed by pathologists on many of these missing people and they provide details that can help identify the individual and confirm the evidence from the commission's records. Additional interviews need to be organised to add to the knowledge about the missing person and, of course, the family needs to be contacted. The task team's standard protocol is to involve the family in the entire process right from the beginning of the inquiry. The model for the investigation is the work of the EAAF on the 'disappeared' in Argentina and the ultimate objective is to give the family and the community closure.

A few TRC grave locations were pointed out during testimony by the police, but by far the largest numbers of 'missing' were actually buried in graves in township cemeteries. During the apartheid

years, the funerals of ANC and PAC members killed in conflict became opportunities for political activism through graveside speeches
and thousands of mourners. The government was infuriated by these
impromptu political meetings and solved the problem by ensuring
that no corpse could be found. No body, no funeral!

In the case of prisoners who died in jail or were executed, the
warders ensured that the body was quickly buried in the cemetery
nearest to the prison, and the family was notified of the death only
after the body had been interred. For insurgents killed in a gun
battle or for those killed by the security police in their secret locations, the trick was to remove all identification from the body and
then to stage the discovery so that the normal police would have no
leads to investigate. Unknown bodies were disposed of as paupers
in unmarked cemetery graves. The Mamelodi 10 is a case in point.

On 26 June 1986, ten men from Mamelodi township outside of
Pretoria boarded a Botswana-bound minibus taxi with plans to
train as ANC guerilla fighters. They were all young activists who
had been involved in township marches and consumer boycotts
and they were eager to volunteer for the real fight as ANC soldiers.
The youngest was fifteen and the oldest only twenty-two.

Unknown to them, the MK guerilla who was their guide was
in fact an informant for the Northern Transvaal security police.
Their trip north was a trap. The excited young men were drinking heavily in the vehicle and barely noticed when it pulled off the
road near the town of Zeerust. Four armed security policemen
in balaclavas pulled them out of the taxi and injected them with
something that rendered them unconscious (the TRC informant
didn't know what was in the syringes). The insensible young men
were tumbled into another minibus, which was driven to a site
near the Botswana border and pushed down an incline into a tree.
Two AK47 rifles were placed in the vehicle, along with a limpet
mine, and the minibus was set on fire with petrol. The limpet mine
exploded and the scene looked exactly like an accident. The burn-

ing vehicle was later found by the local police and the newspapers reported that 'trained terrorists' had been killed in a car accident while trying to infiltrate South African territory.

The severely burnt bodies were examined by a state pathologist at the Ga-Rankuwa state mortuary and buried as paupers by the local undertakers on 31 July. It had taken just over a month to remove ten activists and make them disappear.

The job of the MPTT was to find the graves of the Mamelodi 10 in the Winterveld cemetery just north of Pretoria. Not only were the graves without named markers, but the metal grave numbers were missing as well – stolen in the intervening years by metal thieves. The only way to find the graves was to work out the sequence of burial placement to identify the location of the burials that took place on 31 July 1986.

Even that was hit-or-miss, and several unmarked graves had to be excavated and the remains reburied before the Mamelodi 10 were discovered. The clue to successful identification was the state of the skeletons. The postmortem report from 1986 indicated the damage to the bodies. For example, postmortem case T268/86 described 'a black adult male in a heat charred condition with open compound and heat-crack fractures of the skull bones … and amputation of both fore-arms and legs'. The burning of the vehicle and explosion of the mine had done its job well. The bones from each grave had to be matched against the postmortem reports.

Once they were confirmed as being part of the Mamelodi 10, the skeletons still needed to be identified individually. The bones were laid out in the laboratory and a full forensic anthropology work-up was done for each. That narrowed down the identification, but the bones did not easily give up their precise identity. Madeleine linked up with Neil Leat and Sean Davison at the University of the Western Cape in order to extract DNA from the bones. The burning and poor preservation of the bone made DNA extraction difficult, so the failure rate was high and only four of the samples worked. The families of the missing ten agreed to provide samples of their own DNA, but Neil and Sean were unable to match the four individuals to their living relatives. Still, the postmortem reports confirmed that all but one of the skeletons were members of the missing ten.

The use of DNA techniques has been tried on other skeletons excavated by the MPTT. A single grave from the Winterveld cemetery produced the fragmentary remains of four individuals. The TRC records noted that three of these individuals were murdered in one police interrogation incident, while the fourth was another MK operative who had recently returned to Pretoria from Swaziland when he was picked up by the police. All four were questioned, murdered and then blown up with explosives to hide their identities.

The remains of the four men happened to be buried together in a single casket at Winterveld because their remains had arrived at the morgue on the same day. The MPTT opened the single grave and found all of the fragments of bones bundled together. The presence of four proximal (upper) ends of the left femur confirmed that there were four individuals in the grave.

The laboratory at UWC obtained DNA swabs from the living wives, siblings, parents and children of the victims, and then compared mitochondrial DNA (mtDNA) and Y-chromosome STR (short tandem repeat) data from the four bones to the data from the families. The mtDNA (inherited from the mother) matched a sequence from each of the female relatives, while the STR data (inherited from the father) gave a 99 per cent certainty of a paternal relationship for the children of two of the victims. All four individuals were effectively identified using the DNA data.

The task of identifying individuals who were not buried in a pauper's grave has been even more difficult for the task team. Post Chalmers was a government-owned property about twenty-five kilometres from Cradock in the Eastern Cape. At one stage in its recent history it was a regional police station, but the station was moved in 1972 and the farm and its buildings were mothballed.

Its anonymity was ideal for the Eastern Cape security branch, who reopened the property in the early 1980s as a 'safe house' where they could 'debrief' detainees. The euphemisms mask its true purpose – it was a torture and execution location and it was the last place where the Pebco Three were seen alive.

Early in the evening of 8 May 1985, Sipho Hashe, Champion Galela and Qaqawuli Godolozi were abducted from the Port Eliza-beth airport, where they had been lured by a police informer. The three were leaders of the Port Elizabeth Black Civic Organisation (Pebco) and they had been instrumental in mobilising consumer boycotts in the Eastern Cape. The order came from Pretoria that, because they were making the Eastern Cape ungovernable, they had to die.

A team from Vlakplaas organised the kidnapping and delivered the three to Post Chalmers. They were tortured, interrogated and then killed by Lieutenant Gideon Nieuwoudt and other policemen from the Eastern Cape security police. All three were drugged, shot in the head and then burnt on an open pyre. Nieuwoudt had had experience in this practice. He had burnt the bodies of Siphiwo Mthimkhulu and Topsy Mdaka three years previously at Post Chalmers, and he knew that it would take between six and eight hours with plenty of firewood. The job in 1985 took six hours.

The testimony of the police at the TRC hearings was unsatis-factory. There was confusion about who was responsible for the murders and what had happened to the burnt remains of the bodies. Apparently, some of the remains were dumped into the Great Fish River, but the disposal was incomplete.

In August 2007 the MPTT visited Post Chalmers and began a full-scale excavation. The burn sites were examined, but so was the content of the septic tank into which some of the bones may have been washed. The team removed 260 kilograms of material from the farm for closer examination. Over the next three months the team sorted out the bone fragments from the charcoal, metal and other material. In the end they had winnowed out 12.1 kilograms of burnt bone for the last level of analysis.

The search for the missing persons of the apartheid era is a very public activity and the Post Chalmers investigation was no exception. Madeleine phoned me to ask if she could do the last analysis in Cape Town at the medical school, and I readily agreed. She came down in May 2008 with her permanent team and Steve Symes, who was visiting Pretoria. Steve is an American expert on burnt and cut bone from forensic cases and he was ideal to have around for the analysis.

This team joined my students (many of whom were part-time members of the team anyway) and we laid out the whole collection onto clean white sheets of paper on the dissection tables in the anatomy hall. We then spent two finicky days trying to assemble as many pieces as possible.

An eye for detail was required to recognise a join between two small fragments of bone, and each announcement of success was like the shouting of a win at Bingo night in the old-age home. We knew that we would not be able to confirm the identity of these people from the tiny fragments of bone, and the burning of the remains removed the possibility of using DNA.

However, the two days of painstaking work delivered two conclusions: 1) the vast majority of these bone fragments were human; and 2) three individuals were represented in the sample. Theoretically, there could have been more than three, but we could confirm that there were no fewer than that.

Madeleine had called the press and we had half a dozen reporters on site looking at the bone scraps and asking questions. This was Madeleine's job and the rest of us kept quiet unless asked a specific question. But carefully stage-managed publicity doesn't always work out as planned. The following day two of the journalists suggested that the presence of fragments of burnt tyre in the septic tank meant that the Pebco Three had been necklaced by the Eastern Cape security police.

Poor Madeleine had to go back and restate the findings based on our evidence, which did *not* include necklacing. All that the bones indicated was that three individuals had been disposed of at the location and that the remains had been burnt. This was consistent with the TRC evidence.

Visiting the Winterveld cemetery north of Pretoria to search for the bodies of the Mamelodi 10 was one of several occasions on which I was involved with the MPTT, but my role was a relatively minor one. Much more important has been (and continues to be) the involvement of my students. Nearly all of my postgraduate students have been part of the excavations and analyses. I've simply had to get used to the idea that Madeleine contacts the crew and a sheepish-looking couple of students pop into my office to tell me that they won't be available because they are off for a week or so to Mafikeng, Pretoria, Venda or KwaZulu-Natal. Actually, I am very pleased, because I cannot offer better training than this. Even better is that the students have also participated in the reburial ceremonies. They have been there to see the families gain closure on the horror of the past, and the students understand the value of their work.

The reburial ceremonies are a critical aspect of the work of the MPTT but they have not been without controversy. Jay Aronson from the Department of History of the Carnegie Mellon University in the United States has been an independent observer of the process over the past few years. Jay has emphasised that families seek to recover more than just the remains of their loved one. He suggests three forms of recognition: biological, which identifies the remains of the dead; social, which brings closure to the family of the victim; and collective, in which the community acknowledges the victim.

Collective recognition requires a formal ceremony for reburial and can provide a form of reparation not only in financial terms, but also in terms of acknowledging the importance of the deceased to the community and the nation. The first reburial was that of the MK soldier Reginald Kekana, whose service was used by the Department of Justice to launch the task team's public activities. The ceremony at Freedom Park was with full military honours and the guest list included prominent politicians, military officials, and famous leaders of the struggle.

Kekana was praised as a military hero who died to free his people and his country from colonial rule. Speeches were made by the Minister of Justice and Constitutional Development and the Minister of Defence. The Kekana ceremony set a precedent for the families of the subsequent reburials and they have demanded the same formal recognition from government and the community. This has not always been possible, given the political friction within the ANC.

The ceremonies have also given families the platform to speak of their unhappiness with the broader process of reconciliation. Many have been angry about the decision to grant amnesty to perpetrators without substantial interaction between victims and the perpetrators.

Jay Aronson points out that the women of the families do not want presidential pardons for the perpetrators; they would prefer prosecution. Their definition of reconciliation includes more than remorse from the aggressors and they demand both redress and accountability. The reburial ceremonies remain a 'work in progress'.

FINDING THE VICTIMS OF VIOLENCE

At first glance, the TRC excavations are not about South African heritage. The graves exhumed so far have mostly been of individuals killed by state forces and disposed of as paupers in municipal cemeteries. The MPTT initially believed that their largest role would be to give closure to the families of the dead, but the reality is that the families want more than simple closure.

Jay Aronson's analysis has shown us that a key issue for the families of the dead is the placement of their names on a role of honour recognising those who died in the fight against apartheid. Seventeen years of democracy have not erased the anger about the past, and it often lies just below the surface, waiting to burst forth if the surface is scratched.

The Heritage Act of 1999 defines graves from the past as being those that are older than sixty years. This pretty much excludes nearly all police forensic cases that fall under the Inquest Act, but the Heritage Act does provide a special category of graves for 'victims of violence'. No time frame is given and the victims could be from colonial history, the South African War or from the fight against apartheid. The commonality is the recognition that these graves are part of our heritage and need to be seen, in Jay Aronson's term, as 'the collective sense of acknowledgement of the past'.

Sometimes it is not about truth; it is about treating the dead with honour. The truth is not only what lies beneath the ground, but what people believe exists there. The United Nations (UN) forensic teams working on mass graves in Bosnia have already discovered this. Families of the dead sometimes resist the excavations, not because they fear what they will find, but because they fear what they will *not* find.

A case in point from our South African experience is the excavation of the mass grave at Laingsburg. The loss of 104 lives on 25 January 1981 had nothing to do with politics. A soft, penetrating rain had been falling for several days over the normally arid Karoo about 300 kilometres north-east of Cape Town. The dry ground could not absorb this wealth of water and the run-off began to swell the river valleys upstream of the small town of Laingsburg. On a Sunday afternoon, the Buffels River finally burst its banks and a mass of water reached the railway bridge just south of the town. Uprooted trees, dead farm animals and other debris clogged the space under the bridge and the water had nowhere to go but over the bridge and into the town. A five-metre-high wall of water erased a school, a church, an old-age home and many houses. In total, 104 people, including children and babies, died, but seventy-two bodies were washed downstream and never recovered.

The natural disaster of the Laingsburg flood would have ended with a commemoration of the lost dead if it were not for the inequities of the apartheid government. More than half of the dead were from the coloured community living close to the river, but the government provided compensation only for the white victims. For twenty-two years the injustice of this decision burnt in the minds of the families and finally flared up at a council meeting in 2003.

Accusations were made that the old government had collected the bodies of the coloured dead and buried them in black plastic bags in a mass grave. Eyewitnesses remembered seeing council workers dumping black bags in a trench behind the abattoir. With no bodies, there was no closure. The small community was split along racial lines and the provincial government was called in to help.

The provincial government of the Western Cape decided that, at any cost, the mystery of the black-bag burials needed to be resolved. An initial survey of the dump site with ground-penetrating radar was inconclusive, so the University of Pretoria's forensic archaeology team was called in. Coen Nienaber, the archaeologist attached to the unit, used earth-moving equipment to dig a series of trenches at the site and each trench was carefully examined by the archaeological team.

After several days' work, they concluded that no human remains were present. Bones were found, but all were of animals. It was clear that the dumping at the site was of animal carcasses from the nearby butchery and from drowned animals found on the river bank. The cost of the exercise was nearly a quarter of a million rand, but the money was well spent in terms of human rights.

The provincial and municipal governments decided to facilitate a process of healing and reconciliation by planning a fitting memorial that would include the names of all of the dead. The outcome was the building of the Flood Museum, which was officially opened on 23 January 2011 – two days short of the thirtieth anniversary of the flood. The seventy-two bodies are still missing, but a form of closure has finally come to the community. In the same manner as the TRC, a step has been made to correct the inequities of the past.

The Laingsburg incident occurred only thirty years ago, but many of the historical wounds are much older. Chief Fadana was one of eight Xhosa leaders imprisoned on Robben Island in the 1860s, and it was his lot to have died there. During the winter of 2005, his direct descendant in the Transkei, also known as Chief Fadana, dreamt that his illustrious forebear came to him to ask that his body be brought back to the Transkei for burial. The younger Fadana approached the Robben Island Museum and SAHRA to ask how this feat could be accomplished, and in September 2005 a joint team from the Universities of Pretoria and Cape Town spent a week on Robben Island searching for Fadana's remains.

With the museum's facilitation, the team worked closely with the family and their sangomas to search the ground where Fadana's dream had indicated that his body was buried. We (and the sangomas) knew that the Xhosa prisoners had been camped on the east side of the island in the 1860s, but there were no records of historic graves at the site nor were there any obvious graves visible on the grounds. The Fadana family was working strictly from what the sangomas could find by divination, but, sadly, three excavations in four days failed to locate the body.

I spoke to the chief on the last day of excavation and he was still upbeat. He said the problem lay with our inability to understand the message from the ancestors and he would like to try again some time in the future. When I reported our failure to find the body under the direction of the sangomas to my colleagues in the Department of Human Biology during tea, most of them thought this was hilariously funny and wrote off the expedition as a failure.

But I begged to differ. Not only did we set a precedent with the Robben Island Museum paying the costs, but my students spent five days on a national monument staying in the old guards' houses with free access to all sites on the island. When I asked my fifteen colleagues in our tea room how many of them had even been to Robben Island, only two of my South African co-workers had done so. Most important of all, the group of us from Cape Town and Pretoria were not involved in some academic exercise, but were part of a process of cooperation between science and traditional belief.

This same spirit of cooperation was present ten years earlier in the much more politicised case of Hintsa's head. Early in 1996, a sangoma from the Eastern Cape, Nicholas Tilana Gcaleka, hit the news headlines when he travelled to the United Kingdom in search of the skull of his clan ancestor Paramount Chief Hintsa. Hintsa was the hereditary leader of the Gcaleka clan of the Xhosa in the Eastern Cape. During the conflict of the Sixth Frontier War, Hintsa was captured and then murdered by a sergeant of the 72nd Regiment on 12 May 1835. Documents from the time suggest that an attempt was made to take his ears and prise out some of his teeth as trophies.

Subsequent Xhosa legend has suggested that his body was decapitated and his head taken to England. There is no documentary evidence of the decapitation, but actually it is not surprising that such views would be held, because the British certainly *did* do that from time to time in the nineteenth century. Sir Stephen Lakeman, writing of his Eastern Cape experiences during the Ninth Frontier War in the 1870s, penned the following rather frightening passage:

Doctor A--- of the 60th had asked my men to procure him a few
native skulls of both sexes. This was a task easily accomplished.
One morning they brought back to camp about two dozen heads
of various ages. As these were not supposed to be in a presentable
state for the doctor's acceptance, the next night they turned my
bath into a caldron [*sic*] for the removal of superfluous flesh.
And there these men sat, gravely smoking their pipes during
the live-long night, and stirring round and round the heads in
the seething boiler, as though they were cooking black-apple
dumplings (Lakeman, 1880: 94–5).

Nicholas Gcaleka not only believed that Hintsa's head had been
cut off and taken to the UK, but he had a vision that led him to an
estate in Scotland where he located a cranium, which he declared
to be that of Hintsa. This was done in the full light of publicity,
and a photograph showing Gcaleka holding the skull appeared in
newspapers throughout Britain and in South Africa.

Gcaleka proclaimed that he had found and returned Hintsa's
head, and that by doing so he had put Hinta's soul to rest, which
would usher in an era of peace in the new democracy. His claim was
not refuted by South Africans at large, but was instead challenged
by the traditional leaders of the Eastern Cape. At an *imbizo* (council
meeting) held at the Great Place of the then current paramount chief
Xolilizwe Sigcau, it was decided to 'confiscate' the skull and send it
for forensic analysis.

Gcaleka's demand that the Queen of England apologise to the
descendants of Hintsa raised the matter to an international level,
embarrassing the British and South African governments. The
demand must have had a major influence on the outcome of the
imbizo. Gcaleka's self-proclaimed status as 'chief' in the British
press would not have gone down well at the court of Sigcau.

I had become involved with the case by this stage, acting as an
advisor to Mda Mda, who was the legal advisor for the paramount

163

chief, Sigcau. I advised him to let the forensic procedure go ahead through the police, but in our conversations I did raise the issue of a possible excavation of Hintsa's gravesite. This would immediately confirm whether or not the head had been taken from the body in historic times and it would settle that aspect of the investigation.

In the meantime, the Eastern Cape bureaucracy ground on exceedingly slowly and when the skull finally arrived in Cape Town, I had already left on a six-month sabbatical in the United States. The task of examining the cranium fell to Deon Knobel of UCT Forensic Pathology, Vince Phillips, then of the University of Stellenbosch Oral Pathology, and Phillip Tobias, the emeritus professor of anatomy at the University of the Witwatersrand.

Their opinion was that the cranium was anatomically inconsistent with a middle-aged African male, but looked instead most like a female with significant European ancestry. Their pronouncement effectively stifled the claims of Gcaleka, but I thought at the time that it had dealt only with the physical aspects.

At a paper I presented at the African Studies Association in San Francisco in November 1996, I said that this kind of case is complex and the solutions to the problems presented cannot be couched in terms of historical realism alone. I was surprised that no one had delved more deeply into Xhosa myths, the role and status of the traditional chiefs and historical perspectives.

Shortly after my return to South Africa, the three professors presented a poster at a meeting of the Anatomical Society of Southern Africa (ASSA) in Stellenbosch. The presentation was done in the form of a forensic report that did not consider anything other than the morphological identity of the skull. Unfortunately, racial identification techniques were used in a very rigid way.

Nicholas Gcaleka had heard about the conference and he came to see the poster and hear the discussions. Clearly he was not impressed and argued that it was not the role of scientists to take an interest in the ancestors of the Xhosa. I caught him in the corridor later on and had a personal (and fascinating) chat with him, during which he told me that 'it didn't matter what the skull looked like, the spirit of Hintsa was in the skull'. I certainly was not qualified to question that belief.

Very recently, Premesh Lalu of the Department of History at the University of the Western Cape completed a thorough examination of these non-forensic issues. He does not deal with the forensic question of the skull's identity, because to him it is a minor point. The bigger issues are about historical interpretation and the presentation of post-colonial and post-apartheid history in South Africa.

Although I don't think I could have stretched it to the 269-page argument that Lalu does in his book, this is a key point I raised back in 1996. Lalu hints that the original information gathered by the British military inquiry in 1836 was biased and possibly inaccurate, and he is also disparaging about the Knobel/Phillips/Tobias report. He and I would agree that the forensic report was fundamentally unsatisfying because of its failure to look beyond the simple identity of the skull, but I wouldn't go so far as to say (as he does) that 'a significant incident in the colonial past was surrendered to the terms and categories of a forensic procedure that reduced history to mere epidermal difference' (Lalu, 2009: 3).

It entirely depends on the question you want to ask. Science is not very good at interpretation of historical facts, but it can be used to check them. The question posed in this case is not 'What colour was the person represented by the skull?', but 'Is this skull likely to be that of Hintsa?' The forensic report asked and answered that question.

A period of 150 years has not resolved the anger felt by many traditional Xhosa-speaking people over the way they were treated by successive colonial, union and apartheid governments. Stories about the mutilation of their dead leaders continue to appear. Such a tale emerged in 2004, when it was said that the head of King Sandile had been cut off when he was killed in battle in 1878, taken to England and buried on a farm.

This allegation was taken just as seriously as was the story of Hintsa, and a delegation was sent to England to verify it. On their return, the current king, Maxhoba Sandile, decided to open the grave of the historic Sandile to find out if the skeleton had been tampered with. The University of Pretoria team under Maryna Steyn, Coen Nienaber and Louisa Hutten carried out the excavation and they were able to confirm not only that the skeleton was complete and undisturbed, but that the bones were almost certainly those of King Sandile.

Anger over events during the colonial era has also surfaced in Namibia, but in an even more dramatic way. Two mass graves with hundreds of bones exposed on the surface have come to light in the last fifteen years or so.

In November 2005, Namibian authorities were notified of the discovery of human remains during the building of a sewage dam near the old main South African military base about 110 kilometres from the town of Oshakati on the northern border of the country. The site was not officially examined, but soon the word was out in the newspapers that the bodies were those of South West African People's Organisation (SWAPO) soldiers and that cloths representing blindfolds were found with the bodies. Other reports said that the bodies were those of women and children brought back from Angola for questioning and execution by the police before independence. Within a week, the previous chief of staff of the United Nations mission in Namibia recounted the results of his own investigation into the events of April 1989.

SWAPO fighters had infiltrated the northern border area just before the arrival of the UN troops. The object was to place themselves in strategic locations while the South African troops were confined to bases waiting for the arrival of the UN peacekeepers, but South African troops and police attacked them and at least 100 of their fighters died.

If any of the allegations published in the newspapers were true, then an investigation was desperately needed. In fact, the Namibian

The sangoma's shack in Cape Town where the remains of a five-year-old child were discovered in 1994

The lower jaw of the child, attached to the wall of the shack with some wire

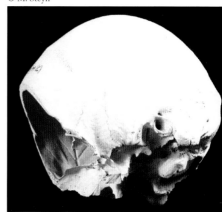

Decorated pots from the sangoma's house in Pretoria, as they were discovered by the police and labelled from left to right as Objects C, A and B. The pots labeled C and B were found to have been made from human skulls

The skull that formed the pot in Object C

The Missing Persons Task Team in May 2008. From left to right: Laché Rossouw, Sipiwo Pahlane, Steve Symes (consultant bone-trauma expert), Tshiamo Moela, Nonhlanhla Dlamini, Kundisai Dembetembe, Madeleine Fullard, Morongwa Mosothwane, Claudia Bisso (consultant from the EAAF), Thabang Manyaapelo, Nicky Rousseau and Kavita Chibba (kneeling)

© K. Dembetembe

© A. G. Morris

Exhumation of the graves at the Mafikeng cemetery as part of the MPTT excavations in June 2006

MMB-OI
G 607 SK1
SA 22 06 06

© A. G. Morris

Exposure of the skeleton at the Mafikeng cemetery as part of the MPTT excavations in June 2006

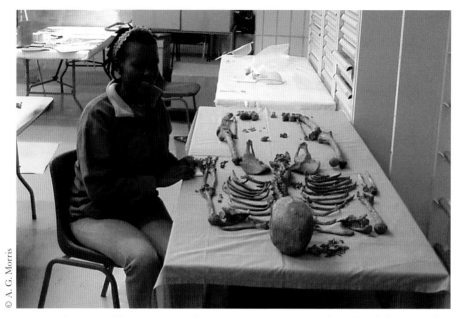

Morongwa Mosothwane analysing the remains of one of the TRC victims in the lab

The MPTT team showing the remains of an identified individual to his family as part of the team's efforts to ensure that victims' families are engaged throughout the entire process of search, excavation, identification and reburial

Ceremonial handover of the remains of Reginald Kekana from the NPA to his family, Freedom Park, Pretoria, July 2005

© A. G. Morris

© M. Fullard

Excavations at the dump site outside Laingsburg

The author arriving on Robben Island, September 2005

Excavating possible sites for Fadana's grave on Robben Island, September 2005. Jacqui Friedling is doing the hard work on the ground with Coen Nienaber standing. No grave was found at this site

Nicolas Gcaleka in Scotland in February 1995 with the skull he was bringing back to South Africa

Clea Koff's visit to the bone room at UCT in April 2005. From left to right around the table: Tasneem Salie, Lauren Joshua, Jacqui Friedling (obscured from view), Thabang Manyaapelo, the publisher's representative, Nhlanhla Dlamini (obscured from view) and Clea Koff

The disturbed prehistoric grave at Noetzie outside Knysna. The bones have been dug up and placed in a heap beside the construction trench

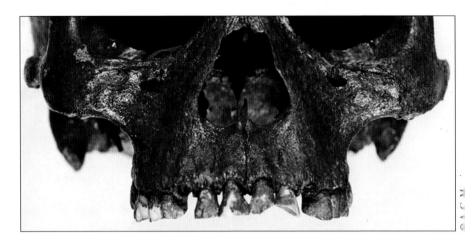

The face of NMB 1408 from Abrahamsdam in the Northern Cape province showing clear evidence of a pipe smoker's wear on the crowns of the left central and lateral incisors

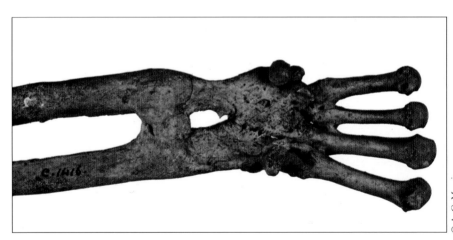

The right arm of NMB 1416 from near Augrabies Falls, showing the bridging between the ulna and radius, along with the infective damage to the wrist and palm of the hand. All of these bones are joined by new growth of bone triggered by the infection

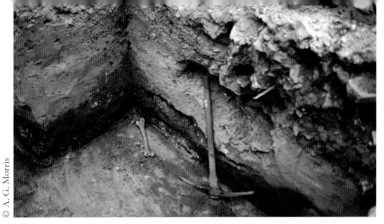

Exposure of skeletal remains in the foundation trench of the new building at Cobern Street, Cape Town, 3 October 1994

Excavations in progress at Cobern Street, December 1994

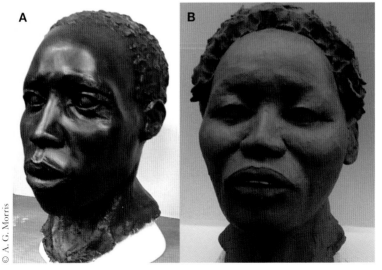

Reconstruction of some of the faces from Cobern Street by Rosendorff and Phillips. A: the face of a man between the ages of 30 and 35. He was in a coffin burial with a bone-handled knife and a clay pipe as grave goods. B: the face of a woman who died between the ages of 35 and 40. She was also buried in a coffin, but without any grave goods

Delegates to the Khoisan Identities and Cultural Heritage Conference in Cape Town, July 1997. Chief Adam Kok V is fifth from the left in the second row from the front (wearing an orange cap and sporting a white moustache). The author is on the extreme left of the picture

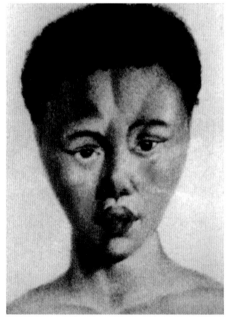

A close-up of a drawing of Sara Baartman in life. The original was painted at the Jardin de Roi in Paris at the request of George Cuvier in October or November 1815. She died a few weeks later

© G. Cuvier

The 12th thoracic and 1st lumbar vertebrae of UCT 317 from Quoin Point on the Cape South Coast. The arrowheads can be seen penetrating the back of the thoracic vertebra and entering into the space of the spinal cord

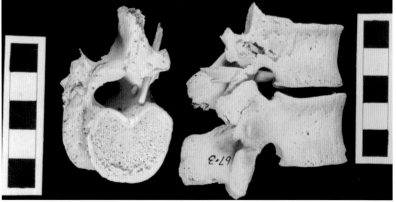

authorities briefly liaised with the MPTT about the possibility of visiting the site, but then all went quiet on the northern front. To date nothing more has happened, but it appears as if the Namibian government is reluctant to begin the investigation process. Namibia has not set up a TRC process like that of South Africa, and those individuals who were in the South African Defence Force at the time have not made any statements before the TRC in South Africa in reference to Namibia, so there is no information on the South African side that would help.

It is also possible that the Namibians fear that an investigation will get too close to their own secrets in Angola and in South African–occupied South West Africa.

Even more recently there has been a resurgence of an older claim of evidence of atrocities committed by the Germans during their colonial period in Namibia, but there are some doubts about the validity of the evidence. In April 1999 I received a call from the eTV news presenter Jane Dutton, who asked me to look at some video footage they had shot near Lüderitz in southern Namibia. They had rented a helicopter and filmed a field of bones sticking out of the sand. They wanted to know if I could see any signs of violence on the bones, specifically signs of gunshots.

Working from video footage is not ideal, but I told them that the holes I could see on the bones were consistent with erosion and not gunshots. I also told them that I had not seen anything like this before because the bones were all jumbled and didn't look as if they came from orderly skeletons. eTV also interviewed Dieter Noli, an archaeologist working in the area, who told them that the site was an old cemetery linked to a town called Charlottental that was part of the diamond-mining works between 1900 and 1930. The town was now deserted and the loose sand of the cemetery was exposing the historic burials.

eTV went ahead with a piece quoting both of us, but suggesting instead that this was the burial place of Herero people killed by the Germans in the war of extermination between 1905 and 1908. Neither Dieter nor I had provided any information in support of this theory.

I had forgotten entirely about the site until a while ago, when a new book titled *The Kaiser's Holocaust* was published. In it appear photographs of the same site and it is unambiguously stated that these are the remains of Hereros murdered in the concentration camp at Shark Island in 1906 and 1907. I was rather surprised, as I thought I remembered Dieter telling me that the site was not near the coast and was actually linked to a historic town as a formal cemetery. Not so according to the new book. So I rang Dieter Noli to ask him what evidence there was to link this to the German colonial concentration camp on Shark Island.

The town of Charlottental was established in 1909 (after the Herero War) and was occupied until the early 1930s. During this time, thousands of labourers, drawn from places as far away as Ovamboland in the north and the Cape Province in the south, were employed at the mine. Even normal mortality would have placed a large number of individuals in the local cemetery every year, but the area was particularly hard-hit during the 1918 Spanish flu epidemic.

In general the Charlottental burials are fairly shallow and the wind-blown sands have exposed the bones. I can vouch for this, as I have seen the phenomenon before with prehistoric skeletons that I have worked on from the Kuiseb River mouth near Walvis Bay. At some point in the 1960s, an employee of the Kolmanskop Diamond Mine used a front-end loader to cover up the exposed part of the graveyard, which would account for the disturbed state of the bones. Wind erosion continues to expose the bones on a regular basis.

The 'exposé' by eTV in 1999 resulted in a renewed interest in the site, and the Namibian government brought an archaeologist down from Windhoek to look at it. This archaeologist had almost no experience with skeletons and none with historic cemetery remains, yet he reported that he could see bullet holes and blood stains. These were not verified by anyone qualified as a physical anthropologist or forensic pathologist. Shortly after this, Dieter hosted a 'fact-finding mission' for politicians from Windhoek. He showed them the features that identified this as a formal cemetery that had been disturbed by erosion. He stated his disagreement with the previous archaeologist about the identification of the signs of violence.

The authors of the book on the German war atrocities visited the site in 2006, and it is they who initiated the latest interpretation of this as a holocaust site. As a result of their publicity, the Namibian government removed the exposed bones in 2010 and reburied them as part of the twentieth Heroes' Day commemoration in Luderitz as the remains of 'gallant Namibians who died in German concentration camps between 1904 and 1908'. Evidence to the contrary was ignored, so the lesson to all of us once again is that we see what we want to see, with or without evidence.

All of this digression into the politics of violence and reconciliation is important because it teaches us that the interpretation of bone from forensic or archaeological contexts is not always about science. This was brought home to me and my students once again during 2005, when we had a visit from a young woman named Clea Koff.

Clea had recently published a book of her experiences as a United Nations forensic anthropologist in Rwanda, Bosnia and Kosovo. She was on a sponsored world tour to promote the book and I discovered that she would be visiting Cape Town. My initial approach to the publisher to bring her to the Department of Human Biology to meet my team was rebuffed with the statement that, as Clea's time was limited, we could come to her book launch instead.

Fortunately, my message reached Clea and she insisted on making time to come to us. I fetched her, along with the local book company representative, and she spent nearly three hours with us in the bone lab. We all gathered around the table and talked bones and forensics. What impressed me, and what I know impressed the students, was Clea Koff's fantastic motivation to do more than just skeletal biology. She was the best ambassador for human rights in forensic science that I have ever met.

6

Archaeological Remains

Perhaps the most frustrating event in a bone case is the delivery by police of a black plastic bag containing a load of broken bone pieces that are obviously archaeological. Unpacking the bag reveals that the breaks are fresh (nice white-coloured broken edges compared to the dirty brown of the bone surface itself) and that many of the newly broken pieces are missing.

Right away I know that the skeleton is old and that it has been damaged during the process of removal. It is not the fault of the police. Often they are called out to a construction site and the workers show them a neat pile of bones on the periphery of the site, so it is already too late to call in an archaeologist. The police should log the case as an investigation and stop all construction, but sometimes it is so obvious to them that it is not a forensic case that they simply tell the construction crew to collect all of the remains and continue work. Thank goodness this has been happening less often over the years, resulting in the less frequent loss of important archaeological sites.

Looking through the fragments of bone tells me a great deal about the deceased person, but I know that I am missing most, if not all of the cultural clues telling me who the person might have been. The secrets of the grave structure itself are gone and, if the people at the discovery site have not been careful, then the associated cultural material is lost as well.

This is precisely the reason why I am prepared to put so much time into talking to the police constables and the mortuary technicians as well as the senior police and pathology personnel. I want them to realise that archaeological burials are as important as forensic cases. It is a bit of a losing battle because policemen are busy people and they know that their job does not include sorting out archaeological cases, but my experience is that they are all fascinated by the origin of their own communities and want to know about the past as much as anyone else – they simply don't want to add to their paperwork.

I think I am winning because fewer 'black bag' cases have been coming my way over the years, but also because the recent heritage legislation that protects prehistoric graves is finally being applied at the local level. All I really ask of the police is to make sure that the destructive work on the discovery site is stopped and that an archaeologist be called before the entire burial context is lost.

The worst-case scenario is the decision of the construction company to destroy the site because stopping work and calling in an archaeologist will be too costly to the project in terms of time and money.

Such a situation occurred in Knysna on the southern coast Garden Route in July 2006. The area between Mossel Bay and Port Elizabeth has long been recognised as one of the most beautiful parts of South Africa, and this isn't only a recent acknowledgement. Archaeological discoveries along the coast tell us that people thousands of years ago felt the same way. Cave sites, beach middens and stone fish-traps provide evidence of people living there continuously for over 100 000 years. The natural beauty and rich coastal resources mean that the land remains highly desirable, but where a few thousand years ago the demand was from prehistoric fishermen, it now comes from well-heeled golfers.

The Pezula Private Estate was developing the site at Noetzie just outside of Knysna and needed to dig a hole for a swimming pool in the new hotel complex. Despite the fact that they did not have approved permit plans, they drove a trench through a prehistoric midden, even though they were aware of its archaeological importance.

The damage was already done by the time archaeologists were called in, and no amount of legal action will bring back the information lost at the site. This is a battle between heritage and progress, and it is being fought on many fronts. Although there will always be greedy developers, education about our archaeological past through alerting everyone to the importance of preserving what we can is needed.

The issue of development is critical. Not only is our population expanding but it is becoming wealthier, and this translates into more building. The coastal sites are under tremendous pressure because of their picturesque settings, but the development is even more marked in the urban centres, where prime building land is sometimes already occupied by cemeteries. The excavation of cemeteries and the disturbance of prehistoric archaeological burials have resulted in conflict over cultural heritage, but have also provided opportunities for learning.

In an apparent paradox, the rise in public interest in forensic anthropology and the medico-legal investigation of the recently dead has been paired with a reluctance to allow archaeological investigation of earlier peoples. The paradox arises because the methods of the two activities are identical and the questions posed by the researchers in both cases are similar. Evident in this debate is the politics of heritage and especially the anger of communities that have been abused in the past and now wish to claim proper respect for their ancestors and restitution for past injustices.

More of this later on, but what it does force us to ask is whether we really do need to do forensic-level analysis of archaeological skeletons and why we should keep archaeological human remains in collections for research.

The total number of archaeologically derived skeletons in South Africa is currently being assessed, but my guess is that there are approximately 3 000 of these skeletons in museums and medical schools around the country. At least four university departments currently have research students working on these remains, which have provided, and continue to provide, a valuable resource for students training in human origins, human variation and forensic anthropology.

There are also about 5 000 modern human skeletons from medical-school dissections in the country. The question arises as to why we can't simply use the cadaver sample to study human biology and leave the more contentious archaeological skeletons alone. We can and do study skeletal biology using modern skeletons. Much current forensic research involves understanding degrees of sexual dimorphism and accurate estimates of age at death. For these questions we do need skeletons of known identity like those originating from medical-student cadaver dissections. But the medical-school collections do not necessarily represent all of the people of southern Africa.

The cadavers come from two sources: donations and paupers. The donations are overwhelmingly from Christians, and some-times from reform Jewish people: nearly all come from relatively wealthy urban communities. Muslims, Orthodox Jews and Hindus do not generally donate cadavers because their religious beliefs demand burial or, in the case of Hindus, cremation. Similarly, there are virtually no people who come from an ethnically African background. Although the majority of these people are Christian, traditional African beliefs in the need for burial are powerful and, under normal circumstances, these people do not consider donating their bodies to medical education.

The pauper burials are nearly entirely (but not exclusively) black.

An unclaimed body is held at a mortuary for a fixed time and then released for a pauper burial or donation to a medical school. Such people are either from the poorest of our communities or have lost touch with their families and remain unclaimed. The cadaver collections therefore consist of two segments: a wealthy, predominantly white Christian group, and an overwhelmingly poor, black and urban group. Any study using these skeletons is biased by this demographic reality.

Although we can still examine some issues of sex and age, we need to understand that generalisations will be difficult. We know that socio-economic welfare affects growth, maturity and sexual dimorphism. The two commonly represented groups are not comparable and neither group represents the full range of variation in its own community.

Archaeological samples give us special opportunities to understand much more about the peoples of southern Africa. One such opportunity is that we see a wider range of southern African peoples whose bodies would be excluded by the cultural selection factors that determine who ends up as a medical-school cadaver. A second is that we can see the remains of people who represent the social and biological mainstream of their communities. This is critical if we want to understand how to interpret the modern variation that we see in forensic cases. A third opportunity provided by archaeological skeletons is that they give us a chance to see evidence of the natural history of disease when it was not influenced by the surgical and pharmacological treatments of Western medicine.

Whether or not we wish to rely on alternative or Western medicine, it is undeniable that Western medicine has alleviated the suffering of much of humanity. It has reduced child mortality to levels never seen before in human history and, although thus far it has been unable to extend the human lifespan by many years, it has dramatically improved the quality of those years.

Scourges such as leprosy, syphilis and smallpox are now treatable or, in the case of smallpox, eradicated completely. In order to under-stand the natural history of these diseases in the present, we need to find evidence of them in the past, before modern treatments became available. Often archaeological skeletons are our only source of information.

Lastly, and perhaps most importantly, we need to study the past in order to understand our history. By its nature, forensic anthropology is concerned with the present or the recent past, but our knowledge of forensic anthropology comes from our broader knowledge of the human species and its origin. Why do we look the way we do? Why do some of us look different from others? What is the commonality that we all share? These are questions about origins, and our key to learning the answers must be found in the remains of our ancestors. The need to understand the past is not simply an academic pastime. All of us need to know about our roots.

EXPEDITIONS AND EXCAVATIONS

I am not a forensic anthropologist by training. My background is in zoology and anthropology. My decision to study in South Africa dragged me away from the study of fish – the topic of my under-graduate research in Canada – and into the realm of humanity.

I arrived in Johannesburg in January 1975 and immediately began to work on an idea for a PhD project, but it was a slow start. The topic that I eventually chose was actually my third choice. The first proposal was an attempt to find a relationship between body weight and structural features of the femur, pelvis and lower vertebrae with the idea of predicting the living weight of a person from the structure of his bones. I soon discovered that my idea wouldn't work. There was so much variation in the structure that it was impossible to find predictable patterns, so I gave up after eleven months and started looking for a new project.

My second attempt was more archaeological. While I had been working on the first idea for a thesis proposal, I had been reading about African archaeology and had discovered that the origin of the Khoekhoen was still unknown. Were they the original sheep herders who had come down from East Africa with their herds, or were they locals from the northern Kalahari who had been fortunate enough to be the first southern Africans to learn of the pleasures of keeping livestock?

If the first option were true, then the Khoekhoen were foreigners, bringing new genes and cranial shape down from the north. As I pondered this problem, I received some bad news. Philip Rightmire from the State University of New York at Binghamton had arrived in the country with one of his PhD students and had given her the very topic that I was considering.

Alice Hausman was already in Cape Town and was starting to measure skulls. I didn't know what to do. It was certainly possible for us to work on similar projects, but it would end up as a race to see which one of us would finish first. Alice was ahead of me, so I decided that I would drop the idea and see what else could be done.

In conversation with Philip Rightmire, I discovered that there was a large set of excavated human skeletons stored at the museum in Kimberley. Over eighty burials had been excavated from along a fifty-kilometre stretch of the banks of the Riet River, and none of the skeletons had ever been studied. The odds were very high that this represented a single population from just before the arrival of Europeans in the region. Not only that, but there was a similar set of skeletons at the museum in Bloemfontein from further down the river beyond the confluence with the Vaal, and this would double the size of my sample. I could also add the skeletons stored at Wits from the Griqua site at Campbell because they were roughly from the same time period and quite close geographically.

What these skeletons had in common was that they represented the people living in one particular historic region of the country called the 'Northern Frontier' between roughly 1500 CE and 1850 CE.

The movement of European missionaries, farmers and adventurers into the Northern Cape and southern Highveld took place in the latter part of the eighteenth century, and therefore the skeletons covered the period before contact, during early contact and later colonisation.

My project was going to be a new approach for physical anthropology in South Africa. The prime interest was not in race or identity; it was to be an attempt to look at the life and times of people in one place over one historic period. I gave it the appallingly boring title 'An Osteological Analysis of the Protohistoric Populations of the Northern Cape and Western Orange Free State, South Africa', but when I eventually published the completed project, I gave the book the much more palatable name *Skeletons of Contact*, because that described much of what it was about. What made this project new to South Africa was its 'bioarchaeological' approach. Previous studies of South African skeletons had concentrated on the issue of racial identification and basic parameters of age and sex, but my study would encompass diet, lifestyle issues, signs of past disease and demography, all in conjunction with the historical and archaeological record.

I worked on my PhD from 1977 until its submission in 1984, but the project ended up being greater than the study I had initially proposed. Many unanswered questions popped up as I worked through the skeletons in Bloemfontein and Kimberley. The most important of these were about the original excavations, especially in reference to the collection of skeletons from along the Orange River near Kakamas in the Northern Cape.

The Riet River burials had been carefully excavated during the 1920s and 1930s by the amateur archaeologist William Fowler. Fowler had been meticulous in making notes about each grave and had included descriptions of all discoveries inside the black box that housed each skeleton.

The same was not true for the Kakamas graves. T.F. Dreyer

and A.J.D. Meiring, both zoologists with an archaeological interest, were intrigued by the publication in 1935 of the journal of
Hendrik Jacob Wikar. Wikar, a Swedish employee of the Dutch
East India Company at the Cape of Good Hope, had made two
journeys into the northern frontier of the colony in 1778 and 1779
respectively, and had not only made notes of his experiences but
had also produced a hand-drawn map of the region.

Dreyer and Meiring were very impressed with his description
of the Khoekhoen people he met on his travels, and in June 1936
they set out on 'an expedition to collect Old Hottentot Skulls'
using Wikar's map and his notes describing where he met native
peoples. Dreyer and Meiring were neither discriminating in their
choice of site location nor in their technique of excavation.

They rapidly surveyed the banks of the lower Orange River
from Augrabies Falls to Upington and beyond, and excavated any
concentration of graves that they could identify as such. In the space
of three weeks they opened 112 graves and accessioned sixty-nine
human skeletons to the collection of the National Museum, Bloemfontein (NMB). Their interpretation of both the graves and the
skeletons was coloured by their typological racial views, and all
of their subsequent publications focused only on the issue of the
identity of the people. In fact, they had already decided that these
were the remains of the original north-east African Hamites and
that the best preserved graves contained the skeletons of 'pure
Hottentots', because the high burial cairns represented 'undegen-
erated Hottentot culture'.

Their fieldwork was pretty close to archaeological rape and their
interpretation reflected the rigid link between biology and culture
that was common racist thought at the time. I needed to follow
their footsteps to see if I could locate other burial cairns. This way
I could find out if their observations had been correct.

I led my own expedition to the Orange River in 1984. Instead
of following Wikar's map, we followed Dreyer and Meiring's. We

carefully surveyed two locations where a large number of cairns had been excavated in 1936 in order to find more undisturbed cairns. On the farm Omdraai on the north bank of the Orange River opposite Renosterkopeiland, we found six intact cairns, while on a side branch of the river just to the north of Augrabies Falls on the farm Waterval, we found twenty-five stone burial cairns, including one location with eight badly disturbed cairns – evidence of the activities of Dreyer and Meiring fifty years before. We carefully excavated three graves at Omdraai and two graves at Waterval, and our conclusions were very different from those of our scientific predecessors.

It was obvious to us that the preservation of the burial cairns was linked to two features – the age at death of the person buried there, and the proximity of the grave to the river. Our largest two cairns covered the skeletons of adult men, while a slightly smaller cairn covered the body of a woman. The two smallest cairns were both over the graves of children.

Careful checking of the analysis of the skeletons in Bloemfontein against the rough-and-ready field notes made by Meiring showed the same pattern – the cairns with the largest number of stones (even if they were dispersed) invariably covered the graves of adult males.

More important was that the highest cairns were just on the edge of the flood plain of the river and remained high and well packed because they had escaped the worst of the annual flooding of the Orange River. There was no link between burial style and 'ethnic purity'.

Our careful excavation of the five cairns revealed that care had been taken over the burial of these people, as reed mats were used to cover the bodies. Grave goods were not commonly placed near the body. The burial pattern largely matched the ethnographers' records for historic burials of Khoekhoen people throughout the region. The bones themselves gave evidence of gene flow between the local

Khoesan and the neighbouring black African peoples immediately to the north. This was a dynamic population trading and mixing genetically with the Tswana peoples beyond the Orange River.

The careful notes compiled by William Fowler and some very detailed archaeological surveys by Tim Maggs and Tony Humphreys meant that I did not have to visit the Riet River to confirm the original observations. Maggs and Humphreys had already demonstrated that these people were pastoralists with cultural links that suggested San (Bushmen) rather than Khoekhoen, and that they were also in a trading relationship with the neighbouring Bantu-speaking Sotho groups to the north and east of the Riet River.

But the skeletons did provide a surprise that made the Riet River sample very different from the one from Kakamas. Whereas the pattern of gene flow between the Khoesan and their Bantu-speaking neighbours was readily visible in the shape of the skulls from Kakamas, there was no gene flow visible in the skulls from Riet River. Their morphology was distinctly Khoesan and they would have been lost in a sample of !Kung San from the Kalahari. This posed an interesting question: Why were neighbouring groups sharing an intimate relationship far deeper than social calls on the Orange River but keeping strictly apart on the Riet River only a couple of hundred kilometres away?

I proposed as an explanation the theory of 'unidirectional gene flow'. The social anthropologists had long been aware of something they called 'hypergyny', which they could see in the caste system of India. Gene flow follows social class lines, with high-status men taking brides from lower castes, while high-status women never marry below their rank. We were seeing evidence of this in historical South Africa.

Along the Orange River, two groups of people met who had similar world views and wealth systems – the pastoralist Khoekhoen and the pastoralist Bantu-speaking Tswana. The two groups had trade relations as equals and that meant that wives (and perhaps the occasional husband) were chosen from both groups. The people along the Riet, by contrast, were foragers who were looked down upon by nearly all of the neighbouring Bantu-speakers. They had learnt some animal husbandry and kept flocks of sheep and goats, but their social relationship with their neighbours was unequal. Riet River women were sometimes chosen to join Tswana groups as brides, but there would have been active social pressure preventing Tswana women from joining the San.

The analysis of the 200 or so skeletons that formed the basis of my PhD thesis produced some extremely interesting information, but I was aware that it did not answer all of my questions about the people of the Northern Frontier, especially those about the early historic times when the region was being actively transformed by immigrants from the colony in the south. Through Professor Andy Smith of the Department of Archaeology at UCT, I was introduced to a farm called De Tuin about fifty kilometres west of the town of Kenhardt. Although De Tuin has been a stock farm with just a few people living on it for the past half-century or more, it had a brief historical moment between 1863 and 1868 when it was the Northern Cape residence of the people known as the Rehoboth Basters.

The Dutch word *baster* has all sorts of negative connotations when translated into English as 'bastard', but in the first half of the nineteenth century the Dutch word had a different meaning. The Basters were people who claimed a genetic and cultural heritage from both the European settlers and the Khoekhoen. They spoke Dutch as a home language and practised the Reformed Protestant religion of the colonists. Most of these people lived along the northern border of the colony and many were relatively wealthy stock farmers.

As the nineteenth century progressed, the Basters became increasingly disenfranchised. Pressured by white *trekboers* moving into the Karoo in the 1840s and 1850s, many of the Baster families came together to begin their own trek out of the colony and into the 'open' lands to the north. At one stage over 500 people were living at De

Tuin. They had a stone church and their own Rhenish missionary, but the Northern Cape in the 1860s was not a happy place to be.

Not only were white farmers impinging on the land from the south, but the political disruption along the Orange River had triggered a wave of lawlessness throughout the region. Finally, in 1868, the people at De Tuin literally pulled up stakes, put all of their belongings into their wagons, and began what is almost certainly one of the least studied and most difficult nineteenth-century migrations in the history of South Africa.

They crossed the Orange River and moved through the Kalahari up to central Namibia, where they asked permission from the Afrikaner family in Windhoek to settle at Rehoboth, about 100 kilometres south of what would become the Namibian capital after its conquest by the Germans. This epic voyage took three full years over some of the most difficult terrain on the subcontinent.

I carried out an initial survey at De Tuin in 1982 and discovered two large clusters of graves that were undoubtedly linked to the Baster occupation of the 1860s. I contacted the Rehoboth community through Dr Beatrice Sandelowsky in 1989 and in 1994 relaunched my investigation at De Tuin with the blessing of the Rehobothers in Namibia.

The excavation of graves from the historic burial ground at De Tuin will probably be the last time an archaeological project that specifically excavates human remains for research purposes is allowed in South Africa. We mapped over eighty graves, and fourteen were opened between 1982 and 2002 to identify who was buried there.

By 1999 I had turned over the De Tuin excavations to Tanya Peckmann, who incorporated the information into her PhD project. Tanya picked up where I left off in 1984 by extending the historic Northern Cape sample to include burials from Colesberg and other sites. Her project specifically looked at the health and dynamics of the people of the region and she also included some serious palaeopathology, looking for signs of the dreaded smallpox that we knew had ravaged the region in the second half of the nineteenth century.

One of Tanya's conclusions was that the childhood mortality among the Griqua and Basters was extremely high and that many of the children were affected by porotic hyperostosis and cribra orbitalia, signs that their immunity was low and that the populations were under stress.

To me, one of the highlights of working on the hundreds of skeletons from the Northern Cape and adjacent areas was the personal stories that I could find in the bones. Earlier studies had been lost in the identification of race, but each individual was a new case to me, providing evidence not only of biological origins but of the life history of that person. There was an element of surprise every time I opened one of the skeleton boxes in the museums, as I did not ever know what I would find.

I frequently discovered signs of disease or anatomical variations that marked the person as an individual. There are dozens of examples I could give you but I have selected only two, as they are good examples of how we learn about individuals from their bones.

NMB 1408 (referring to its number at the National Museum, Bloemfontein) was one of the skeletons disinterred on the farm Stinkwater near the village of Abrahamsdam in the Northern Cape. I am still not sure why Dreyer and Meiring decided to excavate here, because it is distant from the Orange River and does not appear on Wikar's map, but they collected fourteen skeletons from two farms in the Abrahamsdam district. All of the graves are early historic and may very well represent Griqua residents from the second half of the nineteenth century.

NMB 1408 was the well-preserved skeleton of a man, distinctive for his front teeth: between the first and second incisors on the left side of his mouth was the distinct channel caused by habitual pipe-smoking. The shape of the channel was perfectly round, telling me that this was the classic nineteenth-century clay pipe, but he was over a thousand kilometres from the nearest place where he could have bought a pipe. Nineteenth-century clay pipes were cheap and brittle and did not travel well over the long wagon treks from the Cape.

The man from Stinkwater either had his own supply of pipes as a result of travelling to the Cape frequently, or he had spent a long enough time in Cape Town to erode the hole in his smile by smoking a pipe. One simple dental feature had the power to tell us something about this man, his habits and his travels.

NMB 1416 was a skeleton that came from one of the large graves near the Augrabies Falls. It was a young adult man whose skeleton appeared relatively healthy, except for his right arm. At some point, a few years before his death, he had had a terrible accident and his arm had been crushed in two places. Damage to the palm of his hand was extreme and it had become infected. All of the small bones in the wrist and the palm of the hand had fused.

At the time of his death the disease process had stopped, but he must have experienced extreme pain before the healing finally relieved him of his agony. In the end, bending his elbow must have hurt him and he would have had no movement in his forearm or in his hand, except for his fingers. He could use the hand to bear weight, but only on his second and third digits because his fourth and fifth fingers had begun to waste due to lack of function.

What had caused his mishap? Well, of course we will never know the details, but the kind of infection that destroyed his hand is typical of a penetrating wound that has gone septic. In addition, his ulna, one of the two long bones in the forearm, had been broken and new bone growth had bridged across to his radius, the other long bone in the forearm. My guess is that the two breaks happened at the same time. He learnt to live with his disability and whatever killed him in the end had nothing to do with the damage to his arm and hand.

The Northern Frontier project was really a pioneering study of bioarchaeology in southern Africa. Since then a number of similar studies that examine the life history of people have been undertaken. Many of these projects have been conducted by my students. Mary Patrick looked at the Later Stone Age people of Oakhurst on the southern Cape coast, while Maryna Steyn examined the large sample of skeletons from the Iron Age of K2 village at Bambandyanalo. Anja Meyer, who is being jointly supervised by Maryna Steyn and me, is looking at the historic Chinese miner skeletons from Johannesburg, and Nhlanhla Dlamini is currently exploring the people of the fourteenth to the sixteenth centuries in southern Congo.

These southern African projects are part of a worldwide change in approach to skeletal biology that started in the 1950s and 1960s with what is now called the 'New Physical Anthropology'. Instead of race being the central focus of study, the New Physical Anthropology concentrates on the process of variation. Issues of diet, growth and disease – and not the cataloguing of racial variation – become the point of the study.

Susan Pfeiffer of Toronto has also been active in the study of skeletal biology in southern Africa. She has published several papers with her students and in collaboration with southern African partners, mostly involving various aspects of Stone Age hunter-gatherer health, adaptation and biomechanics.

What started in 1977 as a project to look more broadly at skeletons from one particular archaeological sequence on the Northern Frontier has now turned into a major research field exploring all of the archaeological populations of southern Africa. The common feature of all of these projects is that race is not an objective of research for any of them.

FIELDWORK AND DESCENDENT COMMUNITIES

The Northern Frontier project gave rise to both my PhD and extensive experience working with skeletons in museums and in the field. Most of the work involved the painstaking and detailed anatomical examination of the bones, and I spent many hours reconstructing broken bones so that reliable observations could be made. I learnt not only anatomy and statistics; the fieldwork also brought me into contact with the descendent communities, especially in relation to my work at De Tuin.

My initial survey of the site in 1982 was followed by a long period in which I chose not to continue to work there. I had needed to obtain the permission of the landowner, Mr du Plessis, before we could begin the work in 1982. I had contacted him and he had given us permission, but there was a rider. Mr du Plessis would not allow any students of colour onto his property.

I agonised over this at the time, but since it just so happened that all of my science students that year were white, I decided to go. In hindsight I recognised that I had made the wrong decision and I resolved not to go back. Finally, in 1994, I realised that it was extremely important to complete the research. I had worked in Rehoboth in Namibia 1989 and 1990 and members of the Rehoboth community had been strongly supportive of the De Tuin project and wanted me to continue.

I wrote back to the farmer – this time determined not to be bullied into a decision that excluded any students on the basis of their skin colour. It transpired that the old man had retired and left the farm to two of his sons. Riaan and Henry were not pleased with the idea of radicals from Cape Town conducting research on their farm, but in the end they relented. As I mentioned earlier, Tanya Peckmann took over the De Tuin project in 1999 when she joined me to do her PhD, and between us we took a multicoloured group of over twenty students and colleagues to De Tuin over the years.

Tanya's expanded Northern Frontier project studied quite a number of skeletons of Griqua people, including the set of thirty-five skeletons from the historic Griqua cemetery at Campbell, which was excavated by Phillip Tobias and his students from Wits in the 1960s. The skeletons were stored at Wits but no research could be carried out on them without the written permission of the Griqua people of Campbell. My contact among the Griqua in Kimberley was Martin Engelbrecht, a member of the Griqua National Forum (later the National Khoisan Forum and later still the National Khoisan Council).

Martin had been very supportive in the past, and although he envisioned a formal reburial of all of the Griqua remains, he was keen to allow us to learn as much as we could from the skeletons before the reburial. Unfortunately, the politics of the local Khoesan communities in South Africa is complex and one is never sure who is 'in' or 'out' at a given time.

When I wrote in support of Tanya's proposal in 1999, I discovered that Martin was 'out'. I had to write directly to the royal house of Adam Kok V[3] and was unsure of how my letter would be received. The new advisor to the royal house was Mr Barend van Staden, and I outlined the details of Tanya's project for him. In particular, I emphasised the need to record the things that happened during a person's lifetime, as this could give us an understanding of the life of everyday people in the nineteenth-century Northern Cape. To my (and Tanya's) great pleasure, the response was positive and Tanya was given permission to continue her studies. In fact, this spirit of cooperation is something I have found in my dealings with nearly all descendent communities. Where there is friction

---

3 Griqua politics is notoriously complex. The original community in the Northern Cape was led by the sons of the founding Kok family, but there was a major split when a large part of the group migrated to the Eastern Cape in the 1860s under Adam Kok III. His descendants remain the main group in the Eastern and Western Cape and form the majority in the Griqua National Conference. A small group remained in the Northern Cape and was led in Phillip Tobias's time by Adam Kok IV and in the late 1990s by his son, Adam Kok V.

it is usually caused by people who claim the right to speak for local communities but have a much larger political agenda.

My work in the museum collections also introduced me to the scientific racism that has existed in my profession in the past. As I worked through the various museum catalogues, I found reference to how the skeletons were acquired by the institutions. Many of them were from archaeological contexts – sometimes intentionally excavated, but just as often they were chance discoveries.

Other skeletons were accompanied by documentation that showed a less honourable source. Too many of the collectors were effectively race scientists who collected bones as type specimens. Some, like Scotty Smith, were outright desecrators of fresh graves, while others were amateur scientists like the Reverend H. Kling, who was keen to send 'ethnically known' skeletons to the museums for the advancement of scientific knowledge.

George St Leger Gordon Lennox was a frontiersman known popularly as Scotty Smith in the Northern Cape for much of the late nineteenth and early twentieth centuries. Born in Perthshire, Scotland, he came to South Africa in 1877 and moved to the northern border in 1882. The collection of human skeletons was a money-earning enterprise that he set up in his latter years. The magistrate at Upington even provided him with a permit, valid from 1910 to July 1912, to exhume 'Bushman' skeletons.

Much legend exists about how Lennox came by the bones, and it is even said that he shot the required number of 'Bushmen' whenever he needed their skeletons. Lennox certainly was very familiar with the native peoples of the region, and a more likely explanation is that he excavated graves based on information provided by local native informants.

The Reverend Kling was the minister at the Steinkopf Rhenish mission station from 1893 to 1899 and again from 1907 to 1919. His first appointment at Steinkopf overlapped with the severe Namaqualand drought of 1895 to 1897, and it was during this period that many of the people died whose skeletons Kling later had exhumed and donated to the South African and Albany Museums.

People like Smith and Kling taught me that it is impossible to understand the retrieval and analysis of human skeletal remains unless you understand the political and cultural context in which they were collected.

By this time I was working on a constant stream of reports for skeletons excavated by professional archaeologists in Namibia, Malawi, the Cape south and west coasts, the Karoo, the Northern Cape and Natal, but I hadn't lost interest in the skeletons already in museum collections. I had visited nearly every museum in the country to determine the number of skeletons in their collections and in 1992 I published 'A Master Catalogue: Holocene Human Skeletons from South Africa', which contained the records for over 2 500 people.

Not once in the catalogue did I mention the race of any individual. The object was to sort the skeletons into space, time and archaeological context so that we could better reconstruct the biological history of our country. Glaringly missing from the catalogue were the skeletons collected by scientists as examples of one ethnic group or other.

THE COBERN STREET HISTORIC CEMETERY

In early December 1994 an event occurred that changed the direction of my research focus for a decade. This was the excavation of the Cobern Street cemetery in Green Point, Cape Town.

The first news of the discovery of bones in Cobern Street came on Sunday 2 October 1994. The old house at 4 Cobern Street had already been pulled down by that stage and the contractors were digging deep trenches in the sand for the foundations of the new building. When they started to hit skeletons in the trenches, they did notify the police, but were told not to worry as there would be no investigation. The bones were discarded on the piles of loose dirt removed from the trenches and at least one skull was taken home as a curiosity.

Passersby noticed the bones and it was one of these people who complained to Professor Deon Knobel, head of Forensic Medicine at UCT, on that Sunday. Knobel phoned me on Monday morning and I arranged for Tim Hart and Dave Halkett of the UCT Archaeology Contracts Office to go down to the site on the same day. They gave me an initial report on the skeletons in the trenches, but all they could do was record the location of the bones and note that the skeleton currently exposed in the trench was extended on its back in a coffin – confirming the historic context of the discovery.

That week was hectic for me, as I arranged a meeting of archaeologists from UCT, the South African Museum, the National Monuments Council (NMC) and other people with an interest in the early history of Cape Town. There was great excitement about the discovery, but the archaeologists were angry that construction had begun before the area had been archaeologically surveyed. Duncan Miller and John Parkington of the UCT archaeology department wrote a strongly worded letter to the newspaper complaining about the lack of planning by the City Council and the NMC, but finger-pointing was not terribly useful at that stage. We had a major archaeological site that needed to be excavated before construction at the site completely destroyed it.

The NMC quickly declared the cemetery a protected site. This meant that legally the owner had to stop all work and bring in a team of professional archaeologists to explore the area and excavate the discovery. This would take months and the owner, Herbert Jung, was furious. I had the unenviable job of trying to come up with a workable plan. Jung was threatening to take the NMC to court, but he was keen to find another solution if one was possible. We made an agreement that he would stop work for a few days while we surveyed the area already trenched and damaged, and then he would demolish the house on the other half of the site and remove the rubble so that we would have the time during the December/January builders' holiday to excavate. He would also provide space and pay for a small museum display in the foyer of the new building that would tell the history of the site and the excavations. I then had to obtain a permit to excavate, arrange money to cover expenses and find a crew – all before the end of November.

My request for funding from the City Council and the NMC was unsuccessful, but Syfrets Limited, as the trustees of the Lorenzo and Stella Chiappini Charitable and Cultural Trust, came up with R2000. Despite its earlier refusal, the NMC eventually offered me an additional R3000 along with the necessary permit to carry out an archaeological excavation. The money allowed me to hire Tim Hart and Dave Halkett as the official archaeologists on site. It would be their job to map the site and properly record each discovery as it was made.

The local branch of the South African Archaeological Society sent out a notice to its members asking for volunteers and I had nearly thirty people contact me to offer their services. I even managed to secure a small pot of money from the university to hire students, and one or two students who had not gone home for the holiday agreed to come down and help. I also roped in my twelve-year-old daughter and one of her friends for a few days. We had only three weeks to complete the dig and I needed all hands on deck.

Over three weeks in the stifling heat of summer we excavated 108 square metres of sandy soil and identified sixty-three burial features, including eleven disturbed scatters of human bone, from around the site. Although the majority of the formal graves were orientated in the same direction, some graves appeared different in placement, and there was also a large number of isolated bones unrelated to any specific burial. Newer graves had disturbed older graves and we frequently found loose bones packed around the outside of coffin burials. It was evident that the grave diggers had collected the bones that they had disturbed and buried them on the margin of the grave shaft for each new burial.

But there were also loose bones everywhere – sometimes a skull or two, sometimes isolated single bones, and in one case a small hole that was packed with the jumbled bones of one person. This disruption was almost certainly caused by the construction of the now-demolished house that had been built in 1862. The old house did not have deep foundations, but the land must have been levelled at the time and disturbed many of the shallower graves. Our later search through the archives indicated that by about 1800 the cemetery had fallen into disuse and that it was finally sold to one of the city councillors in 1827, but left fallow until the redevelopment of the whole street in the 1860s.

FIGURE 11: Map of burial sequence at Cobern Street

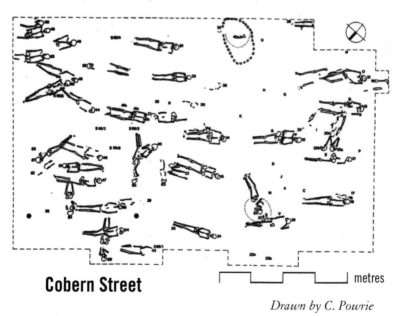

Cobern Street

metres

Drawn by C. Powrie

Back in the laboratory we began the analysis of the individual skeletons. There were fifty-two formal undisturbed graves containing fifty-seven individuals, and at least an additional sixty-four individuals were represented by the disturbed bones around the site. Kundi Dembetembe later worked on the preservation of the bones and calculated that the maximum number of individuals at the site was likely to be about 162.

Most of the formal graves contained coffins and were facing the same direction. These graves often had grave goods buried with them. We found long tobacco pipes, eighteenth-century 'matchboxes', beads, buttons, and two beautiful silver artefacts in the grave of a young woman. These looked like make-up boxes and one had the initials 'MHK 1764' scratched on the back.

Five other graves were buried at right angles to the main sequence and contained neither coffins nor grave goods. The grave styles reflected religious differences in the community at Cobern Street. Our archival search indicated that these were indeed the 'invisible' people of the colony. The burying ground was unofficial and most likely contained slaves, 'free blacks', non-Christian immigrants and anyone else who was not formally recognised by the Dutch Reformed or Lutheran Churches that held sway in the colony until the arrival of the British.

The most recent artefact we found in association with these graves was a British one-penny coin dated 1793. Our biggest surprise came when we located two stone cairns at the lowest level of the historic graves. Upon removal, we found that each cairn had covered a Later Stone Age double burial complete with Khoekhoe-style pottery. Radiocarbon dating confirmed that they were from around 1 000 years ago, and their presence in this location was unrelated to the historic cemetery that was eventually placed on top of them.

Our work on the Cobern Street project has been ongoing, but it is now being tied up with one final publication, we hope. The skeletons will then be permanently housed in the ossuary for historic skeletons in downtown Cape Town. At least six students have received higher degrees for work they did on the Cobern Street cemetery. They have analysed the burial pattern, the diet as seen in the biochemistry, the preservation of the skeletons, the teeth, the pathology, and the bone strength and activity patterns. I have continuously emphasised that we are looking at burials from a tremendously exciting time in the history of Cape Town, when a new amalgamated identity of settlers, slaves and Khoekhoen was being forged in this urban environment at the tip of Africa. These are the people *not* seen in official documents. They have been excluded from the textbooks of history. Our job has been to learn as much as we can to help put them back in their place in local history.

One of the things that I was determined to try was facial reconstruction. These reconstructions would be different from forensic reconstructions because the accuracy of individual identity was not the primary objective; the attempt would be more to find the most likely facial appearance. I wanted to try to make a connection with the living people of Cape Town. The use of facial reconstruction, although we have to acknowledge the impossibility of checking its accuracy, allows people to visualise the archaeological site as a place where real people lived.

The Cobern Street excavation overlapped with the resurgence of coloured, and, particularly, Khoesan, identity. Cape Town hosted two exciting conferences that for the first time in our history included the very people that the conference was discussing. In August 1995, the Institute for Democracy in South Africa (IDASA) convened a conference titled 'National Unity and the Politics of Diversity: the Case of the Western Cape'. We all called it the 'Coloured Identity Conference' for short. I was an invited delegate. My job was to listen and to learn, and I did precisely that. Nelson Mandela gave the opening address and the speakers were a mix of academics and politicians, most of whom would have been classified 'coloured' under the old political dispensation.

Debate from the audience was openly encouraged. The crux of every argument was how to deal with ethnicity in a non-racial society. The delegates divided into two broad camps: those who saw any form of racial categorisation as a perpetuation of apartheid racial discrimination, and those who wanted a separate identity for coloured people in South Africa. The conundrum for the first group was how to apply redress and redistribution if racial categories were no longer accepted.

The second group needed to consider how a rigid racial identity could be morally justified after forty years of apartheid racial engineering. I was fascinated, especially by the groups who supported a separate coloured identity and even lobbied for ethnically based political parties.

Two years later, the University of the Western Cape, along with UCT and the National Monuments Council, organised a conference at the South African Museum titled 'Khoisan Identities and Cultural Heritage'. It was actually the third in a series of academic conferences on Khoesan peoples and I had attended the previous one in Munich in 1994. In Germany the delegates with Khoesan cultural or biological heritage could be counted on one hand, but in Cape Town nearly half of the invited delegates came from the various Khoesan communities around southern Africa. Only a few presented papers, but all were involved in discussions afterwards.

This time I was not a silent delegate. I presented a paper showing the disjunction between the biological and cultural/historical identity of the Griqua. I argued that the Griqua were not indigenous in the sense of being an unchanged remnant of a prehistoric Khoesan group, but *were* indigenous as a uniquely South African ethnic creation formed by the dynamic reshaping of our society starting in the historic period and continuing today.

I showed that it was impossible that the number of Griqua in the 1985 census could have increased naturally from the original 1860s groups, and that the Griqua actively attracted new members and were continuing to forge their identity. This might sound like the kind of academic argument that is of interest only to scholars tucked away in a university, but it had immediate implications for debates at the conference. The reason was that the Griqua National Conference (GNC) had chosen this gathering to begin its claim to represent all Khoesan people, and to demand the return of the remains of Sara Baartman to South Africa.

THE SAD STORY OF SARA BAARTMAN

The story of Sara Baartman is a long and sad one that has now been published many times, so I will give you only the briefest outline of her history. Baartman was born somewhere in the Eastern Cape in the second half of the eighteenth century. She was Khoekhoen in ethnic origin, but it was a bad time for her people and most were living as shepherds or farm labourers in the service of colonial farmers. She moved to Cape Town and entered domestic service, but in 1810 she was taken by an English doctor to London, where she was exhibited as 'The Hottentot Venus'.

Sara was the subject of a court case in London to determine if she was enslaved or free, and although the court decided that she was not enslaved it was probably a moot point. Her (and her manager's) income was based on the British public's fascination with the exotic, and it was her 'native costume' and projecting backside that attracted the customers. In 1815 she and her new manager moved to Paris, where she died of an 'inflammatory and eruptive malady' in December of that year.

That would have been the end of the sad story, except that her presence in Paris had attracted the attention of the famous comparative anatomist Baron Georges Cuvier. Cuvier had had Baartman drawn in life, and after her death he obtained her body for dissection. He had a cast made of her body, carefully removed her brain and private parts, and then boiled down the rest of her body's flesh to extract her skeleton. Her brain, sex organs and skeleton were accessioned to the Musée de l'Homme, and that was where she was in 1997.

The presence of Sara Baartman's remains in Paris was not a secret and several writers in the 1980s (including me) had drawn attention to her story. The tale of the abused Khoesan woman who died far from home and whose remains were kept in a museum struck a major chord with the GNC, and the council, under its legal advisor Mansell Upham, demanded her return.

The Musée de l'Homme at first refused, fearing that this would open a floodgate of demands to return other colonial treasures, but the GNC persisted and, after a five-year battle involving both the French and the South African governments, the remains of Sara Baartman were finally repatriated in May 2002.

The GNC's claim to represent all Khoesan peoples in the battle to bring Baartman home needs to be seen in terms of the political context of the mid-1990s. The new African National Congress government in Pretoria had initiated a process of land claims to redress the injustices of the past, but they had made a specific decision to limit their considerations only to those who claimed land taken from them after 1913. That was the year that the Union of South Africa promulgated the Land Act, which segregated land ownership into 'black' and 'white'.

The courts and government papers kept a record of removals and resettlements from that date, which meant that there was a paper trail for the Land Claims Court to follow. But the Khoesan people of South Africa were dispossessed long before 1913. Because of this, the only legitimate claim that anyone could make for restitution of land taken from them before 1913 was to demonstrate a link to traditional tribal leaders of groups whose names appeared in the old historical records. The Griqua was one such group.

The original Griqua communities of the Northern Cape were a mixture of Khoekhoen, San, Basters, Tswana and others united under the leadership of the Kok clan in several small settlements north of the Orange River. The glue that held them together was the Griqua Church, which aligned itself with the London Missionary Society after a visit by Reverend Campbell in 1813. They had called themselves Basters before this and it was Campbell who suggested that they find a new name that was, in his opinion, less demeaning.

The people chose the title Griqua because it was a shortened version of the name of the Khoekhoen clan that formed a large segment of their community. Ignored by successive South African governments, many of these people began to identify themselves as a special group in the 1910s and 1920s. Under the leadership of A.A.S. le Fleur, whose ancestors were part of the Griqua who had trekked from the Northern to the Eastern Cape in the 1860s and who was married to one of the granddaughters of Adam Kok III, they attempted physically to set themselves apart from 'Europeans' and 'natives'.

To Le Fleur and his followers, 'Griqua' became a synonym for 'people of mixed heritage' rather than a specific historical entity. Le Fleur started new communities throughout the southern Cape Province that attracted many 'coloured' South Africans who preferred to identify themselves as Griqua, because it gave them historical roots at a time when the apartheid government was trying to define them as a racial category.

The GNC was created to unite these disparate communities. Whereas in the past Griqua communities emphasised their 'mixed' heritage, the GNC began to emphasise their Khoesan heritage after the 1997 conference in Cape Town. 'Griqua' had therefore moved from a political category in the late nineteenth century, to a social category in the early and mid-twentieth century, to an ethnic category in the late twentieth century.

The claim of the GNC to inherit Sara Baartman emphasised the Griqua as an ethnic identity. This strengthens their argument for the official recognition of their leaders in the same way that the tribal leaders of the Bantu-speakers have been recognised else-where in South Africa. Ethnic recognition results in government stipends for the leadership and the possibility of legal claims for land long lost.

The body parts of Baartman were returned to South Africa in May 2002. They were given a formal burial with Christian rites at Hankey in the Eastern Cape on Women's Day, 9 August, that year. In her death, Baartman has become a symbol not only of Khoesan people, but also of oppressed Africans and oppressed women in general.

Despite her great importance to South Africans of all origins, we actually know precious little from the historical record about this woman. The most complete picture of her identity has recently been published by Clifton Crais and Pamela Scully in a book called *Sara Baartman and the Hottentot Venus*, but this is a rather strange book that is effectively an imaginary rather than a real biography. The authors do provide some important information about her life from the documents they found, but often the detail is based on historical context rather than fact.

They imply, for example, that she was beaten and ill-treated by her employers, but only because it is likely that a woman of her class in domestic employment probably *was* beaten by her employers, and almost certainly by the men with whom she cohabited over the years. Would an examination of her bones help to add more concrete evidence to this conjecture?

From a scientific perspective, Sara Baartman has not been given the respect she deserves as an individual. Cuvier saw her as a racial specimen and an example of primitive humanity. Subsequent researchers have made no comment about her in the published literature. Instead, they have simply used her measurements in a database of Khoesan human variation. As a physical individual, Sara Baartman does not exist in any of these anthropological re-ports, with the exception of Cuvier's racial description. So allow me to use my own notes on her skeleton to correct this by looking at the evidence provided by her bones from the perspective of forensic anthropology. I won't describe her identity, as that is not an issue of debate, but I can add information about her life experience and her state of health at the time of her death.

Cuvier stated in his report that Baartman was twenty-six years old when she died, but Crais and Scully argue that she must have been at least a decade older. The state of her skeleton indicates that she was unlikely to have been older than thirty-five years at death. The medial clavicular epiphysis (the inner end of the collar bone) is united to the shaft of the collar bone. This normally happens at between twenty-five and thirty years of age, but there is no sign of the fusion line on the bone that would indicate that the union was still in progress. This implies that she was certainly not younger than twenty-five, but the completion of the epiphyseal union means that she was probably thirty or older. Crais and Scully might be right on this one.

Cuvier measured her height when he met her in the autumn of 1815 and recorded that she stood four foot six inches (137.2 centimetres) tall. This is an exceptionally short stature, even for a person of Khoesan genetic heritage, and it does not match the evidence of the bones. A ratio of 3.745 multiplied by her femur length of 39.2 centimetres gives an estimated stature of 146.8 centimetres. This generic femur/stature formula sometimes produces distorted values in very short people, so we can double-check our estimate by using John Lundy's more specific formula for South African Negro women. This formula, although not based on the body proportions of Khoesan women, also gives the value of 146.0 plus/minus 2.8 cm. Cuvier measured Baartman's height in life, so in theory his measurement should be more accurate, but none of the surviving illustrations of Baartman suggest that she was so small, so Cuvier could have got it wrong. One possible reason is that Cuvier would almost certainly have been using metres rather than feet and inches, and it is possible that his conversion was incorrect. The only way to solve this mystery is to measure the height of the body cast that is still in Paris. Then we will know whether the mathematics or Cuvier is wrong.

Sara Baartman's dentition presents a somewhat confusing picture. In general, her dental health was quite good and there are no caries in any of her teeth. This in itself is not really surprising if she was raised in a family practising a hunting-and-gathering lifestyle, as that generally promotes excellent dental health, but what is surprising is that the occlusal (chewing) surfaces of Baartman's teeth are almost unworn, indicating that she never had the very abrasive diet of a hunter-gatherer.

Baartman may well have had three different dietary regimes during her lifetime. Where she spent her childhood would have been critical to her dental health. The coastal regions of South Africa tend to have very low levels of fluorine in the drinking water, which means that the teeth are poorly protected against caries, but if Crais and Scully are right and she spent her childhood on the southern edge of the Karoo, then it's likely that the more fluorine-rich ground water would have given her some protection against caries. Her diet at this time was probably very low in sugars and may well have contained at least some gathered foods. This would have promoted good dental health and a low incidence of cavities.

As a teenager or young adult she moved to Cape Town, where her diet would have been very different. The Cape Town natural water sources are fluorine poor, but Baartman's tooth crowns were already formed at this point of her life and would have been unaffected by the new hydro-chemical environment. The poor of Cape Town probably ate a diet with significant fish protein, balanced with bread or root vegetables. Whatever foods she was eating, none of them abraded her teeth.

Although sugar would have been more available in the colonial town, it was a fairly expensive commodity and therefore not a regular feature in the diet of the poor. Bread made from finely ground flour can promote caries, but roughly ground bread may not be so cariogenic. As long as sugars were avoided, rough bread and fish protein would have promoted fairly good dental health.

Sara's arrival in England in 1810 would have exposed her to a diet that promoted rapid tooth decay and subsequent tooth loss. Sugar and milled flour were easily accessible and were common foods of the poor in London and Paris. Despite this, Baartman's dentition does not appear to have been affected. Unfortunately, the dental evidence does not give us any clues to her diet in Europe, although it seems very unlikely from the state of her teeth that sweetened foods were a frequent occurrence.

One other dental observation does provide a statement about her habits. The alveolus (gum line) on her lower jaw at the base of the incisors is severely resorbed. Because there is no accompanying tooth decay, it is most likely that whatever was affecting the gums did not affect the teeth. The culprit is almost certainly tobacco. Smoking was done with clay pipes in the early nineteenth century, and excessive smoking causes periodontal disease but also helps to prevent tooth decay.

In a strange paradox, smoking keeps the teeth healthy until they fall out because the bone of the alveolus retreats and the sockets are exposed. Contemporary pictures of Baartman in Europe almost always show her smoking.

Do Baartman's bones give us clues about her health condition in the years before her death? The illustrations of Baartman not only show her as being steatopygous (with enlarged buttocks), but clearly indicate that she had substantial body fat and could not be defined as undernourished. In addition, the roofs of the orbits of her skull are free from cribra orbitalia, a frequent sign of nutritional- and iron-deficiency problems. Radiographic analysis of the proximal (upper) and distal (lower) ends of the tibia show the presence of two Harris lines on each end. Harris lines are signs of growth arrests during the development of long bones, like those in the leg. When a child has a particularly nasty illness, the body slows down its growth in order to marshal its resources to fight the disease. This results in a thin line of bone visible in a radiograph.

In the case of Baartman, the lines are very near to the ends of the bone, indicating that growth was nearly over when the illness struck. This implies that the event happened when she was fourteen or fifteen years old.

No scars of parturition are visible on the dorsal aspect of the pubis, nor are they visible as a sulcus in the preauricular region of the ilium (hip bone). These are scars that form when the ligaments joining the three large bones of the pelvis are pulled away from each other during the first stage of labour. The ligaments soften and allow the bones to pull slightly away from each other in the midline of the pubis and also where the hip bone joins the sacrum at the back of the pelvis. This is an interesting non-observation because the historical records indicate that Sara Baartman gave birth to children during her lifetime (Cuvier says two, but Crais and Scully say three). The scarring on the pubis and ilium are usually signs of multiple childbirth, but it is quite possible for a woman to have had a couple of children without generating these signs. Whether that would extend to a third child is unknown.

The arch of Sara Baartman's fifth lumbar vertebra (the last one before the pelvis) is separated from the body of the vertebra. This is known as L5 spondylolysis. There is a debate in the literature about how this anomaly comes about. Some suggest that it is a sign of excessive bending and physical activity, while others propose that it is a genetic rarity that is unaffected by posture. This feature has been recorded in as many as 7 per cent of Griqua but is otherwise fairly rare in southern African populations. Baartman was probably unaware that she had the defect, but modern clinical cases tell us that such patients are at risk of lower back pain if the ligaments loosen and allow the body of the vertebra to move forward (spondylolysthesis).

Baartman's skeleton provides evidence of at least two events of physical trauma in her life. The left orbital process of the maxilla (the side of her nose) demonstrates a healed fracture on the edge of the left nasal bone and just above the nasal aperture. This is clear evidence of a blow to the left side of the face between the cheekbone and the nose. No change in contour is perceptible and the healed fracture was probably not visible in life. The state of healing was well advanced at death, but it is not really possible to suggest a date for the traumatic event, although the injury must have happened in adulthood after the reshaping of the middle face by growth. My guess (and it is a guess) is that the injury probably happened within the last four or five years of life.

A second healed fracture is present towards the lower end of the right ulna. This is seen as a well-healed callous, and radiographic examination shows that it still had fairly extensive trabecular development in the marrow cavity. This is consistent with an event date probably two to five years before death. A fracture at this location is often referred to as a 'parry fracture' because it typically occurs when the victim raises her arm to defend herself against a blow. It may also occur during a fall, but often this involves both of the bones of the arm or only the lower radius.

One last observation needs to be reported. The periosteal surface of the lower shafts of both tibia show extensive activity in the months before death. Such activity is often the sign of a low-grade infection that affects the bones. A second patch of periosteal activity is present as a small depression on the frontal bone of the skull.

Although non-diagnostic, these two sites and their associated features are suggestive of the early stages of the treponemal diseases, such as syphilis and yaws.

Yaws is a tropical disease and is historically unknown in the

Cape, but venereal syphilis was indeed present both at the Cape and in Europe. The problem is that the signs on the bones are so diffuse and at such an early stage that it is extremely difficult to confirm this as a diagnosis. The disorder could just as easily represent a non-specific infection.

So, looking at the bones does give us some new information about Sara Baartman. We are now certain that she was both older and taller than stated in the original Cuvier report. We know that she had a childhood illness serious enough to slow her growth when she was in her early to middle teens. Her dental health was pretty good, but she had a problem in her lower back that could have resulted in serious pain or disability had she lived longer. She was struck hard enough to break bone – once in the face and a second time on the arm, and these are likely to have happened during her stay in England. This would certainly increase the likelihood that her response to the court that she was 'happy and free' was coerced.

Lastly, there are the signs of general infection on her leg bones and on her scalp that might possibly be evidence that she was suffering from the early stages of skeletal syphilis at the time of her death. No information regarding the final cause of death can be identified from the bones.

THE POLITICS OF OLD BONES

Times have certainly changed for skeletal biology in the past couple of decades. Although the forensic aspects of anthropology have grown in leaps and bounds, access to archaeological skeletons has become more difficult. One could lament the loss of the easy access to bones in museums that scientists had in the past, but I prefer a different take. I think the field has been enriched by scientists having to engage with the descendent communities. The thought that goes into proposals for study is now much deeper and included in proposals are ways in which the results can be disseminated to those outside of the scientific community.

Guidelines have been drawn up to encourage dialogue between scientists and descendent communities. The Heritage Act of 1999 legislates a sixty-day period in which effort must be made to identify any person who might have an interest in the discovery (as a descendant or not). No longer can a developer object to carrying the cost of excavation and providing time for thorough investigation. However, all has not run completely smoothly because, besides giving due respect to the dead and acknowledging living relatives, other contentious issues exist.

In 2000, Martin Legassick and Ciraj Rassool published a short book outlining the trade in skeletons practised by the likes of Scotty Smith. As historians, they had sifted through the museum letter files and discovered details of which even I was unaware. Austrian researcher Rudolf Pöch had passed through the northern Cape between 1907 and 1909 and had left in his wake an unscrupulous assistant who spent his time digging up fresh bodies of deceased San and boiling them down to bone for shipment to Vienna.

The McGregor Museum in Kimberley sponsored a workshop in September 2001 to discuss what to do about skeletons in museums that had been collected in an unethical manner similar to the disinterments arranged by Pöch's assistant. The curators of the major skeleton collections were invited, along with a wide range of Khoesan representatives from the northern Cape. Once again I found the people of Khoesan communities firm in their desire to rebury their kin from the past, but open to learning as much as possible about them before the reburial took place.

Not so with Rassool and Legassick, both of whom desperately wanted the collection curators to dig in their heels and refuse to consider reburial. For them it was a battle against the race scientists, and they were distinctly disappointed when the curators simply said that the collection of bodies in such a manner was morally wrong and that it was a great idea to plan a reburial.

In 2003 a second large historic cemetery was disturbed by development in Green Point in Cape Town. Once again the burial ground was an unofficial one representing the poorest communities of Dutch colonial Cape Town. The discovery of the Prestwich site was nearly identical to that at Cobern Street eight years before, but this time there was a legislative plan in place to deal with the process. All construction was stopped and a sixty-day period was called to search both for descendent communities (if they could be identified) and other interested parties.

SAHRA allowed excavation to resume at the end of the sixty-day period, but this time there was opposition from a group based at the District Six Museum. They argued that the dead should not be disturbed and they created a public advocacy group called the Prestwich Place Project Committee to hold vigils in protest. Ultimately their motivation was not primarily about the disturbance of the graves, but about the development of Cape Town and how communities should be empowered to control the development.

No real alternative to excavation was provided by the group. They suggested turning the building site into a grass-covered open space with a memorial to the dead buried there. The debates took on a distinctly racial overtone by implying that it was white colonialists who had oppressed these people in the past and now white developers were going to make money out of the land on which they were buried.

The archaeologists were painted as villains who wanted to dig up the dead as research objects, yet the entire project was triggered by development, not research. Eventually the acrimony resulted in the Minister of Arts and Culture having to make a final decision. The excavation was allowed to proceed, but the developer had to fund the construction of a mausoleum for the storage of the human remains that would also act as a memorial museum to the people of the old District One in Cape Town.

Sadly, the one area excluded from this agreement was the study of the human remains. The activists bluntly refused to allow even the most basic assessment of who was buried on the site. Science was equated with development and I was curtly told by Bonita Bennett, the acting director of the District Six Museum, that physical anthropology could not provide any information about history.

My students and I tried everything we could to show them how we could decipher a wealth of information about health, lifestyle and demography from the skeletons, but to no avail. The same kind of attitude was not evident elsewhere. My student at the time, Jacqui Friedling, gave talks at schools in her home suburb of Belhar and was overwhelmed by the interest and response of both the students and the teachers.

The Prestwich Street cemetery sample now rests in the mausoleum in the city but remains unstudied. My guess is that eventually there will be a request for analysis of the remains as the activists who fought the excavation move on to other projects and people in the descendent communities want more information.

There is currently a proposal at a national level to regulate the collections of human remains throughout the country. Although reburial where possible is clearly a motive for the proposal, there is room in the plan to allow museums to continue research on skeletons where it is deemed to be important for the advancement of our knowledge, but research projects must comply with ethical and professional standards. Research must be conducted in a manner consistent with the interests and beliefs of the members of the genealogical and cultural descendants.

My experience so far with the various Khoesan communities outside Cape Town has shown me that not all descendent groups are anti-science and that ways of accommodation can be found.

FIGURE 12: Tony Grogan's 'Crack of Dawn' cartoon showing me lamenting
SAHRA's decision not to allow scientific examination of the Prestwich remains

"Alas, poor Yorick, Sahra
wont let me know you
well!"

OLD BONES IN A FORENSIC CONTEXT

The fields of skeletal biology and forensic anthropology are so closely
aligned that it is sometimes difficult to know which is which. Both
involve skeletal detective work and the mystery of the unknown,
but their immediate objectives differ. Forensic anthropology is
concerned with the very practical issue of individual cases, where
skeletal biology tends to be more interested in groups of people and
its research questions tend to be broader. Skeletal biology constantly
searches for new techniques that can be applied to archaeological
problems. These new techniques, honed on archaeological samples,
can then be applied in a forensic context.

The isotope laboratory in the Department of Archaeology at the

210

University of Cape Town is a special centre of skeletal biology research focusing on the identification of past diets from ancient bone. The laboratory was started in the early 1970s by Nick van der Merwe, who did extensive research on stable carbon isotopes. He was joined in the 1980s by Andy Sillen and later by Julia Lee-Thorp, who extended the range of isotopes examined. Since the 1990s the laboratory has been run by Judy Sealy, who has started to ask broad questions about prehistoric diet throughout the region. The essence of their work is the biochemistry of the non-radioactive (stable) variations of common elements in the diet – in particular carbon and nitrogen, but also rarer elements such as strontium.

Radioactive carbon (^{14}C) is unstable and disappears at a fixed rate over time. This makes it a perfect tool for estimating the age since death of an organism by analysing the amount of ^{14}C in the bone and comparing it to the amounts that should have been present when the animal was alive. Stable carbon isotopes (^{12}C and ^{13}C) are not lost after death and therefore can't be used for dating, but the ratio of ^{12}C to ^{13}C in bone is dependent on how the carbon was incorporated into the bone through the food ingested in life.

The most common form of carbon is ^{12}C, but it is mixed with small amounts of ^{13}C at a fixed ratio in atmospheric carbon dioxide (CO^2). Plants use this CO^2 to manufacture carbohydrates during photosynthesis, but differences in the photosynthetic pathways they use result in different amounts of ^{13}C being found in the sugars they produce. Most plants, trees, shrubs and temperate grasses and some marine plants use the C_3 pathway, which incorporates lower amounts of ^{13}C, but tropical grasses that grow in high summer temperatures use a C_4 pathway that is 'enriched' with ^{13}C. Tropical grasses include maize, sorghum and some other mainstays of human agriculture.

Animals that specialise in eating plants from different photosynthetic pathways reflect the same pattern of differences, as do the plants themselves. For example, the black rhinoceros is a browser that tends to eat the leaves and stems of woody plants, while the white rhinoceros is a grazer that eats almost exclusively high-summer-temperature grasses. The $^{13}C/^{12}C$ ratio for the white rhinoceros is therefore 'enriched' in comparison to that of the black rhinoceros, even if the two species live in exactly the same area.

Humans show the same pattern according to their diets. A person who has a diet heavy in meat and the milk of cattle will have an 'enriched' $^{13}C/^{12}C$ ratio because his diet is based on animals that eat C_4 grasses. A person who subsists on gathered foods such as berries and roots, along with animals such as small buck and tortoises that eat similar kinds of foods, will have a 'depleted' $^{13}C/^{12}C$ ratio. This gives the archaeologist the opportunity to differentiate between hunters, herders and farmers based on the biochemistry of their bones.

The system would be perfect if it were that easy, but there are many complications. People don't eat single-food diets, and there-fore a human diet may be a mixture of grass seeds, seafood and root crops – resulting in a confused isotopic signature. Seafood has $^{13}C/^{12}C$ ratios that tend to be midway between grazing and browsing diets because many marine plants have a different photo-synthetic pathway to the two main land-based ones, but the seafood analytical problem can be solved by using nitrogen ratios.

The stable isotope of nitrogen is ^{15}N and the metabolic pathway that fixes nitrogen into animal and plant tissue draws in more ^{15}N in a marine environment. Therefore high levels of ^{15}N in human bones provide a reliable clue to the marine components of that person's diet.

Strontium levels in the bone are not direct indicators of diet. In the same manner as carbon and nitrogen, strontium has stable isotopes that can be measured, but these reflect the amount of iso-topes in the rocks and soils of the environment, not the metabolic pathway of digestion. $^{87}Sr/^{86}Sr$ ratios are lower in the oceans, which represent an averaged value of strontium washed into the sea, but the ratios can be much higher on land depending on the amount of ^{87}Sr in the parent rock.

Plants get their strontium from the water and soils in which they grow, and animals derive their strontium levels from both their drinking water and the plants they eat. All in all, the $^{87}Sr/^{86}Sr$ will reflect the environment in which a human has lived, and therefore different $^{87}Sr/^{86}Sr$ ratios between individuals will indicate different points of origin.

This biochemical evidence has the potential to be used directly in single archaeological or forensic cases where issues of origin and individuality are being questioned.

During the early 1990s, historic archaeologists began work at Vergelegen, just east of Cape Town and near the town of Somerset West. Vergelegen is historically important because not only is it one of the oldest wine estates in South Africa, but it is also the location of our first case of civic corruption. The governor of the Cape in the early years of the eighteenth century was Willem Adriaan van der Stel. He was entrusted by the Dutch East India Company to ensure that local farmers could provide food as needed for the company's ships on their way to the Dutch colony in Batavia, but in the way of many government employees (if not all, depending on how cynical you are), he worked the system for his own benefit.

He diverted the best building supplies to his own farm, Vergelegen, used government slaves for his personal building projects, and made sure that his produce was sold first and at the highest prices when the company ships pulled into Table Bay. The corruption became so bad that the Free Burgers (settler farmers) revolted and in due course Van der Stel was recalled to Holland in disgrace and his property was sold.

The historical records note that Vergelegen had a large slave lodge that was remodelled in the middle of the eighteenth century and finally demolished at the beginning of the nineteenth century, when slavery ended. As the archaeologists excavated the foundation of the building, they found one single burial right in the middle of the floor plan. The grave had been dug through the remodelled floor but was sealed by the debris of demolition. This dated the grave to the second half of the eighteenth century, similar to the time of the burials at Cobern Street.

The burial contained the body of a woman who had died in her fifties. The grave was Christian in style, with the body lying on her back in a coffin made of yellowwood. The nails that sealed the coffin were of varying lengths and seemed to have been scavenged or reused, suggesting limited access to resources. The locale of the grave in unconsecrated ground as a single burial was most unusual.

I wrote up a detailed report on the skeleton. Although I could provide a great deal of information about the woman, I could only give limited information about her origins to the archaeologists. This was because the lid of the coffin, which had collapsed onto the skeleton as the wood had decomposed, had produced an acid local environment where the wood touched the bone. Since she was lying on her back, the acid had destroyed her face, sternum, scapula, the ventral aspects of the vertebrae and her pelvis.

The shape of the remainder of her skull showed none of the characteristic features seen in Khoesan populations, so I was only able to say that I thought she was unlikely to have had a significant amount of Khoesan ancestry. Otherwise, I had no idea of the origin of her ancestors. Her long-term health seemed to have been good, as there were no signs of growth arrests during her childhood and her diet in adulthood had been adequate. She was not strongly muscled, but the muscle markings were well delineated, suggesting that she was fit and strong. Most interesting was that she had obvious squatting facets on her tibia, telling us that she had used the squatting posture since childhood. Her latter years had not been fun, as she had suffered very badly from arthritis in her hands and her back. The damage to the vertebral column was so severe that she must have been substantially disabled towards the end of her life.

Judy Sealy took over the analysis at this point by carefully extracting a small amount of enamel from the teeth and a small sample of bone from her rib and femur. The reason that Judy chose both teeth and bone to analyse is extremely important. The enamel of the teeth forms during the growth of the child. The dental enamel never remodels after its formation and therefore the biochemistry of the teeth can tell us about diet during the first ten to fifteen years of life depending on the teeth chosen. The bone tissue, on the other hand, is constantly remodelled by the body and its biochemistry tells us about the last ten years or so of the person's diet. Judy's sample would tell us about our mystery woman's childhood and her old age.

The report from Judy Sealy's analysis was fascinating. The data from the teeth showed that our woman had eaten tropical grains with little, if any, seafood as a child. Her diet in adulthood was very different, in that seafood was an important component of her food for many years before her death. The strontium values were higher than those seen at the Cape, telling us that she had come from somewhere far away.

So who was this woman? Why was she given such special treatment in terms of her burial? Her diet tells us that she was not born at the Cape but came from a tropical land far from a sea coast. The slave importation records reveal that the most likely source to fit this description is the inland region of the Malaysian peninsula, India or Madagascar. Historical research points most strongly to Madagascar for female slaves.

She is unlikely to have been Christian at the time of her arrival, but again the records tell us that many of the slaves at the Cape were baptised during their captivity. Her job is unknown, but her bones suggest that she was unlikely to have been a field hand. The squatting facets suggest instead that she was involved in domestic service, probably tending the fire and preparing food.

The historic homesteads at the Cape had their hearths set at ground level, and activities at the fireplace would have required a great deal of time spent on one's haunches. She could not have been much help in the kitchen during her last years of life, but the special placement of her grave suggests that she had earned substantial respect from those who were responsible for her burial. During their archival research, the historic archaeologists discovered that many of the families who still work as labourers on the Vergelegen estate are descended from the families who lived there at the beginning of the nineteenth century. This meant that our lady in the floor of the slave lodge was almost certainly a direct ancestor of the living farm staff. The decision of the current owners of Vergelegen was therefore to rebury the unknown woman on the farm at a ceremony attended and conducted by the local community, which comprises the current residents of Vergelegen.

PREHISTORIC MURDER

Trying to catch a murderer a couple of thousand years after the crime was committed sounds like a waste of time, but it may be of some use if it helps us to understand why people commit murder.

One of my very first publications dealt with the death of a woman about 2 000 years ago at Quoin Point on the Cape south coast near Hermanus. The skeleton had been excavated some years before by John Parkington in a Later Stone Age context near the beach line. During the analysis we found two bone arrowheads stuck in one of the vertebra. The victim was a young female and a very young infant was buried with her. There is no obvious cause of death for the infant, but the double burial is suggestive of the fact that the two died together.

If the young woman was the mother, then there can be little doubt that the baby also met a violent end. The arrows struck the woman from behind at the level of the twelfth thoracic vertebra (just above the small of her back) and both arrows penetrated the spinal canal. There was no sign of healing, so it is likely that the damage occurred at the time of her death.

Were these the fatal wounds? I can't be sure, except to say that had she lived she would have been crippled, but it is almost inconceivable that someone with a penetrating wound to the vertebral canal could have escaped infection without treatment. Infection of the wound would certainly have killed her. The entry angles of the arrowheads also confirmed that she must have been lying facedown on the ground with the person who shot her standing at her feet. This was definitely not an accident.

FIGURE 13: Lower surface of the last thoracic vertebra of UCT 317 showing the trajectory of the two projectiles. The smaller arrow point was deflected off the rib before it pierced the spinal canal

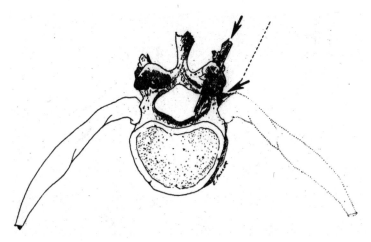

Drawing by E. Fuller

FIGURE 14: Side view of the articulated vertebral column of UCT 317 showing how the arrows entered the body when the person was prone rather than standing upright

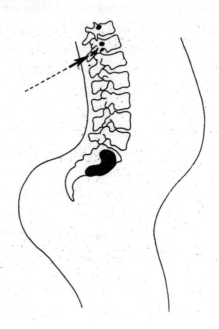

Drawing by E. Fuller

Susan Pfeiffer of the University of Toronto has been working independently on the question of violence in the Later Stone Age, and between us we have now documented ten individuals from LSA archaeological contexts who met a violent end. Men, women and children were all victims, and in some cases the wounds suggest that there could be no other reason for the violence except to kill the person.

One case that Susan has described involved a single grave containing three children at Modder River on the West Coast of South Africa. Each child was killed by cranial trauma caused by an implement that is consistent with an LSA digging stick. This archaeological evidence does not fit the picture that we have been given of the Kalahari San over the past thirty years. The San are often described as the 'Harmless People' and are seen as gentle hunter-gatherers with an egalitarian lifestyle in which disputes are settled by people leaving the band and joining another group to avoid conflict.

Something simply isn't right. The social anthropologist Richard Lee has calculated a murder rate among the Dobe !Kung San of Botswana. The number of murders is small, but so is the size of the population he studied. When scaled up to compare with modern homicide rates, it works out to over thirty killed per 100 000 people. Putting this into perspective, this murder rate is three times higher than that of New York City in the 1970s and more than half of the current spectacular murder rate for the Western Cape in South Africa during the past decade or so. The choice of weapon also needs to be explained. In a world where the poisoned arrow was the ultimate arbitrator of arguments, why kill your neighbours with the violence of the bludgeon?

What can we make of these South African archaeological cases? Perhaps it is possible to argue that a few of these cases might just represent the unlucky individual who was 'in the wrong place at the wrong time' and who sustained a serious cranial injury in an accident, but other cases leave no doubt that the person involved was executed. The two bone arrowheads in the back of the woman from Quoin Point were shot into her while she was lying prone on the ground. Why kill the children at Modder River, who must surely have been too young to have been guilty of sexual or ritual transgressions? That leaves us with the possibility that perhaps they were the victims of inter-group rather than intra-group violence dynamics.

Tony Humphreys of the University of the Western Cape has provided a radical proposition that challenges our entire view of hunter-gatherers around the world. He says that the rich linguistic variation across the Kalahari is inconsistent with regular contact and intermarriage (gene flow) between groups. It only makes sense if territory is fixed and language is being used as an ethnic marker.

His argument is rooted in behaviourial ecology in which genetic relatedness and rigid ethnic identity would be more important than reciprocity and altruism between strangers. Violence would be a regular occurrence between bands as they contest territorial ownership. If this is the case, then the individuals that Susan Pfeiffer and I have been seeing in the archaeological record have been guilty of nothing besides being part of the opposite group at a time of territorial disagreement. If Humphreys is correct, then we need to rethink our view of the nature of humanity. We have visualised simple societies as gentler and kinder than our own, but people in all societies are violent in this world view.

IN SICKNESS AND IN HEALTH

I have concentrated on two forensic-like questions in this last discussion about archaeological remains. The methodologies of skeletal biology can be applied equally effectively in forensic anthropology. There is another field that falls into both disciplines: palaeopathology. I have already written about the difficulty in diagnosing disease from bones. Modern pathology relies heavily on physiological testing and, ever since the days of Rudolf Virchow in the late nineteenth century, we have accepted that the roots of pathology are in cells, not in large body structures.

What this means is that most diagnoses of disease based solely on the appearance of bone (in gross structure or histology) are bound to be unreliable. We can make intelligent guesses as to the process that was occurring just before death, but the precise cause of the disorder is likely to elude us. What we can often see are signs on the bones that tell us about the symptoms that the patient was suffering. We can describe arthritis very accurately from bone, and although we may have to debate the precise origins of the disease, we can be very precise about the symptoms the patient has experienced.

A few years ago, a group of physical anthropologists and demographers based primarily at the Ohio State University in Columbus began a study they called the 'Global History of Health Project'. Their idea was to measure the health of whole communities over the past 10 000 years of human history. The data would come from archaeological skeletons but, instead of dealing with the difficult problems of diagnosis of specific diseases, they chose instead to look at the common disorders on bone that tell us about the symptoms rather than the disease. They created a 'Health Index' incorporating seven observations on the skeleton in order to do this. Ideally, an assessment of health should look at length of life along with quality of life, but sadly the calculation of demographic numbers from archaeological samples is not very reliable, especially if the skeletons are from isolated sites rather than cemeteries. The Health Index therefore focuses on 'quality of life'.

The Health Index combines stature of adults (calculated from long-bone length), growth disruption as seen in the hypoplasia of tooth enamel, the presence of anaemia as represented by porotic hyperostosis on the cranial bones or cribra orbitalia in the roof of the eye sockets, dental health (caries, antemortem losses and abscesses), periostitis on the surface of the long bones, degenerative joint disease and antemortem bone fractures caused by trauma. An individual with tall stature and none of these minor miseries of life seen in the bone was deemed to have had a high quality of life.

As an experiment I tried to grade myself on this Health Index scale. I am tall (one point) and don't have signs of anaemia or bone infections of which I am aware (a couple more points). However, I don't do so well on the balance of observations. I have one healed fracture of my right radius, which I broke when I was five by falling down the stairs in my parents' home, and I have an interesting bump on my head where my father accidentally dropped me when I was two.

My teeth have no abscesses, but I have lost one antemortem from disease (four were also removed by an overzealous dentist who wanted me to avoid impacted wisdom teeth) and I have several molars with filled cavities. I can definitely feel at least one linear hypoplastic line on my left lower canine.

I do have incipient hip joint arthritis on my left side and suffer from joint pain from time to time, although I don't know how much that has marked my bones. Whew – all of that and I still consider myself to be relatively healthy.

The Ohio State team has already guided and collated the collection of data on over 12 000 skeletons from the western hemisphere. Nearly 80 per cent of the skeletons are from Native Americans, but the remainder includes both Euro-Americans and Afro-Americans, so the range of populations includes both prehistoric and historic samples. The team is now engaged in triggering the same kind of data-gathering in Europe and the last I heard was that they expected to gather data on 55 000 past Europeans.

The focus is now on Africa and I am hoping that we will be able to put together a large database for them. Of all of the reasons for allowing the study of human remains before reburial, this is most valuable. The object of the study is *not* to look at remains of 'colonial' or 'primitive' people. The object is to put together the biggest picture yet of human health and fitness over our history. This is an ongoing project, so keep watching.

7

Death as a Growth Industry

Chibondo, Zimbabwe, March 2011. Hundreds of decomposing bodies have been brought to the surface of a remote mineshaft north of the capital, Harare. The exhumation of the skeletons has been orchestrated by a group of Zanu-PF party loyalists who call themselves 'The Fallen Heroes of Zimbabwe Trust', and the government-run media have blamed the former Rhodesian rulers for blatant human rights violations in the murder and disposal of these bodies of guerilla forces from the Rhodesian War of the 1970s.

The government has announced that no forensic tests or DNA analysis will be carried out. Instead, traditional African religious figures will be called on to perform rites to invoke the spirits to identify the dead. The Zimbabwean public broadcaster has urged ordinary citizens to come to the disused gold mine to witness the horror of colonial atrocities.

But there is a problem. Why are bodies dumped in the gold mine forty years ago still dripping body fluids and displaying skin, hair and body tissues? Why is the stench of death from the mine so overwhelming when decomposition should have done its job of cleansing the bones decades ago? Are these the sad relics of violence of forty years ago, or the evidence of something that happened much more recently?

Will the courts in Zimbabwe accept identification based on the word of a sangoma? I doubt it, when the forensic anthropological expertise is available and a scientific approach could be taken. The procedure would be very straightforward as a police case. The skeletons would be analysed for basic demographic parameters and the postmortem interval would be estimated. The separate cases would then be sorted in relation to possible identities from the missing persons' reports, and finally DNA matching would be done against living relatives of the missing. But of course this is not a police case – it is political.

Already Amnesty International (AI) has put out a press release decrying the damage done by these unofficial exhumations in Zimbabwe, saying that only a full forensic investigation will bring out the truth. It strikes me that over the next decade we will see many more cases like this. Leaders may try to take their secrets to the grave, but it is the graves themselves that tell us the stories.

The forensic community in South Africa is fully aware of the fact that mass grave sites will come to light over the next few years in the countries to our north. This has long been a topic of conversation among my students, especially those who have been involved with the MPTT in Pretoria.

A couple of years ago the students proposed the creation of a group that they suggested be called the 'African Forensic Anthropology Team', or AFAT. It would be modelled on the Argentine Forensic Anthroplogy Team, the EAAF, but it would be staffed by Africans (of all definitions) and its primary focus would be to discover the truth about the events of the past throughout the region, thereby bringing closure to the families of the dead.

Funding such a group would be an interesting exercise because there could be conflict of interest between governments. It seems so straightforward in South Africa when following up the TRC testimony of the apartheid police, but the situation becomes hazy when we try to go beyond the activities of the security police of the 1970s and 1980s.

The ANC has admitted that its past was not perfect and that torture and executions did occur, but the organisation did not give the TRC free rein to delve into that past, and there remain both missing persons and open questions. We know that the situation in the Angolan and Ugandan camps was bad and that the brutalities of the liberation leaders in the camps led to mutinous behaviour.

The mass graves of Zimbabwe and beyond remain to be investigated, but only if the politicians cooperate. In the meantime we still have the police inquiries that are the meat (or, more appropriately, the 'bone') of forensic anthropology in South Africa, along with the continuing TRC cases being examined by the MPTT. Our methods of investigation are the same as those elsewhere in the world, but the local context makes the practice of forensic anthropology distinctive in South Africa.

Much work still needs to be done on the assembly of local osteological standards for African populations, including Africans of Asian and European genetic origin. It would be a false premise simply to assume that people whose families emigrated here two or three centuries ago are still biologically identical to their cousins who remained in Europe or Asia. Scientists should never assume – they need to check their facts.

Are there lessons in South African forensic anthropology for the rest of the world? South Africans are particularly obsessed with the idea of race within our society precisely because it still has an impact on us. We continue to think in rigid apartheid terms when it comes to placing people in racial pockets and this is enforced by the need to rectify the inequalities of the past. It will be wonderful when biological and cultural differences no longer have meaning and are simply quaint records of historical origins, but those days are still far off. For South African scientists to divorce themselves from the social context of race to focus simply on physical identity will be a big mistake when the reality is that identity takes on many forms that are not physical. The complexity of our society is a fantastic workshop in which to explore these issues.

We are not alone in trying to solve the riddle of redress; many other countries face the same issues.

South African scientists, like other scientists around the world, are still learning how best to deal with the changing landscape of archaeology and skeletal biology. The new proposals by the National Heritage Council of South Africa to regulate the storage, study and reburial or repatriation of human remains provide challenges and opportunities. The proposals do not rule out research and study, but they require that this be done with the knowledge and cooperation of non-scientific parties.

One of the challenges that we as bone specialists must face is the need to explain why studies of bone are so important and how skeletal biology intersects with forensic anthropology. All of us have acknowledged the wrongs of race science and we are seeking ways to find an accommodation where ethical research will continue to be allowed for the benefit of all, including descendent communities where those are traceable.

In his recent autobiographical book *Steeped in Blood*, South African forensic practitioner David Klatzow argues that forensic evidence is neutral and that forensic experts work for neither the prosecution nor the defence. The forensic scientist 'endeavours to get as close to the truth as humanly possible using scientific methods'. This is wonderfully idealistic, but we do need to temper it a bit. The nature of scientific data is not always so clear-cut that we can see the truth as clearly as David proposes. This is especially true in the world of statistical variation. Sometimes the truth comes in shades of grey. When this happens, we must recognise what is possible as much as probable, and the most honest answer to a question may be 'I am not sure'. A scientist needs to be able to recognise the limits of his knowledge. Knowing when to say 'I don't know' is part of science training. To me, that is the most important aspect by far of my job.

Interest in forensic anthropology and skeletal biology is growing, and I have no shortage of students. I am certain that my colleagues in Johannesburg and Pretoria are experiencing this increase in interest too.

From the perspective of science training, death is indeed a growth industry. I hope that developments that have been in discussion over the past two or three years come to fruition in the near future. The University of Cape Town is launching a master's-level programme in biomedical forensic science that will include forensic anthropology, and several institutions around the country are building forensic genetics curricula. We need to ensure that these new programmes embrace as wide a definition as possible to include not only basic science research, but also human rights.

I said in my introduction that I hope to leave a legacy as a forensic anthropologist through my students. I want to restate that here because, of all the hats that I have had the opportunity to wear, the one labelled 'educator' is the most important to me. Wherever my research interests take me in the future, I am hopeful that my greatest bequest will be the research done by my students.

Glossary

Adolescence: That period of behavioural transition from childhood to adulthood.

Ankylosing spondylitis: A progressive form of arthritis primarily in the vertebral column where the vertebral bodies are bridged over by bony outgrowths. The ultimate result of this process is a fused and entirely immovable spine. The exact cause is unknown but it is not related to normal ageing of the body.

Articulation: The junction between bones. In freely movable synovial joints, the surface of each contact (or articular) surface is covered by a thin layer of cartilage that protects the bone surface from wear and tear. The whole joint is enclosed in a tough capsule and filled with a fluid that further projects the joint.

Bakkie: A light motor vehicle with a separate cab and open rear cargo area. Known as a pickup truck in North American, South Africa is the only place where it is known as a bakkie.

Biltong: Traditionally prepared dried meat in the form of long strips. From the Dutch for 'strip of rump'.

Braai: A word in South African English meaning 'barbecue'. It has been borrowed directly from the Afrikaans word meaning 'to cook on an open fire'.

Calcification: The process of deposition of calcium salts (hydroxyapatite) during the formation of the tooth crown and root. The term is also used to describe the deposition of bone-like material into diseased or foreign tissue as a defence response by the body.

Cerebrospinal fluid: The fluid that surrounds and protects the brain and spinal cord.

Cranial bones: The bones of the skull. The bones on the base of the skull pre-form in cartilage to support the growing brain, but the bones that cover the vault (or top) of the skull develop from ossification centres within the covering membrane. See frontal, occipital, parietal and temporal bones.

Cribra orbitalia: The presence of small pores piercing the outer layer of bone in the upper margin of the eye socket (or orbit). This is a sign of increased activity and expansion of the red bone marrow inside the orbital bones as part of a response to iron deficiency anaemia.

Dentition: The full set of teeth in the mouth. In young children these are referred to as 'milk teeth' or deciduous dentition, and consist of 10 teeth. The adult set of 32 teeth is called the permanent dentition.

Diaphysis: The shaft of a growing long bone. The process of ossification begins in the middle of the shaft and moves towards both ends. See epiphysis and metaphysis.

DNA: Deoxyribonucleic acid. The complex double helix molecule that stores the information required for inheritance in all living organisms. The chemical struts that bind the outer helix are made from only four kinds of bases and their sequence is the code that determines inheritance. No two individuals will have an identical sequence and it is therefore the identification of these specific base sequences that is used in DNA fingerprinting.

Epiphysis: The secondary ossification of a knob of bone in the cartilage at the end of a growing long bone. This develops at the site of articulation with the neighbouring bone and eventually unites with the diaphysis when the child reaches adulthood. See diaphysis and metaphysis.

Fascia: The sheet-like connective tissue that surrounds and delineates the muscles. From the Latin for 'band'.

Faunal analysis: The analysis of non-human animal remains from an archaeological site. It will include not only the species list, but also all signs of butchering and human use of the bones.

Femoral neck fracture: The fracture of the upper end of the thigh bone across the anatomical neck between the head of the femur (which fits into the socket of the hip) and the shaft of the bone. This fracture is common in the elderly when the internal supporting trabeculae have been resorbed and the bone is weakened.

Foramen magnum: The hole in the base of the skull where the spinal cord leaves the brain.

Frontal bone: The bone that forms the front (or anterior) part of the brain case.

Fundi: A word in South African English meaning 'expert'. It has been borrowed from the Bantu root word meaning 'someone who is learned and teaches others'.

Genome: The complete set of hereditary information in the DNA of an individual. It includes both the genes that code for physical features and the non-coding sections of DNA that are duplications of genes and non-functioning 'junk' DNA.

Hamites: The old name for the biblical peoples of North Africa. Included would have been the Berbers of the Atlas Mountains and the ancient Egyptians. They were believed to have migrated into sub-Saharan Africa bringing domestic animals and specific cultural beliefs, such as circumcision, with them.

Hypoplasia: Incomplete or deficient growth of bone or teeth. This is visible in the teeth as a small channel on the surface of the enamel known as a 'linear hypoplastic line'. It represents a short period when growth has slowed or stopped during the formation of the tooth crown.

Khoesan: The term coined by German researchers in the late 1920s to include both the Khoekhoen (Hottentots) and San (Bushmen). Originally spelt 'Khoisan'.

Lumbar vertebrae: The lowest five vertebrae just above the sacrum.

Lytic: Literally 'to cut'. Refers to the active pathological processes of destruction of bone tissue at a bone infection site.

Mastoid process: The large projecting process behind the ear that forms the seat for several neck muscles. The interior of the process is filled with sinus spaces. The process is larger and more prominent in males.

Metaphysis: The growth zone in a juvenile long bone. It is made up of a band of cartilage at the end of the diaphysis. The bone grows in length by adding new cartilage. The metaphysis is obliterated by ossification when the bone reaches adulthood. See diaphysis and epiphysis.

Metastasised tumours: Disseminated cancer foci in the late stage of the disease. Found anywhere in the body and they tend to be lytic (i.e. tissue destructive).

Mitochondrial DNA (mtDNA): Small loops of DNA found inside the cell organelles called mitochondria. These structures are known as the factories of the cell, as they are responsible for converting chemical energy from food into a form that can be used as energy in the body. Since they are not part of the chromosomes and are found only in the cytoplasm of the cell, they are inherited solely as part of the egg and therefore only from the mother. MtDNA is used to track female lineage in anthropological and forensic research.

Muscles of mastication: The muscles used in chewing. The two major ones are the masseter and the temporalis, both jaw closers.

Nuchal muscles: The muscles of the neck. These are strap-like muscles that run along the arches of the neck vertebrae and insert onto the lower portion of the occipital bone.

Occipital bone: The bone that forms the back (or posterior) part of the brain case.

Occlusal surface: The chewing surface of the teeth.

Ossification: The process of deposition of calcium salts (hydroxyapatite) in the formation of bones. Long bones and bones that support weight usually pre-form as cartilaginous models and are then infiltrated by bone-forming cells in the process of ossification.

Palaeopathology: The study of ancient disease. Palaeopathology uses preserved bone and dry tissue to assess anatomical evidence of disease, unlike pathology, which is primarily a physiological and cellular-based medical discipline.

Parietal bone: The pair of bones that form the sides (or lateral part) of the brain case.

Periosteal: Anything to do with the periosteum, which is the membrane that covers bones in life. The periosteum protects and feeds the surface of the bone. Periostitis occurs when it becomes infected and inflamed.

Pharmacopoeia: The drugs available to a medical practitioner.

Porotic hyperostosis: The presence of small pores piercing the outer layer of bone along the parietal and occipital bones of the skull. This signifies the presence of a major anaemia in a similar manner to cribra orbitalia, but the disease process is much more severe.

Puberty: The attainment of sexual maturity that is marked by the production of sperm and ejaculation in males and menstruation and release of eggs in females. It is the biological parallel to adolescence, but the two do not necessarily have to occur at the same time.

Pubis: The pair of bones projecting towards the midline in the pelvis. They can be felt directly above the external genitalia on the front of the pelvis.

Resorbed: A technical term referring to the absorption of bone material by the body when a bony structure is no longer used. The normal physiology of the body will recycle the bone material when the structure is no longer biomechanically stressed. A good example is the sockets of the teeth, which will resorb if the tooth is lost and the action of chewing no longer innervates the bone. This is different from the absorption of bone salts during osteoporosis in old age where the structure remains but the bone material itself is weakened.

Rheumatoid arthritis: This is a form of arthritis that is a generalised and chronic inflammation of joints throughout the body but usually starting with the hands and feet. The exact cause is unknown, but it is most likely to be an autoimmune disease unrelated to the ageing process.

Sacrum: The triangular bone in the lower back formed from fused vertebrae below the lumbar region. Together with the pair of hip bones, the sacrum forms the bony pelvis.

Sciatic notch: A deep anatomical notch on the back (posterior) of each hip bone. In females this notch tends be very wide, but in males it is formed by a much tighter angle and is therefore useful in identifying the sex of hip bones.

Sexual dimorphism: Literally meaning 'two shapes for sex'. These are distinct anatomical differences between the sexes caused by differences in bony structure or distribution of fat and hair.

Sickle-cell anaemia: This is a genetic disorder found frequently in sub-Saharan Africa caused by the presence of one sickle-cell gene (allele) from a parent. The disorder is mildly debilitating if it is caused

233

by one allele, but if a child inherits both genes (one sickle-cell gene from each parent), then the serious disease known as sickle-cell anaemia is caused. Porotic hyperostosis is a common sign of sickle-cell anaemia in bone samples.

Temporal bone: The pair of bones that form the lower side and part of the base of the brain case. The upper part is thin and connects to the parietals that cover the brain on each side. The lower part is heavier, forms as part of the cartilage of the base and contains the inner ear and the large mastoid process.

Testosterone: The sex hormone present in males. It is required for normal sperm production but also enhances masculine secondary sexual characters, especially those that reflect increased muscle mass.

Thalassemia: A similar disorder to sickle-cell anaemia found in the peoples along the margins of the Mediterranean Sea.

Trabeculae: These are internal bone projections found inside the ends of long bones and in bones that support weight, such as the bodies of the vertebrae. The trabeculae form bony struts that follow the lines of force coming down the bone to give it strength.

Trekboer: Descendants of the Dutch settlers in South Africa who migrated into the interior of the country in the 18th and 19th century. They initially moved with their herds following the pasturelands, but progressively became more settled in the 19th century as the frontiers closed.

Treponemal disease: Highly infectious diseases caused by the micro-organism *Treponema*. The most important of these diseases are 'Yaws', which is a tropical disease spread by direct skin contact in crowded conditions, and 'syphilis', which is a venereal disease. Syphilis was a common and often debilitating disorder before modern treatments became available.

Umkhonto we Sizwe: IsiZulu for 'The Spear of the Nation'. This was the name of the armed wing of the ANC during the liberation struggle.

Y chromosome STR: An STR is a 'short tandem repeat' of base pairs on a DNA molecule. The STRs on the Y chromosome are often used in forensics, paternity testing, and in genealogical surveys to trace the male lineage in cases of interest.

Bibliography

CHAPTER 1

Blau, S., and D.H. Ubelaker. *Handbook of Forensic Anthropology and Archaeology*. Walnut Creek, CA: Left Coast Press, 2009

Gordon, I., and M.R. Drennan. 'Medico-legal aspects of the Wolkersdorfer case', *South African Medical Journal* 22, 1948, pp. 543–549

Krogman,W.M., and Y. İşcan. *The Human Skeleton in Forensic Medicine*. Springfield, Illinois: Charles C. Thomas, 1986

Singer, R. 'Estimation of age from cranial suture closure', *Journal of Forensic Medicine* 1, 1953, pp. 52–59

Tobias, P.V. 'The problem of race identification: Limiting factors in the investigation of the South African races', *Journal of Forensic Medicine* 1 (2), 1953, pp. 113–123

———. 'Memories of Robert James Terry (1871–1966) and the genesis of the Terry and Dart collections of human skeletons', *Adler Museum Bulletin* 13, 1987, pp. 31–34

White, T.D., and P.A. Folkens. *The Human Bone Manual*. Elsevier Academic Press, 2005

CHAPTER 2

Adhikari, M. 'Not White Enough, not Black Enough: Racial Identity in the South African Coloured Community', *Ohio University Research in*

International Studies, Africa Series No. 83. Athens: Ohio University Press, 2005

Burns, K.R. *Forensic Anthropology Training Manual*. New Jersey: Prentice Hall, 1999

Cohen, M.N., and G.J. Armelagos. *Paleopathology at the Origins of Agriculture*. Orlando, FL: Academic Press, 1984

Davies, C.J. *The Cape Flats Smile: dental mutilation in the Western Cape*. Third-Year Science Project, Department of Anatomy and Cell Biology. Cape Town: University of Cape Town, 1990

Dlamini, N., and A.G. Morris. 'An investigation of the frequency of squatting facets in Later Stone Age Foragers from South Africa', *International Journal of Osteoarchaeology* 15, 2005, pp. 371–376

Edgar, H.J.H., and K.L. Hunley. 'Race reconciled?: How biological anthropologists view human variation', *American Journal of Physical Anthropology* 139, 2009, pp. 1–4

Ferembach, D., I. Schwidetzdy, and M. Stroukal. 'Recommendations for age and sex diagnoses of skeletons', *Journal of Human Evolution* 9, 1980, pp. 517–549

Forensic Anthropology 2000: 13th Annual Forensic Anthropology Course. Armed Forces Institute of Pathology. Bethesda, Maryland: National Museum of Health & Medicine, 2000

Friedling, L.J., and A.G. Morris. 'The frequency of culturally derived dental modification practices on the Cape Flats in the Western Cape', *Journal of the South African Dental Association* 60 (3), 2005, pp. 97-102

———. 'Pulling teeth for fashion: Dental modification in modern-day Cape Town, South Africa', *Journal of the South African Dental Association* 62 (1), 2007, pp. 106–113

Gerasimov, M.M. *The Face Finder*. (Translated from the German by Alan Houghton Brodrick). London: Hutchinson & Co., 1971

Howells, W.W. 'Cranial Variation in Man', *Papers of the Peabody Museum of Archaeology and Ethnology* 67. Cambridge, Mass.: Harvard University Press, 1973

———. *Skull Shape and the Map: Craniometric Analyses in the Dispersion of Modern Homo*. Cambridge, Mass.: Harvard University Press, 1989

Maclennan, B. *Apartheid: the lighter side*. Cape Town: Carrefour Press, 1990

Nafte, M. *Flesh and Bone: An introduction to forensic anthropology*.
Durham, North Carolina: Carolina Academic Press, 2000

Ousley, S., and R. Jantz. *Fordisc 2.0: Personal Computer Forensic Discrimination Functions*. Knoxville: University of Tennessee, 1996

Sanders, V. *An Assessment of Muscle Insertion Sites and Biomechanical Beam Analysis in Living Subjects*. MSc thesis. University of Cape Town, 2002

Seekings, J. 'The continuing salience of race: discrimination and diversity in South Africa', *Journal of Contemporary African Studies* 26 (1), 2008, pp. 1–25

Smith, M.C. *Gorky Park*. New York: Pan, 1981

CHAPTER 3

Brummer, L. *Waking the Dead: An Analysis of Physical Anthropological Cases at the University of Cape Town from 1980–2008*. Unpublished Special Studies Module for MBChB II, Faculty of Health Sciences. University of Cape Town, 2008

Steyn, M., J.H. Meiring and W.C. Nienaber. 'Forensic anthropology in South Africa: A profile of cases from 1993 to 1995 at the Department of Anatomy, University of Pretoria', *South African Journal of Ethnology* 20 (1), 1997, pp. 23–25

CHAPTER 4

Boonzaier, E., and J. Sharp. *South African Keywords*. Cape Town: David Phillip, 1988

Bryant, A.T. *Olden Times in Zululand*. London: Longmans, 1929

Dawkins, R. *The Greatest Show on Earth: The evidence for evolution*. London: Bantam Press, 2009

Hammond-Tooke, W.D. *The Bantu-speaking Peoples of Southern Africa*. London: Routledge & Kegal Paul, 1974

Mason, R. *Origins of black people of Johannesburg and the southern western central Transvaal AD350–1880*. Archaeological Research Unit, University of the Witwatersrand, 1986

Murray, C., and P. Sanders. *Medicine Murder in Colonial Lesotho*. Edinburgh: Edinburgh University Press, 2005

'Muti doctor arrested for killing boy', *Cape Times*, 6 October 1994

'Mutilated boy identified', *Cape Times*, 6 July 1992

Scholtz, H.J., V.M. Phillips, and G.J. Knobel. 'Muti or ritual murder',
    Forensic Science International 87, 1997, pp. 117–123

'Second muti-murder suspect', *Cape Times*, 11 October 1994

Steyn, M. 'Human pot burial from Greefswald', *South African Journal of
    Ethnology* 18 (2), 1995, pp. 87–90

———. 'Muti murders from South Africa: A case report'. *Forensic
    Science International*, 151, pp. 279–287

Steyn, M., A. Meyer, and M. Loots. 'Report on isolated human remains
    from K2, South Africa', *Southern African Field Archaeology* 7, 1998,
    pp. 53–58

Van Schalkwyk, L. 'Wosi: an Early Iron Age village in the lower
    Thukela Basin, Natal', *Natal Museum Journal of Humanities* 6, 1994,
    pp. 65–117

CHAPTER 5

Aronson, J.D. *Social and Political Dimensions of the Search for the Missing
    in Post Apartheid South Africa*. In press.

Davison, S., M. Benjeddou, and M.E. D'Amato. 'Molecular genetic
    identification of skeletal remains of apartheid activists in
    South Africa', *African Journal of Biotechnology* 7 (25), 2008,
    pp. 4750–4757

Dreyer, N. 'No mass grave found for blacks in Laingsburg', *Cape Times*,
    14 September 2003

Koff, C. *The Bone Woman*. New York: Random House, 2005

Lakeman, S. *What I Saw in Kaffir-Land*. London, 1880

Lalu, P. *The Deaths of Hintsa*. Cape Town: Human Sciences Research
    Council, 2009

Olusoga, D., and C.W. Erichsen. *The Kaiser's Holocaust: Germany's
    forgotten genocide and the colonial roots of Nazism*. London: Faber &
    Faber, 2010

Smith, A. 'Excavation starts at Laingsburg "grave site"', *Cape Times*,
    4 July 2003

Terreblanche, C. 'Call for international inquiry into Namibia's mass
    graves', *Weekend Argus*, 20 November 2005

Truth and Reconciliation Commission of *South Africa Report. South African Government Information*. Available at http://www.info.gov.za/otherdocs/2003/trc/

CHAPTER 6

Crais, C., and P. Scully. *Sara Baartman and the Hottentot Venus*. Johannesburg: Wits University Press, 2009

Humphreys, A.J.B. *The Type R settlements in the context of the later prehistory and early history of the Riet River valley*. MA thesis. University of Cape Town, 1972

————. 'A prehistoric frontier in the northern Cape and western Orange Free State: Archaeological evidence of interaction and ideological change', *Kronos* 13, 1988, pp. 3–13

————. 'Behavioural ecology and hunter-gatherers: From the Kalahari to the Later Stone Age', *South African Archaeological Bulletin* 62 (186), 2007. pp. 98–103

Legassick, M., and C. Rassool. *Skeletons in the cupboard: museums and the incipient trade in human remains, 1907–1917*. South African Museum & McGregor Museum, 2000

Maggs, T. 'Pastoral settlements on the Riet River', *South African Archaeological Bulletin* 26, 1971, pp. 37–63

————. *Iron Age Communities of the Southern Highveld*. Occasional Publications of the Natal Museum, 2, 1976

Morris, A.G. *An Osteological Analysis of the Protohistoric Populations of the Northern Cape and Western Orange Free State, South Africa*. PhD thesis. University of the Witwatersrand, Johannesburg, 1984

————. *The Skeletons of Contact: Protohistoric burials from the lower Orange River Valley*. Johannesburg: Witwatersrand University Press, 1992

————. *A Master Catalogue: Holocene Human Skeletons from South Africa*. Johannesburg: Witwatersrand University Press, 1992

————. (ed. A.B. Smith). 'The Einiqua: an analysis of the Kakamas skeletons', *Einiqualand: Studies of the Orange River Frontier*. Cape Town: University of Cape Town Press, 1995

————. 'The Griqua and the Khoikhoi: biology, ethnicity and the construction of identity', *Kronos* 24, 1997, pp. 106–118

————. 'De Tuin, a 19th century mission station in the northern Cape', in N. Swanepoel, A. Esterhuysen and P. Bonner (eds). *Five Hundred Years Rediscovered: Southern African Precedents and Prospects*. Johannesburg: Wits University Press, 2008, pp. 103–118

————. 'The Cairns of Rehoboth', in C. Limpricht, M. Beisele (eds). *Heritage and Cultures in Modern Namibia: In-depth Views of the Country*. Windhoek: TUCSIN, 2008, pp. 155–169

Morris, A.G., and J.E. Parkington. 'Prehistoric Homicide: a case of violent death on the Cape south Coast, South Africa', *South African Journal of Science* 78, 1982, pp. 167–169

Peckmann, T.R. *Dialogues with the dead: An osteological analysis of the palaeodemography and life history of the 18th and 19th century northern frontier in South Africa*. Unpublished PhD thesis. Cape Town: University of Cape Town, 2002

————. 'Possible relationship between porotic hyperostosis and smallpox infections in nineteenth-century populations in the northern frontier, South Africa', *World Archaeology* 35 (2), 2003, pp. 289–305

Pfeiffer, S., and N.J. van der Merwe. 'Cranial injuries to Later Stone Age children from the Modder River Mouth, Western Cape Province, South Africa', *South African Archaeological Bulletin* 59 (180), 2004, pp. 59–65

Sealy, J.C., A.G. Morris, R. Armstrong, A. Markell and C. Schrire. 'An Historic Skeleton from the Slave Lodge at Vergelegen', *South African Archaeological Society, Goodwin Series* 7, 1993, pp. 84–91

CHAPTER 7

Klatzow, D., and S. Walker. *Steeped in Blood: The life and times of a forensic scientist*. Cape Town: Zebra Press, 2010

Shaw, A., and G. Gotora. 'Mass graves in Zimbabwe thought to be Zanu's Handiwork', *Cape Times*, 1 April 2011

Index

cribra orbitalia 71,
184, 221
crime scene 103–104
Crime Scene Unit
(CSU) 18
Crime Stop television
programme 82–83
crutches, users of 56
CSI effect 15–16, 78
cultural markers on bones
59–63
culture 4, 30–31,
45–48, 179
Cuvier, Baron Georges
197, 200, 201–203

Dart, Raymond A. 8
dating of skeletons 17, 211
Davies, Carolyn 61
Davison, Sean 153–154
Dawkins, Richard
141–142
death
beliefs about 124–128
cause 14, 72–74, 78
death penalty 31,
144–145
decomposition in
water 113
degenerative joint disease
(DJD) and individual
identity 59
De Klerk, Marike 47
De Kock, Eugene
144,147–148
Dembetembe, Kundi
36, 194
'demographic' analysis of
bones 25–52
dental caries 64, 67,
202, 203
Department of Health
9, 19
Department of Justice
118, 158

descendent communities
186–188, 206–209, 226
destitute people 107–109
De Tuin farm 182–183,
187
diagnosis of disease
72, 221
diet
and isotopes 17,
211–212
and teeth 38, 63–68,
202–203, 215
dimorphism, sexual 26
Directorate of Special
Operations (DSO)
118–119
'disappeared' persons 151
discriminant function 50
discs, intervertebral
53–55
dismemberment 76,
131–132
District Six Museum
208–209
district surgeons 95
divination 127, 138, 161
Dlamini, Nhlanhla
58, 186
DNA analysis 26, 44,
78–79, 82
in case studies 121, 123,
147, 148, 153–154
Donen, Adv. Michael
144–146
Drennan, Matthew 7, 8
Dreyer, T.F. 178–179, 184
drug trade 118
Dutton, Jane 167
Dyer Island 118–119

Early Iron Age people 132
Engelbrecht, Martin 188
epiphyses 35, 37, 145
ethnicity and race 45–46,
196, 199–200

ethyl and methyl alcohol
108
eTV 167, 168
'exclusion principle' of
racial identity 51, 92
exhumations 148–151
expert witnesses 12–13
eye sockets 70–71, 221

facets, squatting 57, 58,
215, 216
facial reconstructions
80–87, 102, 110, 195
Fadana, Chief 161–162
Federal Bureau of
Investigation (FBI)
118
femur length and height
53, 54, 201
finger amputation,
traditional 131
fluorine 202
'folk' taxonomy 4, 45–48
fontanelle, anterior
32–33, *33*
food *see* diet
foragers 58, 182
foramen magnum 93
FORDISC computer
program 50–51
forensic anthropology
cooperation with
traditional belief 162
definition 11–13
as expert witness 12–13
local nature of 2–5
need for 96
origins and
development of 6–9
and police procedures
18–21
professional recognition
8–9, 96
prosecution/defence
conflict 12–13

Do you have any comments, suggestions or
feedback about this book or any other Zebra Press titles?
Contact us at **talkback@zebrapress.co.za**